Conversations
Out Of
ChAoS

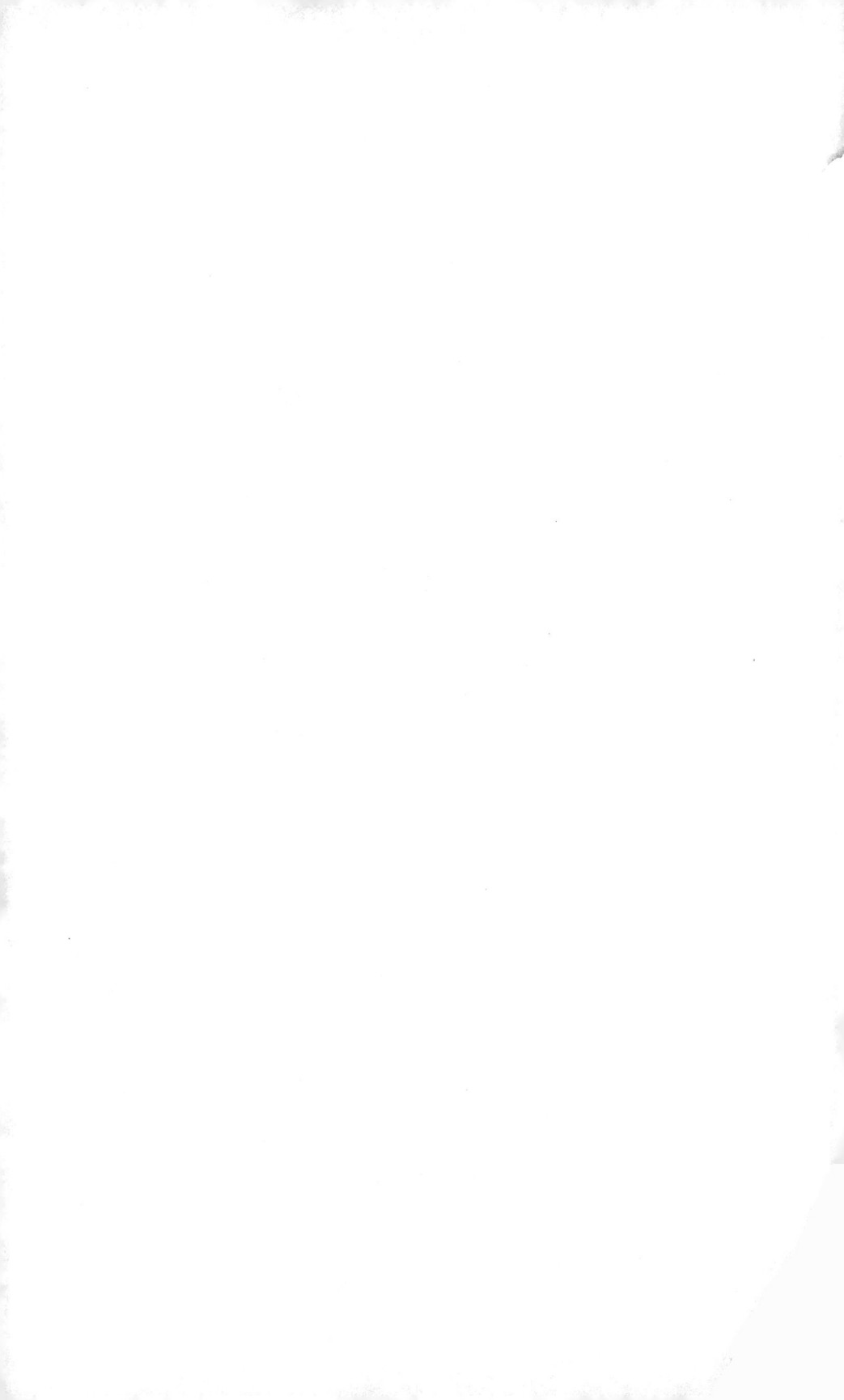

Conversations
Out Of
ChAoS

Imeh Smith

iUniverse, Inc.
New York Lincoln Shanghai

Conversations Out Of ChAoS

iUniverse books may be ordered through booksellers or by contacting:

iUniverse
2021 Pine Lake Road, Suite 100
Lincoln, NE 68512
www.iuniverse.com
1-800-Authors (1-800-288-4677)

ISBN-13: 978-0-595-41637-0 (pbk)
ISBN-13: 978-0-595-85985-6 (ebk)
ISBN-10: 0-595-41637-3 (pbk)
ISBN-10: 0-595-85985-2 (ebk)

Printed in the United States of America

Dedicated to my dad Alvin T. Smith, Tymax, and God.

Contents

PREFACE

This book is a collection of events, mishaps, and adventures in the life of one particular, zany, person. This collection was written on and off over a period of several years. This book was initially outlined in 1998. The outlines, however, were not filled with the detailed events in order. Subsequently, this book was written very out of sequence, in more than 2 different states, many different cities, time periods, and even on 2 different continents.

It's not everyday I walk down the street with people staring at me, but then not everyone is the center of attention or the current attraction in town. This seems to have happened to me. Not everyday, thank God, but I'm currently in Japan writing this while on a teaching exchange program. I'm currently in a Japanese fishing village. Being only 1 of 4 foreigners, and one of darker pigment, I'm like a walking museum.... a walking exhibit. I'll get to that later. As of now, I'm very far from a household name. I'm unfortunately not famous nor rich (as if somehow notoriety and fame equals wealth.) I'm just a single, fat, lonely, female with an **incredible, overactive, imagination.**

MIRACLE FROM THE START

I was actually a miracle right from the start. Perhaps a bound to be famous, known to all, destiny. I don't know; but my mom tried very hard to have children—and I am the only child. She had two miscarriages and a stillbirth before me, and one miscarriage after me. She stopped working and only rested and prepared for my coming. I was the only baby to survive, the only healthy live birth she had. They had my baby shower after I was born just to make sure my mom actually had a successful childbirth.

I don't remember much when I was little, but I vaguely remember falling when I was 3, pre-kindergarten, and kindergarten. I also slightly remember the *Richard Scarry's Best Word Book Ever* and me wishing and pretending to be the characters and traveling across the country with them inside the book. I had a VERY ACTIVE and CREATIVE imagination—and still do. I remember all types of weird, crazy, stuff via my overactive imagination. Like the moon, the man in the moon, the giant hand and so forth, coming inside my room through the window and trying to get me at night. And all types of other weird, exploration of my body that I guess kids do at that age.

I remember going on field trips to the zoo and eating peanut butter and jelly sandwiches for lunch all of the time. I went to St. Anthony for first grade. It was a Catholic school obviously. The only thing I slightly remember there is learning to spell really difficult words like Pterodactyl and other stuff that public schools didn't teach until 5th or 6th grade. I guess it was like any other private or Catholic school. We recited The Lords Prayer and Hail Mary (Full of Grace) prayer. We wore uniforms and the teachers were strict and didn't allow riff raff and misbehaving like that of public schools.

My great uncle on my mom's side use to hold block parties in our neighborhood that took up the whole block—thus a block party. The whole neighborhood would come out. Family, friends, old, young, black, white, American, and foreign (the few foreigners we had in our neighborhood back then). There was a massive amount of food. Delicious pies, cakes, savory ribs, bar-B-Q, grilled, and baked meats and veggies, all types of salads, and plenty of music, games, fellowship, and fun.

I really vaguely remember this old man who lived in our apartment complex. He made this lemon cake obviously with no water nor milk and it must have been dryer than bread. None of the adults wanted any, but I, a child of 5 or so, thought is was tasty and ate all of the cake. On another occasion, he chased my neighborhood buddy and me all over the yard with a switch in one hand and his cane in the other. I have no idea what happened or why he was mad at us. My mom remembers and told me that she was too embarrassed and busy laughing to come down and get us. She said he hopped, wobbled, and ran after us yelling, "I'm gonna beat you … I'm gonna beat you …" but of course he had to catch us first. No person in their right mind would let someone catch them so they can get beat. So we kept on running and he couldn't catch us.

My mom is an artist and makes all types of arts and crafts. She made mini dollhouses out of cardboard and raison boxes. She also made me a playhouse out of cardboard when I was 4 or so. I truly enjoyed playing in the house with my toys. I guess I played so much and so rough, it just fell over. If I remember right, it leaned to the side like the Leaning Tower of Pisa. I enjoyed the house just as much leaning and on the ground as I enjoyed it standing. I remember using it like a sleeping bag and a sled down the grassy hill. My mom gagged and screamed. Her dollhouse was ruined. That was the last one she made for me. I also remember a fun toy as a kid called Sit & Spin. It would make a great aerobic exercise, or at least good for toning your arms. You would sit on this round flat disk with your legs Indian style around this pole. There was a handle at the top and the faster you turned the handle, the faster you'd spin in a circle. Loads of fun, and I'm sure it would be a workout if you are heavy. I guess it could make you dizzy though.

The first Broadway play I remember going to was The Wiz with Stephanie Mills. And I Loved It! I liked it so much that my mom bought me the album soundtrack. I played it so much that my favorite songs became one big scratch. I would play the album and sing and pretend that I was actually in Oz. I soon got a crush on the Tin Man. I would sleep with the album cover under my pillow so I could look at the Tin Man whenever I wanted and needed to through out the night. I must ask a psychologist why I was—and still am—attracted to the worst sorts of characters. As a kid I liked a wild assortment of odd characters. The Tin Man, Blue Bear from the Jungle Book, I also liked the boy in the Jungle Book. Oh my lovely choices of men. I must immediately travel elsewhere to find my husband because now I'm just very lonely.

I am an only child so I usually had to play by myself, thus my imagination is very elaborate and vivid. My mom gave me those wonderful kid books in which you would play the 45" record as you manually read the book and look at the pictures. You're supposed to read along with the narrator and they had music and nice songs too. I would make pretend I'm a character inside the story and I pretended to be there and would imitate the pictures in the book. I would put on my pretty Easter dress and stand and sit on my bed in the same "pose" as the girls in the books. If the author drew them in action like running, jumping, or something then I would pose and put my legs and arms in the same position as the picture inside the kid's books. One of my favorites was "**Richard Scarry's Best Word Book Ever**". I liked that book through out elementary school—even after most kids outgrew the book. I would pretend to be inside the book and act like I was brushing my teeth, eating with the animal family, oh, and my favorite, traveling with them in the city and through the country. And I still LOVE to travel.

My grandma would keep my cousin and me when I was little. I remember wanting to go to school because my cousin, who's only one year older, went, and crying because I couldn't go. Isn't that pure insanity!! Of course, the second I went to school, I regretted it. When I was three I remember walking to school with granny and my cousin Re and then turning and spinning like a mad man then falling and busting open my right knee. I have a scar to this day from that accident. In fact my poor delicate right leg is always in some tragedy. It's my right foot that has a bunion. It's that same foot which first hurts from wearing new not worn in shoes. It is that foot that first gets the corn or new shoe scrap on the back of my heel. It was the big toe on that foot which was attacked by a piece of glass from the liquor store broken beer bottle and needed to get taken out with a long needle. It was the right leg which I fell on and bruised my shin. It is the right leg which hurts along the shin and it's the same knee which banged on a chair and thus again hurting such a precious and delicate gem. Well anyway, shortly after the knee incident we moved from N.E., DC, the city I was born in and my first abode, to Maryland.

My dad's family lives down the country in Virginia. My dad has a big family, many sisters and brothers, and many nieces, nephews, and cousins. They had a big farm with chickens, cats, dogs, a goat, a pig; they even had a little pony at one point. It was a huge farm and back in the day when grandpa and my uncle were living, everyone would come to the house. It was a 2-hour drive from our home in Maryland to my dad's farm in Virginia and I always seemed to need to use the toilet. It is a very old home with no plumbing. There was a leaning outhouse—like my cardboard playhouse that I turned into a blanket and sleigh. My mom refused to use the leaning outhouse, so we took a bucket to go in, as well as clothes, food, beer, $, et cetera. I remember whenever I needed to use the toilet daddy refused to stop so I had to go in the bucket in the back seat. As a 4-year-old in a moving car, I'm sure I got urine on the seat and myself. It's quite humorous though when I think back.

I remember waking up early to see the kid shows like Beth and Bower, Great Space Coaster, and New Zoo Review. I would rush down stairs early Saturday morning just to see it. That was the last time I would happily wake up very early. Outside of Christmas Day when I would rush down stairs to see what Santa gave me and if I got the toy I wanted, I hated waking up early. As I kid I would sleep until afternoon on the weekends and my dad would make me get out of bed. Now I can easily sleep until 4pm.

I also vaguely remember these next sets of events. I somewhat remember jogging all over the mall in downtown DC where the Monument is with my aunt and cousin. We jogged and jogged. We stopped to take a rest at this tree where I remember saying, "Just let me sit and die here." My aunt gagged laughing as I slumped on the ground too exhausted to get up anymore. She said we could stop here. The reason for this activity I don't know. Perhaps we were going for a picnic and sight see, something that my family did a lot of. I have photos of my cousins and me at museums as young as 2½ or 3.

My family would take me to Kiddyland, the Enchanted Forest, and parades—where I was terrified of the loud noises and folks in costumes. I'm sure I wasn't a day over three, but I do vaguely remember the loud terrifying parade noise (maybe they were loud fireworks which I hate the sound to this day), giant costumes, and my mom photographing me being scared of the people in lion and other costumes at the kid's theme park. Mom said I was scared of the giant human dragon consume with the people dancing inside it. She told me how beautiful it looked but that I just kept screaming and wanting her to hold me. I know it's beautiful now, but then I only remember those big, scary, costumes full of feathers. And I was completely terrified! I also vaguely remember the nursery rhyme castle that I was also scared of. I think the animatronics and statues looked fake to adults but too real for me. I probably would be scared of pigs and other animals in real life, let alone a giant singing statue. Animals don't sing, and if one is larger than me and starts singing now, I'm running! Unless it's cute and nice, then I would talk to it.

I remember going to the Smithsonian museums in DC. They are the only set of museum, outside of London, that are free. I was spoiled on this—and perhaps other things too. I was shocked to find out that I had to pay to enter a museum in any other city. The nerve! How dare them charge me, in upwards of $10 and more, to visit a museum. When I first realized I had to pay to enter a museum, I argued and debated with the cashier thinking it was a mistake. I'm sure I embarrassing whomever I was with. My favorite Smithsonian Museum is the Museum of Natural History, and of course, I was scared of things inside that one too. That one is the coolest next to the space museum. It has a woolly mammoth to greet you at the door. It has dinosaur bones and a humpback whale in an exhibit hall and the lights make it look like it's underwater. It has the mummies, cave men, and a cool anthropological mural of all the people and races of the world. It's my favorite, but as a child, I was scared of the dinosaur, whale—in fact I'd start crying asking someone to hold me. I though it was underwater because it looked blue and underwater like.

I slightly remember this event. I was at the Smithsonian Museum of American History. Well, my mom, aunt, my cousin Re, and I were at the boring part. I really don't know what was going on, it was too boring. I do remember being scared of the 1800 train exhibit. Every few minutes the train would sound, start moving, and blow its loud horn. I was terrified. I thought it would actually start moving. This huge, massive, loud machine might hit me. After all, I was probably not a day over four or five. Well we went to the hall of presidents. Re and I were very bored at this point. Who cares about these old, ugly, paintings, let's go to the fun section. After seemingly countless hours there, I asked, probably loudly, "Is this the ugly exhibit!?" I guess my aggravation and question worked. My mom and aunt must have been so embarrassed since all of the other people stared at us. After that, we left that boring section. I can't remember where we went after that, probably to see the scary train.

I remember going to the beach at Ocean City, MD with my cousins who currently live in N.C. I also remember going to the Baltimore zoo with Tony, another cousin, Re, my aunt, and mom. I must have been around 10 at this point. I don't remember much else except the adults got separated or maybe Re and I went with Tony to see some animal. I personally don't like zoo's too much, they stink. With the exception of the Salisbury Zoo, which offers the cutest farm and forest animals—I guess they couldn't afford real zoo animals. Most zoos have big, smelly, dirty animals. The stuffed version of the animal is very cute. The cartoon version can be cute. The real version is not so cute and very smelly, so I can do without zoos.

Well I guess Tony found my mom and aunt so he decided to take a short cut, down this very steep mountain of a hill. He and Re went down fine. When he saw that I couldn't come down the steep hill, he handed me a huge stick and tells me to take my time. I was screaming the entire way. Mom and my aunt heard me before they saw us. They thought it was quite funny, unlike me. They said I looked like Moses with a long his staff coming down Mt. Sinai. Ashamed, I don't enjoy in the laughter.

I actually don't remember this final event, my mom told me about this one. My family went to visit my great aunt. My parents and I went to her house 6 hours from us in Va. I guess I was around 9 or 10. She's extremely religious and superstitious. Like me, she believes in the supernatural. She is a preacher and has a church. It was very small and didn't have indoor plumbing. She had about 8 members, most of which were kids. According to my mom, a few senile members and some kids. She was an excellent pianist and she would sing and preach. Since the church was small I guess we spread out. My mom and dad set on different pews and I sat in the "choir/deacon" seats. She made some comment about, "I wish my 2 brothers would come to church." I was told I whispered, loudly, "Aunt Ruth, Aunt Ruth, are you talking about Grandpa and Uncle Jim?" Daddy loudly hushed me up and she basically ignored me saying, "That there's my niece".

MY CURSED SCHOOLS DAYS/YEARS

My horrific school experience from elementary to high school really didn't begin until I went to MD public schools. Private school has a different caliber of students from public school all together. I remember the horrible students who harassed me in public school had the nerve to talk to me at the private Christian school/church we went to on Sundays. Of course it's not where you live, go to school, or work. As they say, you can move people out of the ghetto, but you can't move the ghetto out of people. And that is basically what my school was, a bunch of poor whites, blacks, and foreigners who weren't able to save up enough money to leave the area. There were a lot of folks that got enough money to leave their DC housing project and move to Md. There are many people, like my family and friends, whom grew up in working class areas to the pit of the ghetto but are normal, professional, nice decent citizens. There are also those people who grew up in nice homes in nice neighborhoods with good families and turn out to be professional juvenile delinquents.

BLUBBER By Judy Blume

My school days, at least in grammar school, reminded me of Blubber, the sweet, tormented, main character in a book of the same name by Judy Blume. I'm sure my school had no more bullies than any other public school or school in general. It wasn't until 3rd grade that kids began harassing me and of course it was then that I begin to hate school. It was also when I began to get fat. I also was an early bloomer and they made fun of my breasts calling me Dolly Parton and laughing. I told mom I wanted to get rid of them, not realizing what an asset it was. I was fat from 8 years old on. I know people who were fat kids and skinny teens or vise versa. They seem to be able to lose weight easier in adulthood. But every person I know—black, Latino, white, man, or woman, if they were fat kids and fat teens, they are still fat. And it seems almost impossible, short of surgery and liposuction, to lose weight. Of course, being fat is one more thing to be picked on in school. Thus, the best part of school were the field trips and the occasional party, everything else.... I hated.

SET POINT THEORY

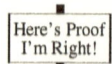

I've done some research on weight loss and weight management and, of course, my findings prove my point and my suspected theory to be correct! "There is a set point theory. The theory states that the human body works to maintain a certain weight. More importantly, each person has an internal set point for fatness that seem to regulate the body's fatness and weight. It seems to regulate fatness by adjusting the person's appetite and energy expenditure, i.e. metabolism. Researches have demonstrated that human and animal subjects put on different diets would only lose or gain up to a certain amount. More so, once the diet ended, eating increases and they returned to their original weight. The body adjusts its energy expenditure by adjusting its metabolism. The further you stray from your usual weight, the harder the force—your set point metabolism—acts to pull your body back to its original desired weight. When dieters lose weight, their metabolism slows down, when weight is gained, their metabolism speeds up. Basically stating, the body resists further weight loss. And the opposite is true for skinny people who try to gain weight naturally. People always focus on the body's resistance to weight loss but rarely think of the body's resistance to weight gain. For example, over eating after Thanksgiving. Overall, however, resistance to weight gain is much less than resistance to weight loss. When a person gains weight and stays that weight for a while, the body tends to defend the new weight and set point.

This is probably the reason why fat kids, who become fat teens, don't seem to lose weight. When obesity develops in infancy or childhood(juvenile-onset obesity)just as that child grows up, more fat cells develop and grow along with them. Outside of having MORE fat cells than someone who was fat only as an adult or a teen but not their entire life, these additional fat cells also blow up like fat balloons. This process results in hypertrophic/hyperplastic obesity." I.e. more fat cells as well as more fat inside each ballooned out cell. In other words, having damn near twice as many fat cells to begin with. Why? Because these annoying cells grew and developed while you were also growing. As well as, having huge, ballooned out fat cells like every other person with a gut, saddlebags, love handles, or flabs of fat. "When obesity develops in adults, only a normal number of fat cells develop, they just contain large amounts of fat inside each cell. Only in extreme cases can adult-onset obesity develop into both hypertrophy and hyperplasic. Unfortunately, once developed, fat cells never disappear." Which is why liposuction exists! "**If adult obesity is both hypertrophy and** hyperplasic, it is more difficult to lose weight than if the obesity is due only to hypertrophy." In other words, it's harder to lose weight because you have twice as many super sided cells full of fat compared to someone who was once fit but now has overstuffed fat cells due to over eating like a pig and no exercise like a slob. "Some evidence indicates that more fat cells increases the body's resistance and reluctance to reduce fat stores. The needs of fat cells may require that they store at least nominal amounts of fat. More fat cells would then result in more fat storage, further complicating efforts to lose weight. The longer a person remains obese, the more difficult it is to correct the problem." Again, the reason liposuction was developed!!! This was taken from chapter 8, <u>Achieving a Healthy Weight</u> page 240–243 out of my Step Aerobics textbook, *Wellness: Concepts and Applications* by McGraw-Hill Higher Education.

Here's another good point and quote from this excellent video, <u>**Never Too Thin**</u> by Willy and Wendy Werby. "Fat people are not alcoholics, drug addicts, or smokers. We can't just say I will never eat again. You need food to survive. The key to losing weight and dieting is gradually changing your eating and lifestyle habits. And most importantly, liking your new habits so you will stick with it."

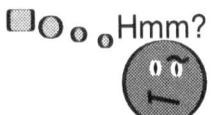

GirL ScoUTs

Well, I joined the Girl Scouts first at my public school then moving to a Girl Scouts at a Catholic school. Between the scouts and the very conservative, right winged church/school that I went to on Sunday's, my eyes were opened to a whole new group of people, friends, activities, and events. The Girl Scouts at the private school went camping, hiking up mountains, camping at amusement parks, and many exciting activities—including the Halloween party when my costume caught on fire from a pumpkin. My long, very flowing costume whipped across the jack-o-lantern on the floor and went up in a blaze. Thank God the counselors reminded me to stop-drop-and roll. Thus covering me with a blanket. Most of my long flowing costume turned into a ragged Flintstones looking dress. With all of that heat, fire, and embarrassment, thank God I only had a little burn on my butt.

The girls at the Catholic school—although one was from my public school that liked to cause a little trouble—they were all very friendly, regardless of race, religion, or age. We all got along, had fun, and learned a whole lot. Unfortunately, I forgot much of the Girl Scout motto like always be prepared.

fuN w/TonY

My cousin Tony on my dad's side came to live with us in the city. It was loads of fun with him around. He was like an older brother. As I mentioned before, I did many things with him. I would play and bother the heck out of him all the time. He was so hilarious. He was very energetic and somewhat hyper. He moved fast and scurried a lot and was always late for work. I must have taken after him; I am constantly late for everything. I need to set my clock and run over an hour fast just to be somewhere on time!!! And many times, I still just make it.

LoSt fOr 6

After finishing my dreaded elementary school, I went to Disney World with my great aunt—whom I must have took after because we both will travel at the spur of the moment, enjoy life, and are free spirits. She came down from Michigan this past summer. Well anyway, I was so excited about the trip, I didn't get any sleep the night before we left. That morning my aunt, uncle, cousins, and me all piled into this station wagon and headed south. We went to the natural bridge museum, a wax museum, over some relative's house in Richmond, and went down to Fl. We stayed with a cousin—her son, in Fl. We went to the beach and then finally went to Orlando, 6 hours away. Once in Disney, my aunt went—and got lost—at Epcot Center. At the same time, my cousin and I got lost after riding a roller coaster in the Magic Kingdom. Like a dummy, I told one of the Disney employees and they took us to this stupid child find place that we couldn't leave, and thus we were lost for 6 hours! Instead of riding on rides and having fun, my cousin and I were stuck in this stupid baby changing room/child find place awaiting our family to tell the police we were lost so they can find us. Our family looked, and looked, and looked for us and then finally told security after 6 hours. What a great way to spend time at Disney! 😦

After we left Florida we went up to Detroit and got lost on the way. In Detroit I got the flu and had the opportunity to look at cable TV. Kid's shows in the morning, adult "R" rated movies in the evening and porno at night. I also kept waking up people to kill the ants that kept walking around the room. I think the ants and my aunt successfully titled me a menace and happily sent me back to DC

It was also during this time that I reached my maximum height of shortness and was the smallest of my teen years. I was still chubby but my round snowman figure turned into a voluminous, big chested, large butt, and the smallest "chubby" waste that I had growing up since 8 years old. After that summer I entered middle school and I only got fatter, but not taller—thus my figure only lasted one summer. I've been basically the same fat size since high school until now. I hate those stupid commercial that say, "loose weight so you can get your wonderful high school figure back" What figure! I was a round ball! What a horrible abomination!!

MUSICAL, BUT CAN'T PLAY AN INSTRUMENT

I guess I'm a true muse and genuine artist. I would have the most elaborate dreams. If you wonder how George Lucas, Rod Sterling, Disney World, and those amazing sci-fi and fantasy authors think of it, it's in their head—literally. Most likely, they had very elaborate dreams and they figured out how to capture them into stories, films, animatronics, and so forth. I write down many of my dreams. I find it interesting that many people either don't dream—as they claim—or have very mundane dreams in which they forget as soon as they awake. Everyone dreams. I guess I'm very left brain (or whatever side the creative thinking is on). I have very elaborate songs in my dreams. I would dream I'm performing a major hit song on stage to millions of screaming fans. Maybe that's just wishful thinking. But I do record whenever I have the chance, whatever song pops up in my head. I understand John Lennon dreamt of Imagine. Songs enter my head through my dreams, listing to other songs, hearing slight melodies in everyday life (like door chimes or engine noise); even listening to the rhythm of a copier can inspire me of a song. I would be good as one of those copyright infringement researchers. I can hear a song and find a melody, harmony, rhythm, and even a drumbeat that belongs or is inspired by another song. Another friend of mine was really good at that too.

> I am now typing back in the states, over 2 years later.

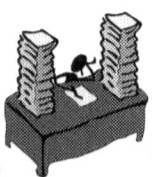

#1 disTracTion ...... mY mInD

It was suggested that I might unofficially have Attention Deficit Disorder. It was said that folks with ADD—outside of having attention and sometimes behavior problems—are very creative, artistic, and musically inclined. I refuse to spend the $1000+ and 6+ hours of time testing to find results that several counselors and I already know. How will an official diagnosis help me? I don't need anyone to take notes for me in class. One, I already have my degree, 2, I can take good notes on my own, and 3, if it's a production oriented class where your final grade is based on a project instead of an annoying written technical term paper and a written exam, I'm good to go. I found it fascinating how few students took my Professor up on the oral exam option. I got a high B in the class. It was an interesting class, Cultural Anthropology, with easy readings and easy papers to do. And I should have gotten an A, he just graded too hard. I asked one student, why he, as well as many other students, chose the written over the oral exam. He said he likes written tests better. Go figure?!?!

I'm very much a visual and auditory learner. I hate stupid network TV however I love documentaries and how-to shows. I never look at sports, except those wonderful girly kinds such as gymnastics, figure skating, and—my favorite— dance competition. I not much of a book person or into reading, unless it's a fun, easy to read, bio or non-fiction. I learn languages by hearing it a million times, not reading it. I learned sign language from my friend, who's completely deaf with no speaking ability. I learned and remembered Japanese characters by seeing them like a cartoon, not writing it a million times. I learn and remember stuff by seeing and hearing, not reading and writing. Some folks—like my current roommate who gets flustered with more than one option—likes to read and do technical writing. She's very indecisive and has difficulty making decisions. They remember that way. She and another roommate allegedly can read, look at TV, talk, and supposedly catch all what's going on. An extreme multi-tasker. I am the extreme opposite. I know exactly what I want and NEVER have a hard time— nor take a long time—deciding. I also am extremely disorganized and very easily distracted. I must have total focus when reading or even watching TV to enjoy, or catch everything. I heard many people with ADD are musically inclined. Even though I can think of a million songs a day, I couldn't play an instrument to save my life. I actually don't know how I got ranting on this topic. I can easily lose my train of thought.

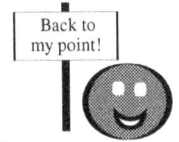

Back to my point!

bacK to tHe muSiC.

One Christmas my Daddy bought me a bike at age 12 and another Christmas he got me a guitar because I played the one at his sister's house. I was too big and embarrassed to learn to ride a very tall 12+speed bike at my age when kids half my age already knew how to ride one. I think I might have been too heavy for my cousin Tony to hold me up. He was the one sanctioned to teach me how to ride.

On that same fashion (bear with me, I do tie things in—especially if I don't lose my point. I just rant a bit) my dad bought me a guitar because I was playing with—not playing on, the one my aunt had. I didn't even know the fingering. I was just plucking and playing with "a toy." Daddy was convinced that I was a natural musician and that I knew how to play a guitar, or could learn easily. Unfortunately it just sat there. I never learned how to play a guitar nor ride a bike, even to this day. I am REALLY not athletically inclined. I hate playing rough sports, ball, softball, et cetera. I really love to dance however. I wish I had the chance and opportunity to learn gymnastics and dance as a child. I think I'm quite flexible, even at my huge size, and I practically lived in dance and house music clubs for a decade of my life.

My mom, on the same music bug as my dad, allowed and insisted that I stay in music lessons through out school. Many elementary schools—before they took music out of school—offered band. I decided to join the chorus and band in 4th grade. I decided to play the flute, because it was small. As you may know, outside of the piccolo and triangles, the flute is the next smallest instrument in an orchestra or band. My cousin played the oboe. That was a bigger instrument. My parents seemed ecstatic of my beginning flute band programs. I guess all parents are pleased to see their kid onstage. They took me to see Herbie Mann, a flutist, in concert. They wanted to expose me to other forms of classical and orchestral music. I, however, never was that good and ended up staying in beginning band for the next three years.

I guess reading music is too math oriented and too much of a foreign language. I would write the letters of the notes above the actual notes—cheating. I never learned to read music. To this day I still can't read music. I, unfortunately, never was blessed to play by ear either. This means that I always need someone who is a musician to collaborate with me to make the music tracks for me to hopefully sing over and perform. For I love to perform, I think I'm a natural. When I went to 7th grade, I had to choose between chorus or band. My mom was quite irate when I chose chorus. "Everyone is in chorus. Anybody can try to sing. Only a few can read music and play an instrument." She is very right. I'm just not one of them. I did join the drama club. And when I went into high school, I stayed in chorus and, like many people, sang in the church choir. My mom started sending me to piano lessons. It was quite boring. Probably because all I did was constantly play the scale. Then I would play these boring songs. I enjoyed playing with the lady's cat more than the lessons. I soon started hiding from her and mom eventually took me out, to both mom and the teacher's disappointment.

WiLLiAm WiRT MiDdLE

Another school that I hated was my middle school, William Wirt. In elementary I hardly had that many friends. There were the kids in my neighborhood that I played such as Belief, Mira, and Sherry. There were some other kids around the neighborhood that I could play with but in school, they would usually hang around their own class or friends. I usually played with Belief, my neighbor Sherry, and my mom babysat Mira.

Because of needing to stop working for me, my mom became a housewife and a stay at home mom until I entered high school. Looking back, it is definitely a blessing. Mostly all of my peers—black, Latino, white, men, women, straight, whatever—come from single parent homes. They were raised by their mom, or grandparent, or something. Even some of my more affluent friends have single parents. Most of the friends that still have both parents are foreign, where the institution of marriage and the attempt to stay together is not a joke. I am blessed to have a 2-parent home. Having a responsible, real man for a wonderful father. He was the one who paid my way through college, took me to Howard's football game while I was still in high school, took me to see baseball, play mini-golf, and many other wonderful activities. My mom was smothering and very overprotective. I guess if you lose several kids you would hold on for dear life to the ones you have. Being that she stayed home, I couldn't easily goof off and stuff during the year. I also would get in trouble when I would come home after dark. It was flat out impossible for me to sneak and get away with ANYTHING! I have no siblings, who can I blame it on?

By middle school on out, most of the people I hung out with were foreign, geeks, nerds, or bamma's. I was unpopular since I had—and still do according to many standards—a bad taste of fashion and could do absolutely nothing with my hair. I had friends in church and Girl Scouts—which my mom took me out of in middle school, saying I was too old and big, even though you can be a scout until you graduate. Brownies are for the little kids, Juniors are for the older elementary kids, Cadets are for middle school kids, and Seniors are for high school. See, I still remember that. Of course, all of the scouts I knew were young and not in middle or high school. My cousin Tony went back to Va. at the same time and I was alone again. The youth in the conservative church, Tony, and the girls in the scouts were nice and someone I could talk to and play with. I hated school and had no one to really hang out with. That is all anyone really wants, young or old, man or woman, someone to talk to, hang out with, and have fun with.

I met more people in middle school who I could talk to and play with. Of course, they all came from another elementary school or from another country. And unlucky for me, practically every person that I met that was pleasant went to a different high school and every rude, mean, obnoxious, ill mannered, lunatic who I couldn't stand followed me to one of the roughest high schools in the county. Oh joy!

thE tRiP tO MAiNe

Before my mom took me out of the conservative church, I had the fun opportunity to go on a 20-hour bus ride to Maine. Although the church is still conservative and my mom disliked the fact they were too right winged and extremists in some issues, in her opinion, the youth group was very fun, warm, welcoming, and packed with plenty of activities. We went to Maine for a one-week summer camp. Our church sponsored the camp and it featured many types of activities, from karate, to gymnastic, to singing, to puppeteering, to mime. It was plenty of fun. The ride up took 20 hours and the trip was just as fun. We packed in school buses and sang, played cards, told jokes, and even put make-up on the first person that fell asleep. Of course he wouldn't realize it until we stopped for food and saw his reflection. It was the first time I heard of a Chinese fire drill. It was so fun. We parked the bus so the driver—who was also the youth leader—could stay awake, and he yelled Chinese fire drill. We would take off running off the bus, run around the bus and then back on. It was hysterical fun.

BlaDEnsBUrG HiGh

It may not have been as bad as I had expected, but it was not good. By this time I had a passion for hating school and not liking the students either. See in elementary and middle school I wanted friends. Someone to talk to, hang out with, and have fun with. By the time high school came, I could care less about most of the students and trying to make friends. I liked them and wanted to hang out with them as much as they wanted to hang out with me. Whether they liked me or not was irrelevant, I could care less by this point. I had a few more "loser," geek, and nerdy friends. Those were my few goofy friends from middle and elementary school.

TRIALS WITH JOBS

Like guys, it seems impossible for me to first, find a tolerable job that actually pays something, and secondly, to keep it longer than a few months—max. There were a few enjoyable jobs, such as working at Greyhound Bus station, the gas station, being a Disney intern, substitute teaching for Baltimore County high schools, and working in Japan. I worked at Tourmobile Sightseeing two summers in a row. I also worked vast telemarketing jobs in which I quit or was fired within a few days or weeks; survey jobs in Roslyn, Va., airline jobs way out at Dulles Airport, and various retail jobs for brief stints each. Office temp jobs for a few days each. Cirque du Solie, twice, UniverSole Circus, and Arena Stage Theater. A torturous Christian camp, Camp Bennett. And my adventures, trials, and challenges of Japan.

CaMp BeNnetT aNd tHe TorTUre

Via the conservative church, I landed this summer job as a camp counselor for "at risk" kids. Take inner city kids, ex-prisoners who need to do community service, a scary, crazy, white man, and his 400 pound wife, way, way, way out in the country, and you have my job. You also have the setting for the next horror film. He walked around with a double barrel shot gun saying he was hunting for possum in the middle of the night while the kids slept. You were forbidden to hear music, see TV or papers, wear comfortable clothes, and sleeveless shirts. You had to eat all of your food or they would only serve it to you for the next meal. If the kids acted up, they threw them head first into a filthy trashcan full of the days food. They would throw a whip cream pie in your face for amusement. It was a boiling hot summer. I got heat rash, black as tar, fat as hell, and had nightmares of him and that awful camp for weeks.

GusSiNi ShOeS

After the torturous Camp Bennett, the next job I remember is here at Gussini Shoes. Nothing really exciting happened except my friend from school, whom I'll call Big T, would loiter there and think of more lies to tell me.

DrIvEr's eDUcaTIOn

One summer I went to driver's education and passed my written test by the skin of my teeth to successfully get my learners permit. I was so happy I jumped and cheered in the test room and the instructor got mad saying people are still testing. One thing I can say about driver's education is that it was at a different high school. Not the best school in the area by far, but way better than my school. I met several new people who were way nicer and well traveled than at my school.

WiLd WoRLd

The following summer I worked at Wild World, the next job in a long line of many different jobs. Wild World, which underwent new management and new names, was a small amusement park near my home. Oh, I didn't keep that one for more than a month either. They supposedly laid me off because of the slow summer. Wild World was not at all what I expected, wanted, or thought it would be.... fun.

SKIPPING SCHOOL & STILL GRADUATING ON TIME

I successfully skipped school several times a week and was late daily. I hooked school and went to the movies and so forth, and still graduated and went to college after high school. I mastered the art of faking sick notes, successfully skipping school 2-3 times a week then begging the teacher to allow me to make up the work. I passed my classes, even if it was with a "D", graduated on time, and successfully went to college.

Big T, a neighbor who followed me through school, would come over to supposedly walk to school with me. Of course, he was using my house as a haven so he could skip school too. He would come over and we would order pizza and play on the phone to our school office and the neighborhood carry out. We would sneak around our nosy neighbor who would tattle to my parents and harass me and say that Big T was my boyfriend.

Most of the high quality students graduated over 1 or 2 years late due to getting arrested or giving birth. Many students join the military, work in salons, raise their kids, go back to jail, or work in their trade. Only some students go to college. In the yearbook, I was crowned "never ever present" and still graduated on time and went to college!

thE "24 HOur LiBRarY" & SCooBy DoO

I just remembered how one summer weekend Big T and I said we were going to the "library" because for some unusual reason, my mom didn't want me to go to the carnival in town. Of course we accidentally caught the wrong train and ended up at the carnival. As usual, Big T acted a fool on the train. After walking forever from the train, we finally arrived at the carnival. I got on many rides. I love roller coasters and fun rides. The first time I rode a roller coaster was when I was 6. I was scared to get on the kiddy coaster named the "Scooby Doo" at Kings Dominion, so my aunt convinced me it was fun and rode with me. I enjoyed it so much, I rode it 12 times in a row!!

Well, we enjoyed ourselves very much. In fact too much, we missed our last train home and of course I only had a train ticket, and as usual, I always carry a lot of money, and was too broke to get home. Of course it was after midnight and we needed to figure out a ride home. Like always, most people I knew were peasants with no car or license. Big T, a compulsive liar, couldn't find any of his rich, famous, beautiful, friends with nice cars who are sooo good to him and always help him out at a drop of a dime. We ended up trying to figure out a way home, and around 2am I decided to catch the last bus into Maryland. With no money, the bus driver let us on. Big T complained about how are we going to pay, with our looks, and ignoring him, I sat down and told the driver we were stranded and needed to get to Maryland.　　　Of course calling our parents were out, we were supposed to be at the library. Well, the bus dropped us off at the end of the line in Md. but nowhere near our house. I finally called my mom since Liar was unsuccessful at finding a ride. Mom comes screaming and Big T told her we were at the 24hour library—which does exists at Md. Univ. but at the time no one knew of it—and of course, she figured Big T was lying again as usual.

BeThel Bible aNd NY

I love to travel and still want a man. I was always lonely and daydreamed of hanging out at the park, on the beach, going on weekend drives, and enjoying myself. I joined another church youth group just to have something to do and somewhere to go on Friday night. My usual Friday night and New Years Eve was miserably spent at home with my parents daydreaming of enjoying myself. Although the atmosphere was very different at this church which was black and slightly more liberal than the other, it was something to do. We even went to upstate New York for this music and art competition.

JoY RiDiNG CaR THiEf

I would sneak out the house at night, borrow my mom's car, and joy ride with Big T and PJ or Aaron—2 useless peasants I met. PJ was one of many in a long string of worthless, no-good men that I met. I successfully hooked school and went to the movies, the mall, and would loiter in other schools. This is how I met PJ, skipping out of my school and sneaking and roaming in his. We would cruise around DC half of the night. PJ was a successful juvenile delinquent. He had a dysfunctional crazy brother who hated me and the feeling was very mutual. His jerk of a brother chased me around his yard with numchucks as Big T tried to be funny and drive off with my mom's car. Big T found humor in that. I, of course, was enraged and terrified.

Another unfortunate occasion with another worthless man got me caught via my parents. Thanks to worthless Aaron, I returned home too late, i.e. morning, and I demanded Big T to accompany me home. I knocked on the door as daddy laughs while looking out of the window at me. He said, "Who is it? Ha ha ha ha … Evett, your child is home. Ha ha ha … Who is it? Ha ha ha." Mom was so mad, she said absolutely nothing, which is the only time this ever happened. Usually she nags and fusses a hole in someone's head. Even when she supposedly had laryngitis, she knew how to muster up nags, and start fussing at daddy and me.

I asked my mom if I could spend the weekend with Big T and his family at his grandma's home in the country. She didn't disagree, in fact she said nothing. So thusly, I went. Their car was full with Big T's siblings and the 2 guinea pigs that left pellets and urine everywhere. There was the cute fat black rabbit, Big T's adorable fat neighbors, and he and his mom fist fighting at the end.

3-Eyelash & My Prom

In the continued tradition of asinine guys in my life and to successfully finish my dreadful high school in style, I was completely ditched by my prom date! To top it off, the guy was less than moderate looking! Get that, some shot to hell looking guy stood me up for my prom! Can you get any worst that that? Only in my life, in this dreadful city, and at that appalling school! I barely remember this dreadful guy. The only thing I remember is that he had 3 eyelashes. What's with that? I know he was a genuine peasant because I probably met him loitering during working hours at Riverdale Plaza. This shows that he was most likely unemployed. This and the fact that he lived with his mom in the refugee section-8 apartment complex behind the plaza. I can almost guarantee he had no car. But what he did have was 3 eyelashes clumped together. You know like those mascara commercials where they say, "You don't want your eyelashes clumped together looking a mess do you? If not, buy our brand." Obviously, he must have used the worst brand of cheap mascara for his eyelashes—or maybe he naturally had shot to hell eyelashes that naturally clumped together in clusters of three's. Not sure.

Well being that he did a no-call-no-show for my prom, and hid like the good roach that he was when my mom and I went looking for him, I ended up not having a date to my ghetto prom. Never fret; I actually went to two other proms, at schools WAY better than mine. I went on a double date to one prom with this silly friend of mine that was stuck at Bladensburg for her freshman year then was lucky enough to transfer to Highpoint High for the remainder of her schooling. I went with her equally silly brother and she went with her boyfriend. I also went to the prom with an intelligent, gentleman, friend of mine who went to Fredrick Douglass High somewhere in Clinton or Upper Marlboro, MD. Both schools offered a better stock of students than mine—especially Douglass, that's one of the best schools in our county—and nether of the guys had 3 or 4 eyelashes clumped together!

UnPAiD JOb

My next unfortunate job was at **American Energy Corporation** as a telemarketer. You may have heard of them. They change names and items every several months—probably to avoid fraud charges and lawsuits. They try and sell everything; from windows to doors to what have you. They allegedly were going bankrupt and went out of business. Thus never paid me and probably a lie. Another joy!

COLLEGE DAYS

UnIvERsiTy oF MaRYlaNd EaSTeRn ShOrE (UMES)

After I graduated high school I went to UMES, the only university that accepted me after graduation because of my SAT score and high school GPA. It was a good school for agriculture or hotel restaurant management. I, however majored in geography at first—which they didn't quite have, then communications and theater—another subject they didn't have. The school didn't have much. I always enjoyed seeing and wanted to be in a marching band. UMES didn't even have a football team. It was a very small school way out in the middle of nowhere. It was surrounded by rednecks and a few stores that closed at dark. A ditch divided us imports, as one local called us, from the town. Everyone left on the weekends because the school had no real social activities. It is a good school to go to, to get away from everything. I, however, never been into anything and I wanted to live and enjoy life, not be trapped in the wilderness. The best thing about UMES was that it was away from home and there was no one from my high school there—thank God!

I remember one of the oh-so-lovely loser basketball players I met while visiting his roommate. He told me to screw him or leave. Since this was one of the first times I had such a rude comment come towards me, I automatically assumed he was just joking and being an A'hole. I gave him back a smart comment and laughed (with one of those nervous type laughs) and stayed there for another few hours. I was supposedly visiting his roommate who was a buddy of mine anyway. He tried to set me up with his non-game-winning roommate as he decided to go talk to this other girl. I guess it was some sort of double booty call, me and his pervert roommate and he and this girl. Well, I guess this shows that wherever you go, or at least where ever I go, I run into all types, styles, and forms of worthless jerks. As I always say, I must go to Europe or Africa to find my husband. With the exception of New York men, who don't like commitment, it's almost impossible for me to find a husband in the states.

FaGS, A HaG, & Va. BeAcH

While at UMES I met this guy who I'll call Dino, a friend I'll call JV, and his wild flamboyant friend, whom I'll call Torch. Dino took me to my first club. It was there that I met JV, who also went to UMES and lived on the campus. It was Trax, a gay club, on black gay night. It was my first time ever to go a nightclub, and I was fascinated. It was like a circus. They danced, pranced, vogued, did ballet, splits, hung from the ceilings and swung on the poles. The music was great and it was very fun. I asked why they were going crazy and getting the "Holy Ghost", he said, they are feeling the beat. From that point, I was addicted to Trax. Back at school Dino would experiment and do my make-up and hair.

JV and I went to Va. Beach, I however only had $5. He drove and once we got there he pumped gas while the car was on. That actually is dangerous and can make something explode, so I turned the car off. "Oh my gosh, why did you do that!" The car wouldn't start back up and we needed a hotel room for the night. I met many guys and they all wanted to come to my room.

Torch was just as festive and flamey as me. His mom said, I'm like a wild girl who's been contained all my life. What an excellent analogy, I couldn't put it better myself. Because most of the people I hung around—with the exception of TW, her boyfriend, and Shelly—and the places I went were gay, Torch called me a fag-hag, a hag that hangs out with fags.

NY & TrAiNhopPiNG

Me and a friend, whom I'll call TW, went to NY over the vacation to see her other boyfriend. While there, I successfully bought wine and drinks with no ID being that I was underage. We also had the unfortunate adventure of accidentally hopping the turnstile and being harassed, detained, and given a ticket, a fine, and a summons to the local court a few months later. Of course we never made it back to court or to see her boyfriend.

TouRMOBiLE & tHE bAR

My next job was a summer job in DC with TourMobile Sightseeing. I started off giving tours on the bus but ended up doing crowd control at Arlington National Cemetery tour bus boarding point. After work I would go to the bar with the other older co-workers and taste samples of sweet frozen cocktails. I would go to the bar at Union Station even though I was only 19 at the time. My mom got the whole family together to tell me to come home before midnight—my usual time home from work. I tried to lie and say it took me that long to come home even though work ended at 6pm. Unfortunately, they didn't go for that.

gREYHOUND bUS aND cA.

My next job was at Greyhound Bus. It was an easy job, I worked the night shift seeing all of the crazies and homeless visit the station. Sometimes I worked in the day passing out flyers and talking to people but the night shift was best. I would call my friends in other cities, talk to the other employees, and most of all, be entertained by all of the lunatics that visited the satiation overnight. Occasionally I would visit TW in Baltimore but my real trip was to Las Angeles. As usual, mom was scared for me to go. My dad was way more slack, like-minded, and relaxed with me. In fact, he was the one who took me to the station. He didn't want to hear mom fuss either, so he told me to leave her a note (as if that would make a difference). I left her a note before I left. My note said "I'm taking the 7pm bus to L.A. and I'll be back in 1 week" Mom asked daddy where I was and he said, "If she's not home by 11pm then she's somewhere in St. Louis, MO headed towards Ca." and mom started screaming.

It was a very fun trip on the bus from DC to LA and I saw many events:

- The crazy man from Mars, Pa. who knew Lonnie Anderson and walked from Tenn. to Pa. and was talking to himself.
- The man diving in the dumpster for trash like it was an Olympic diving contest
- No more blacks or big cities between St. Louis and LA.
- The broken hot bus in AZ full of flies and smokers that kept breaking down.
- And me bumming a ride to the UCLA media conference from the Mexican from NY.

The reason I went to L.A. in the first place was for this one-week media conference at UCLA. I had applied for this conference during that spring semester at UMES. The conference was for 1 week but I stayed for 3 weeks. The 1st week I stayed on campus at UCLA. The 2nd week, I was one of 7 people in a hotel room thanks to Missy from TX who worked for the hotel chain. The 3rd week Missy and I were taken in by this guy who let us use his car, showed us around, and gave us food and shelter. I stayed as long as I could so I could miss the beginning of school and transfer to another school. I finally left after mom told everyone I ran away from home and was lost in LA and having a "nervous breakdown." On the way back, I stayed overnight in St. Louis in route to DC and went up the Arches.

I was fired because I was supposed to be at work that Thursday—even though I was scheduled off for a week. I didn't call or show up until 1 month later. I had to duck and dodge and sneak pass my boss when I finally arrived in DC. When I left Greyhound I was forced to return to UMES.

hOWARD UNiV

The following semester I was finally able to transfer—being that I dropped all of my classes and only took some art classes. My dad was enraged and refused to pay for school the next semester. Since I am an only child and was still a minor, I didn't qualify for financial aid. My mom paid for my first semester at Howard Univ. fearing I was going to "run away" to some far off exotic place again. I lived at home but was never there. I had early classes so to assure I would make it to class on time, I crashed over different friends houses all of the time.

I met many people my first semester at Howard. I met this homeless girl from Ca. during homecoming and we went roaming around the Howard Inn like kids and crashed a banquet dinner. Big T and some other friends of mine met her. We all went out to eat and as usual I had no money and of course she didn't either. One friend bought me lunch and Big T bought his friend lunch. She said, "I can't believe you didn't buy me lunch!!" Big T said, "I can!!"

cHUrCH

I met some really nice people who were members of the Washington, DC chapter of the Church of Christ. This church is different than most churches. Like the Jehovah Witness, they recruit new members and go through this Bible study consisting of 9 or so lessons. Once they feel you thoroughly understand one lesson and you are obeying, they will advance you to the next lesson. Once you finish all the lessons, they baptize you and you are now a member of this church. Many people claim it's a cult. I can see why some may say that, but I feel they are actually practicing what they preach and are no more a "cult" than the Protestant, Catholic, Jewish, Muslim, or any other religion.

In fact, some of the nicest people I met, like my friend Angie (who I still try to keep in touch with today) are members of that church. I used to crash at their apartment all of the time so I would make it to class on time. They lived in the nicest dorms the university had and were very close to the School of Communications. In exchange of constant shelter, I let them use my car and I would drive them to the church meetings way out in Va.

gREAT aDVENTuRES aND N.Y.

I also met another wild girl, whom I'll call Wild D, whom like me, loves to travel at the drop of a dime, and is very wild. We went to NY one week when my mom went out of town and "left me the car." With poor priorities at that time and a major desire to take advantage of the 2-4-1 offer at Great Adventures Amusement Park in NJ, Wild D and I took to the road. I scavenged money from the many worthless men I knew at the time and Wild D did the same. While filling up the car for the road trip at this gas station in Md., I met a future roommate. As a courtesy service, he allowed us to "loot" and get chips, sodas, candy, and stuff, for free.   When we got to NJ we slept in the car at a parking lot and the next morning looked for the closest hotel. I told the maid, "My friend just checked out and left but I didn't get a chance to brush my teeth. I'm sorry, may I please brush them now?" The immigrant, who spoke no English, said yes. She probably didn't care, it wasn't cleaned yet and she had many more things on her mind (like a green card) and many more rooms to clean in the mean time.

Thanks to me, we had free hotel rooms to shower and change. Wild D, via her food stamps, was in charge of finding the 2-4-1 soda cans so we could get into the park and buy breakfast. At this mini mart type store the cashier told Wild D they didn't accept food stamps. Of course Wild D was loud and made an embarrassing scene stating that food stamps are good on food items at all stores nationwide. They consented and we got breakfast and the sodas. We also met some ragged rednecks there. They said their car broke down on the highway and the cops stopped them because they were walking to get help. How stupid, how else were they supposed to find help for their broken car?!

This is something cops are good at. It could be 10 robberies or fights and the cops are NOWHERE to be found. Don't dare pass a stop sign though, 5 cops will run to issue you a ticket. Yes, we have robbers, rapists, terrorists, kingpins, and crack heads lose, but you just turned without signaling correctly, or your head-lights are not properly aligned, so instead of us stopping crimes and making America safer, here is your ticket. No wonder America is so safe!

I'm sure the cops stopped and harassed them because they and their car were the same, dirty and smelly. Anyway, we offered to help them by driving them to their beat up old car on the side of the highway. They finally started it and they too were going to Great Adventures. They paid for our parking in exchange for our help and we offered to take them to NY if their car still wouldn't start. We also got into the park for free using our 2-4-1 soda cans and their full price tick-ets. They bought two tickets at regular price and got two free tickets for us.

What luck, free hotel for bathing, free food for breakfast, free parking, and free admission into the park. When we left we even ran into them and this time their car wouldn't start so we drove them to NY. They paid for gas and tolls in NJ but they didn't know how to get to their house in NY—go figure! At this point they smelled like cigarettes and puke from too much beer. I literally got a headache from smelling them. I held the magic tree incense to my nose the whole trip and Wild D kept laughing as she drove. We used up all of the gas we bought in NJ by the time we got to NY even though it only took 1 tank to go from VA to NJ. We passed several tunnels and bridges, all needing tolls that we didn't have money for. We ended up dropping them off on some street, I guess in Long Island, and left them there since they didn't know how to get home and we ran out of money trying to help them find their house.

Leave it up to Wild D to get something from a man, we stayed at some man's house that we didn't know. Wild D got his number and info from some man that flirted with her at the mall in MD while on our scavenger hunt for money before we left. He was really nice, gave us shelter, food, took us sightseeing and even gave Wild D some money for gas to return home. The damm winch spent it on some shoes. Once home we cleaned and washed mom's car and had it brand new when she finally returned home. Lucky I had some reserve money saved to get back home.

fREAKNiCK

Me, Wild D, Big T, and another friend named Roy, went to Atlanta for Freaknick. I thought it was Morehouse Univ.'s homecoming. Boy was I in for a shock and ill prepared. It was a super freak show exhibiting half-naked women and men following them with video cameras. I was ill prepared with wearing normal clothes and not having some scant hoochie momma outfit to amuse the boys.

This was another trip that I had a major pile of cash on me. I had my Chevron gas card, my visa card and $15 cash. Unfortunately, there were no Chevron stations on most of the trip. Also, Big T claimed to be mad at me because I had no money and threatened to leave me stranded at a truck stop if I didn't "find" some money. He was the one that convinced me to go to Atlanta in the first place. He rented a car and wanted as many people to go as possible to help defer the cost of the car. The car was rented for a few days. I told him I had no money, and for some other reason that I can't remember, I wasn't going to go. He knew I had no money. Anyone who hung out with me knew my budget—broke.

I used my credit card to pay for the hotel and some of the gas. Of course all hotel accommodations were full. Wild D and I were trying for the YMCA, which is cheap, but Big T, and Roy, wanted luxury accommodations. One hotel, ran by some Indians or Pakistanis, said they had one room, then Big T rudely asked how many roaches were there. They immediately said they were full, goodbye. We f-I-n-a-l-l-y found a room at some cheap motel.

pRANCiNG & mY cAR

By this time I had visited many clubs, being under 21 and having my fake I.D. stolen from me. I was a faithful and devoted member at Trax. It was, at that time, the best club by far!! Best music, DJ's, dancing, most fun, and loads of sexy men on "straight" night. I was obsessed at visiting Trax in hopes to find a faithful boyfriend and get my dance and grove on. Besides, dancing is the BEST exercise outside of walking. Anyone can do it. Not everyone can swim, climb mountains, and run. They take a definite level of skill or a lot of stamina and endurance—which I have nether of. And many of those cardio machines can be extremely boring without some blasting, up-tempo music to take your mind off of that exercise. Dance and aerobic classes are always way more exciting, and in this obese, super sized country, we need as much exercise as we can get!! Well anyway, Trax was even free for the first hour. I would go for free when it opened at 8pm and be one of the last to leave when it was about to close at 4am.

I met Lance on my weekly trips to Trax. He and the other "girls" would "walk the runway", march, prance, vogue, and twiddle. It was grand fun. The feminine girly lesbians were great dancers too. They would prance, twiddle, march, split, jump, and I would march, twiddle, and dance with them. I told Lance I knew him from somewhere. I think I was stranded and needed a way home; he however, didn't have a car at the time. He didn't even have a license. He offered me to crash at his house 'til morning, which was near the subway. This sometimes-straight girl and I stayed at his parent's house.

We began to always hang out together at Trax and drove around in my car. We would drive around after Trax with his drag queen friends and go to Denny's 24-hour cafe for breakfast. I supplied the car, he supplied the money and "queens". When we finished sometimes we would sleep in my car until mid morning at the mall parking lot. We were too tired to drive home.

I sometimes felt he was using me for my car and he sometimes felt I was using him for his money. One time he lied and said he had no money and we needed gas. I searched the whole car and all my pockets for money and after 5 or so minutes came up with $1.87. He gagged and laughed hysterically and pulled out a $5 to go along with it. He then realized how broke I really was.

One weekend we went over Miss Mousse' house so he could do my hair. Sometimes he and my other friends took charity in doing it, being that I am, unfortunately, plain and drab without make-up and my hair messed up (being that I can't do hair). My mom wasn't sure what Miss Mousse was, a horrible looking drag queen or funny looking man. Another time Lance and I went to Baltimore with this scary brute female and some drag queens. This horrible looking drag queen showed us some photos of some odd looking men in drag and he said, "some people aren't meant for this." Lance and I gagged and laughed because he wasn't meant for it either.

VolunTERring aT gALLAUDET

I met this girl named Marie and several of her friends from Gallaudet Univ. School for the Deaf, at Trax. Trax was an excellent club for them. In fact, it was an excellent club for anybody. The music was loud, bass really thumping, everyone wild and care free, and like the gays, they and I felt welcome and could enjoy ourselves just the way we are and dance. I would occasionally go there to meet them and hang out. I learned sign language just from hanging out with them. One time I saw a nice jacket from Gallaudet that said "Road Show". What … what is that?! I love to travel, dance, and perform. What is the Road Show? The Road Show was an after school club for the high school students. They would do theater and dances and travel to other schools to perform and educate others about deaf life. They even planned big trips for the summer like to Japan. He said they were always looking for volunteers and the volunteers could soon become an intern—thus free sign language classes, performing, and a chance to travel with them. I immediately called and started to volunteer.

THE LIST CONTINUES

CiRcUs jOB

Cirque du Solie was another job to add to my collection, however this was a fun one. I never heard of them before and they were hiring box office staff. I got a little money, got to see the excellent show "Saltibanco" and bought the tape.

wORLD oF ScIeNce

After the circus left I started to work at the mall next to where the circus was for Christmas help. Mind you it was 1000 miles away from my home in Northern VA.

99¢ MoVie

By now, I had finished my 4th year at Howard. Of course I hadn't graduated yet. I lost over a year's credit hour from UMES when I transferred and changed my major to radio-TV-film with a minor to theater. Remember, UMES didn't have anything close to those majors and my last semester there I dropped all of my important classes, thusly my dad refused to send me back and my mom got me into Howard. My dad kept yelling I'm only going to pay for four years. The reason he liked UMES, it was cheap, we were Md. residents so it was even cheaper—I'm an only child so we didn't get any financial aid. My aunt even joined in on his argument demanding I over load the classes, stop partying, and go to summer school to graduate on time. Graduation is important to them and a degree is important for doctors, lawyers, and such. For many majors like computer programming, theater, music, radio, et cetera, a degree isn't as important as the skills—and more so, connections that you have. It's who and what you know, not how many degree's you have. Well I finished my 4th year and didn't graduate and was very broke. I needed a job so I got a somewhat embarrassing, very easy, laid back, low paying job at the 99¢ movies down the street from my house. It wasn't as embarrassing as a McDonald's drive through, but nowhere near as prestigious or lofty as some cushy desk job.

KiNko's

This is the next in my list of jobs. I was hired on the spot to work the night shift for little money. My boss was the spawn of Satan. Everyone who worked with him cursed him out, quit, or transferred. No one would work with him and the customers dreaded him. This low paying job however helped me get an abode with my lovely rabbit Fufu. I got Fufu over spring break my second year at UMES. While working at Kinko's, I was able to move into this room in this really nice apartment. It was a huge room with a separate A/C—heater set. I had my own bathroom and dressing area, and because of me and my roommates' different schedule, it basically seemed like it was only me. I soon moved from the nice apartment, which was very expensive. I moved into a cheaper, more meager apartment with the gas station guy I met when Wild D and I went to NY and Great Adventures.

NY oN nEW yEARS eVE

I went to NY for New Years Eve and stayed with my old roommate from UMES. I rode Greyhound up and back and went to her cousin's club. I partied all night, took the train to the Greyhound bus station, in DC took the subway to Rockville Metro Station, and made it back in time for work! We did inventory on New Years Day, the only day Kinko's was closed outside of Christmas and Thanksgiving. The most amazing part about this is that I struggle with arriving to work, class, or events on time and I made it all the way from NYC to my job in Md. on time! Sheer amazement!!!

ADVENTURES WITH SWAUTCH

Via one of the guys I used to talk to at Trax, I was introduced to Swautch. We spoke on the phone many times about the music business. He worked for a label, and the mutual friend knew I wanted to do music. After many phone conversations mostly about music I finally met him on the 4th of July. Like Wild D and I, he was a wild one. I met many performers, musicians, and did many wild things with him.

He was the only one who could successfully sneak into movies with me and was good at getting free stuff—movies, food, and clothes. We would go to clubs, movies, and concerts and find ways to get in free. We went to the black people awards and scavenged free food from the vendors there like Pizza Hut, Taco Bell, and the many free cans and bottles of sodas. I got a bag full of sodas and ate like a pig. He, like a fool, filled an empty crate with bottles and cans of soda. We would go to hotels and go to the VIP lounge and get free food and drinks. He knew where the free employee kitchen was, where you could eat all you want. Of course, you're supposed to be an employer. We ate free meals compliments of the hotel employee kitchen. One of the first times we went to a hotel was to get money from the tampon machine for gas. While there he opened a fridge and saw—actually smelled before he saw—some rotten smelly food. It was hilarious.

I met many people through and with him. We met this stinky male prostitute/homeless man one time. We called him Al B Stink because he looked a little like Al B Sure. Swautch rudely put Mr. Smelly in my car trying to be funny and set me up with him. Another time we saw this homeless lady for Swautch and a drunken smelly Puerto Rican for me. The Puerto Rican was actually nice looking—needed a scrub bath, but handsome. I didn't smell him, he was on the passenger side, Swautch can't drive and has no license.

Another guy Swautch introduced me to was this supposed producer. Believing him and giving him the benefit of the doubt, I went to his studio one night. He said he was having a late session, and any musician knows that you're not a true musician until you've done several all niters. So, I went to meet him at his studio during one of his late sessions. His luxurious studio was state of the art all right. He rented a room in this old house with these wild girls and giant, dangerous, flesh eating pit bulls and rockweillers. He had state of the art sound equipment—circa 1982—and a Mr. microphone he got from Sears or some thrift store. He was a decent DJ and had skills spinning records but his music producing skills I listened to were of 1983. To make a long story short, he ended up wanting sex instead of making beats. He, of course, told Swautch that I was scared of his man, which was a lie. I'm not scared of sex, I was scared of those dangerous dogs. I do, however, have standards and refuse to put out after only knowing someone for a few hours. Of course, I was mad that Swautch set me up with another peasant.

KiKi & pOWDER eVERYWHERE

My cousin Re had a baby, whom I'll call KiKi. When she was about 2 years old, I babysat her. With my excellent skills at babysitting, I left her in my aunt's room while I took a shower. She saw the powder I used the day before and decided to use it while I showered. When I came out, there was powder everywhere. The room was covered with powder. I tried to quickly clean up before my aunt returned but she still knew I made a big mess babysitting.

MY WORLD AT DISNEY

My next job was one I tried to get every semester in college. It was a paid internship at Disney. Interns were provided housing and got to meet people from all over America and overseas—they worked at EPCOT's international pavilions. I worked at a dinner theater at Disney/MGM Studios. It was a great job, internship, and experience, and I actually needed an internship to graduate from Howard.

While at Disney World I lived with 5 other girls. Two girls were from Utah, they were really cool. They were one of the first people to call me Hippie. My 2nd cousin called me a "Modern day hippie". My cousin said that only a modern day hippie would buy a car while I only had a part time job in Fl., get personalized plates, and still have those personalized Fl. plates after returning home to DC over 2 years later. Well anyway, one day we all went to Daytona Beach and I fed the seagulls. They were very hungry and very happy that I gave them some food. One of the girls got upset because there was a flock of birds hanging around our blanket. My roommate was from S.C. She was cool too. The other 2 housemates were from Atlanta and went to Tuskegee Univ.

2 Fat 4 Mickey

!!WARNING!!

DON'T READ THIS UNLESS YOU DON'T MIND KNOWING A
PROFOUND SECRET!!

Now I DID warn you!! For those of you who may not have known, Mickey isn't real! Now that we have that out of the way, on with the story. While at Disney I auditioned several times for Mickey. They always look for short people under 5' for Mickey and tall people over 6' for Goofy. I always passed the height—I'm short—and dancing part of the audition but never got the part. One of the ladies who hosted the audition finally told me after my umpteen audition, that I was too fat and busty. Mickey doesn't have any breast nor hips and the costumes are a size 4/6. I've, unfortunately, always been fat.

HoW BackWaRds CaN PeOplE GeT?!

The 2 Atlanta housemates enjoyed cooking and could cook really well. One even helped me buy my current car. One of their friends was this guy with an OK looking face and a tall, dark, slim, solid body. Outside of a nice looking body, he was an official A'hole. They were having a party at his house. It was his first or maybe second time talking to me. He "requested" services from me. When I refused—similar to the pervert from UMES my first semester freshman year—he boasted on how so many girls wanted him and how they would line up for sex with him. That I should be proud and fortunate that he was giving me this opportunity. Then he accused me of having a color complex and that the reason I refused him was cause of his skin. He even challenged me on the issue with my 2 housemates from Atlanta.

I know and understand us up here in the North Atlantic states are backwards, but I was surprised by how much. I guess only those keen, diverse, residents from the mid-west and south truly know and understand true beauty. NOT!!! These girls actually deciphered and analyzed everyone's skin tone and color like a pro. You are 2.5 shades darker than me and she is 1.3 shades darker than you. He has exactly 482 more pigment cells in his skin than us. Wow! Not even seasoned cosmetologist can do that. Perhaps professional dermatologists and cosmetologist who make foundation and make-up learn such anatomy, but these backwards-southern hicks don't. They are just stuck in a reality that was played out in the early 1980's up here in the north.

> Of course, I'm so non-observant, I got a friend's cousin—who she claims is damn near white—mixed up with her sister's ex, who is tan. I even mixed her ex up with her friend when I first met them. Her ex is much darker and WAY taller than her friend, who is almost my height—I guess near midget status. Although I might make an excellent music copyright researcher because I can connect melodies and rhythms to many other similar songs easily; I'd make a horrible detective or person sent to find people or cars. I forget what a person wore the second they leave my sight and always forget what someone's car looks like, let alone the make and model. Unfortunately, I'm very non-observant and horrible at picking up sighs.

PERHAPS PICKY, BUT NEVER INDECISIVE

Anyone who really knows me however knows that skin tone, hair texture, language, and even ability does not determine what turns me on. I am attracted to a solid, vascular, body, a slim, narrow, strong, solid face with a defined jaw line and muscles. And in most cases, dark thick eyebrows and eyes, dark hair, and a long, Roman nose. Also someone subtle who's non-perverted and non-aggressive. Someone who's gentle, fun, and romantic who enjoys driving and doing cultural things and fun activities.

I may be picky, but I know **exactly** what I want and like. Something that he was not in the least! By the way, I had no more dealings with him either, and mutually, he had no more business with me.

One may call me picky, but I know exactly what I want. I'm the **extreme opposite** of those indecisive people who are never sure what they really want and take forever making decisions. I, unfortunately, never take time when I do decide, making quick decisions without fully thinking it all through. Especially if it's something I want and been working hard to achieve. Even when I go out to my favorite places like Cheesecake Factory and such, I buy my usual. Like the $14 salad or $12 shrimp scampi. I never order the special of the day or the listed price. It may be delicious, but since I'm not a gambler, I always go for the sure thing and get what I came for and want.

People say be careful what you ask for, you just may get it. Or people never know what they want, they're so indecisive. Not me! I am one person who knows EXACTLY what I want. I never feel bad for getting something that I requested or asked for. It may not be as good, special, or easy as I may have hoped for or liked it to be, but I still take it and go. Japan, Greyhound, Howard Univ., even Disney, nothing is perfect, but I accept it happily and go. I guess whoever got the Japan job—since I was picked as an alternate—was not sure what they wanted and decided at the last minute to cancel. Thanks, now I have your opportunity.

If I ask for it, I DEFINATELY want it!! Whether it's a man I'm interested in, a job,—both which seem to always change for the worse—a career, an opportunity, a class, a university, whatever. Never say never, but I can almost 99.95% say that I would NEVER be that person that request something or someone and not want it. Most likely, it was that person who had split personalities and changed, NOT me not realizing what I wanted. If someone or some place presents itself as ABC, and when you get there or finally get them, they become 123, they changed—not you. They were a false advertisement!! They claimed they were one thing, then when you get them or it, they switch, like a demon possessed, and become something totally different!

CRAZY JOURNEY HOME

I bought My Friend, a 3 cylinder Geo Metro, while there. When my internship finished at the end of the semester I needed to find someone to help me drive My Friend home. Wild D refused to come saying she was broke and couldn't afford to pay my way home nor afford getting stuck in Fl. and getting fired from her job.

Disney's housing is for interns only. Some French girls let me stay a week with them. If you are caught with someone in your place, you and all of your house-mates could get fired—assuming they're in on it since they didn't tell on you. Of course, none of the girls wanted to risk this. I stayed in the youth hostel in Fl. I met many more foreign visitors while there. When money was short, however, I slept in My Feather AKA My Friend, but it was freezing outside. This was one of the coldest winters Fl. has ever had. It was 30° in the Fl. Keys!! There were big ice and snowstorms along the East Coast and even the airports, bus, and train stations closed down from the ice storm. No one from DC could get to Fl. to help me drive back.

TriP tO nEW oRLEANS

A "friend" from New Orleans had been inviting me to visit her since she moved down there and said she would help me. I met this German at the youth hostel, and together we drove to New Orleans. Like many liars who offer you food, shelter, or invite you somewhere and don't expect you to take them up on the offer, she did the same. She was in no condition to invite people. She lived with her grandmother in a crowed house.

tHE cOVENANT hOUSE

Of course she didn't help me drive home either. She did, however, introduce me to the Covenant House, a homeless shelter for youth. There I stayed, ate, and got clothes for free. I even went to the first day of Mardi Gras. Of course it was small and not like the last day of Mardi Gras, big, wild, and exciting.

While there I met a toothless hillbilly who helped me drive home. He was a compulsive liar. He said he was married, had some kids, the wife and kids died, he was truck driver, he was broke, he was Native American, and many more stories. He was a good driver and he didn't rape or chop me up, so I was satisfied, and so was my mom. In fact, he drove most of the way and My Feather got from New Orleans to DC via Nashville, TN on less than $60 worth of gas.

En-route we visited Opryland, the Country Music Museum, the Gaylord Opryland Hotel and Resort, and we were even guests on a talk show by Bo Duke of the Dukes of Hazard show. We did all of this for free. I think you get charged when you drive up to park at Opryland, but we somehow got around that. We got free food from this food kitchen/church. We even got some gas money from this church in Va. I really wanted to visit my uncle down in the country since we passed his town on the route from TN to DC.

When we arrived back we stayed at home then we went to my aunts home where we visited my favorite club, Trax. While at Trax on gay night, the Hillbilly met some men who offered services that he was interested in. While some clubs had closed, others changed. Trax changed too—it was not as wild and thus less fun.

The hillbilly was supposed to paint my aunt's house and get paid for it. He painted one room and while I was in the bathroom, he roamed around the house and found my aunts money and stole it. He ran out the back door and disappeared. When I left the bathroom I looked for him, not realizing what he did, and drove around the area. When I returned a cop came and asked what happened. Shocked I said nothing. He knew someone ran out the back door and a neighbor saw this ragged white boy run out my aunt's back door and immediately called the cops. When my aunt came home I didn't know what to say so I didn't say anything. She knew what had happened, the neighbor told her. I stayed for a month or so, wore out my welcome—and made a big mess.

EVER CONSTANT EMPLOYMENT TRIALS

Being that I am poor and underemployed, I diligently seek for a job. I even retry Kinko's, Greyhound and many hotels and restaurants. No one would hire me. These stupid hotels and companies would rather hire someone who has no skills and worked for 2+ years as a janitor than someone who has many skills and worked on many jobs and assignments performing the duties of the positions they are hiring for, but for only a few months each. Unfortunately, I never had a job for over a year. Like most artists, actors, musicians, dancers, and so forth, they try to find a job in their field but keep their "day job" until they make it big. Usually their day job consists of coffee bars and waiting tables. In fact, many of my friends are like me, only keeping a job for a few months. The longest that I have ever kept a job before I was rudely and unfairly fired or quit was 9 months. *I eagerly await an anniversary, in employment and marriage!!*

For some reason, unlike my cousin and some lucky people, every job I get seems to not be satisfied with me nor appreciate me. Only a few jobs (and as of now, absolutely NO man) seem to appreciate me such as Disney where I worked on Thanksgiving, Christmas, and New Years while others called in sick; and Greyhound, after the horrible manager—who gave me a hard time daily even though he was the one who hired me—was fired and before I "abandoned my job". Seems like if I don't quit because I don't like the job and I want to stay, they try to fire me and give me a hard time for one reason or another. This is the reason I want a house to rent out rooms so I can live in my own house "for free" thanks to the tenants. I can do like another friend who's an artists and wants to direct theater. Like her, I can do my music and theater full time and not worry or depend on those jobs that don't want me in the first place.

Well anyway, in my pursuit for employment, I landed a low paying part-time job at a gym where I could use the facilities for free. Of course, like almost every job I get, it's nowhere near my abode.

KiKi aND pOPCORN

By this time KiKi was 4 and I again had the pleasure of watching her. Of course she thoroughly enjoyed me watching her because we would play together. I was more like her friend over a babysitter. She would ask mom, "Where is your little girl?" referring to me. Well this day she wanted some popcorn. She tricked me and said she knew how to work the microwave and cook the popcorn. I remember Re cooking popcorn the old style way with oil and a big pot on the stove as a kid. I thought she was about the same age, 5 or so. Besides, microwaves are easy, all you do is push buttons.

Well she went into the kitchen to cook the popcorn and I didn't follow behind her because I figured she knew how to cook it. About 6 minutes later I smelt this horrible burnt popcorn smell. I rush to get the burnt charred popcorn. She had the microwave set for 20 minutes. I told her to go out side and eat it because it stunk. Well, when my aunt and Re returned home, they were upset and wondered how a 4-year-old could trick me into letting her make popcorn.

KiKi anD WiG

By now I moved in with Re at the request of my aunt. My purpose was to help Re with rent and to baby-sit KiKi. Of course KiKi was ecstatic with this. My toys and me came to spend the night and play. KiKi and I watched TV and KiKi would play hair salon and pretend to do my hair, make-up, and nails. I had this wig—that I thought was pretty—and she wore it and some lipstick. I thought she looked cute. Well, like on several other occasions, I was late leaving the apartment to drop off KiKi to Re. When we arrived, Re was upset to see her child walking around the street with a wig on, Halloween wasn't until Oct. She took off the wig and threw it in my car and was mad because KiKi's hair was sticking up like a Pickaninny doll and I didn't comb it (that's because she wore the wig).

I'm still underemployed and poor. I still have my part time, low paying job at the gym and I got another part time, embarrassing job as a giant coffee cup for publicity and promotion for this coffee shop. I would wear this hot costume and pass out flyers on the sidewalks. I also had this part time job as a dancer (that's why I had the wig) where I made my own schedule, worked at will, and got paid in tips only. My purpose for living with Re was to help her with rent and KiKi. Of course when rent was due I was short on cash so I gave Re food stamp for rent, of course she was pleased and I then needed to find another abode.

dRAGON Thief

My next abode was with Ms. Anthony, this fat, so-called butch, gay man who cooks very well and sings in falsetto at gay clubs. He would bring home trade and strays. One night this dragon came and Anthony gave me his money and told me to hide it in my room. He didn't trust his company. At that time, I would always leave my backpack with all of my books, clothes, and car keys in the living room so I can quickly get it when I leave. I should have used common sense and put my bag in my room after he gave me his money and said he didn't trust the thief. I was half sleep when he came in so I was thinking less sharp than usual—if that's even possible.

The next morning the thief cleaned house. He stole his radio, wine, food, vitamins, my bag, and used my car as a get away. I immediately called the cops, searched for My Friend, and prayed to God for help. I remember he said the thief lived on Atlanta St. I searched for over 2 hours, and just when I was about to give up, I prayed again, and BAM, there was the street. I drove up the street and found My Friend, in one piece with a fake tag. I immediately took My Friend and returned Re's car she let me use to find mine.

GOD'S HELP

They say God looks out for the old, babies, and retarded. I'm not sure where I fall in here but I obvious have angels with me as I unwilling get into all sorts and forms of crap. God and the angels definitely work overtime to hinder the forces of darkness around me. GOOD LOOKING OUT and JOB WELL DONE!! I'm not very religious and quite unrighteous, but God always helps me out when I need Him. Unfortunately, He doesn't answer every prayer and give me everything I want (such as a husband) like He's some heavenly flea market, but He helps me out when I'm distressed and when I'm down and out.

One time at Trax I had my nice leather coat with my car keys in the pocket with me. These Indian co-conspirators kept talking to me and this white slut was all friendly and kept complimenting my coat. Like a dummy, I didn't take my coat off of the bench and hide it; I kept it there and kept listening to the camel thieves. When I turned around, the white tramp and her camel friends left with my coat. I ran out looking for her and ran around the club. Just as I prayed to God to help me find my coat, I walked out the door and I found the slut. She was in the passenger's seat of this jeep that pulls up to the light. I opened the door— which just so happened to be unlocked—and yelled give me my coat as I snatched it from her. In fact I was coming from a Church of Christ meeting and a friend told me to go home and get some sleep. I, however, was fiending Trax.

$200 fouND

A few days before I was to leave for Japan I decided to go to the mall for some last minute shopping. My dad told me to stay and finish packing but I urgently needed some blistix and certain clip-on earrings that only a few stores sold. I went to the mall and I stupidly put my four $50 bills inside my bra. Normally that should hold it but for some stupid reason, it didn't. After walking through the mall to the boutique to buy my jewelry, I shockingly realized my money fell! Oh my God!! Where is my money? $200 cash is a HORRIBLE thing to lose! I immediately went searching retracing my steps, of course to no success. I finally decided to ask the info desk if anyone just so happened found and turned in lost cash. I mean, what are the chances of that, 1 in a billion? I have a better chance of losing weight and marring a sexy, rich, husband over someone turning in found cash. I mean, there's no wallet to trace to contact me with. No credit card to can-cel. What are the chances of this happening?! Well the lady asked me how much and I told her. She then called security and they escorted me to the back of the mall to their office. Their boss asked me how much and in what denominations.

Confused, I told him four $50 bills. He said that some man found it on the floor and turned it in to the info booth, who then called them. Oh my God!! Some honest person turning in my money?! And then the employees honestly returning it to me as well!! Now ANYONE can tell you that THIS IS A TRUE MIRI-CLE!!

wHeeL tuRniNg

When I first got my license, I would skip school and drive around, as I mentioned elsewhere in this book. I took drivers education and practiced parking with my dad. I drove on the highway once during drivers' ed. and usually only drove around town. Once I **stupidly** decided to get on Interstate 495 to go somewhere. When I tried to merge onto the highway, an 18-wheeler was rushing right behind me to turn the car and me into a pancake. All I heard was this loud truck horn. Startled, frozen, and shocked, I simply stared in the rearview as this huge truck rushed toward my back. As I sat there frozen, the wheel magically snatched and turned for me to get out the way and drive safely home. 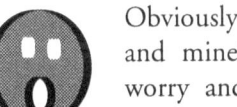 Obviously some invisible force helped save the car's life and mine!! Of course, I never told my parents so they could worry and be upset at me for hooking school and driving in the first place.

stOLeN baCkpAck

When I worked in Florida I met these 2 lovely Latino A'holes who decided to toss my bag out their car window when I forgot it in their car. As usual, they lied and said that we would go to the movies or somewhere, and of course, lied and simply begged for sex. When I constantly refused and was irritated when they refused to show respect and even take me wherever they claimed they would, they happily kicked me out the car and lost my number. Most likely, I lied about inviting them over to my place to relax and unwind simply to get them to take me home. Once they saw the security gate and guard, they happily kicked me out. They kicked me out so quickly, I stupidly forgot my bag. I called them a million times for it. It had no money—as usual—and absolutely nothing of worth for them but everything of importance for me. I had my license, Disney ID, clothes, everything I needed. They refused to return my call. They kindly, like the A'holes they were, tossed my bag out the window in some Florida neighborhood. I tried to figure out how to get inside the theme park and clock in without my ID. A week or so later my roommate said some lady called saying she had my bag. What? What lady and where is she? Go figure, she was visiting her mom and saw my bag lying in the street. When she left her mom's house late that night, my bag was still lying in the street. She decided to pick it up and discovered that it belonged to a Disney employee. She also worked at Disney and was able to return my bag, with all of my ID's and female stuff in it, safe and sound. What a coincidence.... or is it?

$120 rEfuNdeDS

Another miracle was with Bank of America, which is the hallmark of corporate greed. Being that I constantly get bombarded with overdraft fees and bounced checks, I help make millions for that bank. Seems like once a month I get some damn fee. Well, this is no exception. I had this rental car and I wanted to pay in cash. I told the idiots to not charge me until I get there to pay. Since I never showed up, they decided to charge me, which of course, I didn't have all the funds for. I complained and complained about it and told them to refund my fee. I also called the stupid bank to dispute the charge.

I was in an accident and this was an insurance rental I got through the insurance company. (I'll explain later on in this book) The insurance company told me to use this rental company that they work with. The insurance company was mailing me a check and was going to pay them the entire amount for my rental. Since it was through *their* insurance company that they obviously work through and for, I really don't know why they figured their insurance company wouldn't pay them.

It was through that insurance money that I got My Feather repaired from the accident and got my rental. The rental company obviously was not in good communication with the insurance company. Not my fault. The rental company did finally credit my $30 fee, but it was way after I called and disputed it with the stupid bank. Of course, the shiftless bank operator refused to process my dispute at the time to restore my account. Because of her, I got $120 worth of fees! I bought gas, got some coffee, and withdrew $20 from my account. Money that WOULD be there if they DID THEIR JOB AND REFUNDED MY MONEY. Being that they didn't do their job, I had a rack of fees. Technically it was my fault but I did call to dispute that charge.

When I found that my balance was -$130 I immediately called and complained about the fees. Normally, they would greedily refuse to budge and adjust absolutely anything. Amazingly—especially since this happens all too often—they refunded every overdraft fee and the initial charge. I ended up with my usual $75 or so in my account. The reason I say this is a miracle is because getting money and refunds from them is like drawing water from a rock. If I beg, plead, and moan, they MIGHT refund one fee. To refund all four is a miracle from God, not the grace of the bank.

God has also helped and protected me through various mishaps and problems. I am the QUEEN of BAD LUCK but I got this unexpected money for school after they told me I didn't qualify for it. I slipped through the insurance cracks from a car accident. I was even able to save wear and tear on My Feather via a 3-week rental (that I just spoke about) and carpooling to Baltimore with a student who needed extra credit.

When my money seemed to vanish, like David Copperfield, I received a very personal, direct, and exact message while watching a TV evangelist. His show focuses on faith seeds and tithing. I did it because I had nothing else to lose. I asked for a decent job to pay off my debts. I tried it while living in Va. and 8 months later, I landed a job in Japan paying off all of my debt and saving enough money to live off when I returned, as I will mention later in the book.

I did the first faith seed while I was living with this peasant named Eyepatch. Outside of the rack of long distance calls to some trailer park and him not having money for his half of rent nor the phone bill, he AMAZINGLY paid his part of the rent to the landlord. This act of grace and magic is obviously only the result of God. For him paying rent is as likely as a water jug paying for my gas. Because that TV program produced positive results, I always try to watch his show. It was during this TV program seemingly directed towards me that 3 wood chip men appeared on the wood of my door. I even got free food and five dollars just by reading the Bible. I'll explain this later too.

dAVE—N—bUSTER

My next job was at Dave-N-Busters. It's a themed entertainment center and restaurant for adults, like a Chuck E Cheese for adults. I was hired on the spot for this low paying job. I worked in the motion theater and in the midway trying to get people to play the different games. This was another job that wasn't satisfied with me for who knows why and after a few months they fired me. I applied for unemployment. I should be an honorary member of the unemployment office, even though they refused to give it to me. Even if I got it, it wasn't enough to buy a pair of shoes. That was supposed to be my month's salary.

BACK AT HOWARD

At this point, I'm at my wits end in my job search and about to consider the military since they pay for food, shelter, and college. They tone you up—being that I'm still fat after years of countless efforts—and you can travel the world for free. Of course I overlooked all of the negative points. I wanted to study and learn computer programming and foreign languages. An aunt on my dad's side somehow found out about me being at my wits end and about to consider the military, and decided to help me finish school by paying for it. So, I return to college. Being that I've been on my own for several years I qualified for finical aid and thus used loan and grant money to pay for the nice housing that I used to crash in during my first tour of duty at Howard.

NY TriP & cOAT

As always, there is an adventure and a story with Swautch. As stated before, I recently returned to Howard. Before Howard moved me into the lovely apartment style dorms that I used to crash in, they briefly stuck me in this disgusting, supposedly upper-class, "freshman" dorm—far way from campus. Actually you could walk, but it was a hike, especially at night through such lovely and safe crack head neighborhoods and parks. They had a shuttle bus to transport student to and from campus, but it runs just as frequently as the maintenance man works at my current residence. It was supposed to have A/C, I just couldn't feel it. Most of the students were on the meal plan because the kitchen was so luxurious. There was an old, disgusting kitchen for the entire floor. That was my biggest argument, I need a kitchen. I had my private half bathroom but like the kitchen, the shower was for the floor also. The pipes stank of I guess some form of rust. I really never could identify that smell. Someone told me it was of old pipes. Perhaps they're right. My room was as large as my room at home, a closet. I was counting the days before I moved out. They even had someone at the front desk "protecting" us, against the crack heads I guess. They wouldn't receive your packages, however. I stayed there a total of one month, if that long. After that, I started my usual complaining, nagging, and begging to be transferred to a more appropriate dorm for my style and stature, the lovely apartment style dorms.

During that month in squalor, I got to know the girl across the hall. I was telling her my current troubles with men and in particular, this Turk I was dealing with. For some reason, I keep them foreign. Well Swautch told me of the Jamaican/Caribbean day festival in NY. Now for me, I need absolutely NO reason to go to NY. The fact that NY exists is good enough for me. Like going to the mosque with my previously Muslim cousin, I seem to meet sexy men there. Both the mosque and NY offer men containing high levels of sexiness. Of course I'm ready to go, but of course I didn't want to drive. I already had parking problems with my delicate car in this ragged dorm. A friend of Swautch with a car drove and we met some friend of his in NY.

Once there, he parked in front of the usual looking row of old brownstones and told us to wait. Being that he left us in the car forever, Swautch, my neighbor, and I got out to find him. Being that every building looks the same, we split up and simply started knocking on doors. The first few buildings we went to were the wrong building. We finally encountered on a door that actually opened. Once inside it seemed like some storage. My neighbor realized that it was a store. I decided to help myself to a nice pleather jacket and left. I immediately put it in the car. By this point Swautch saw my prize and wanted one too. The guy finally returned. They insisted that I show them this store. We took them to it but now someone decided to come to work, after leaving the back door open for our convenience. "Can I help you?" "Oh we're lost, sorry." To bad for them. We ended up staying at some guy's house. We went to the Caribbean Festival the next day, and—like usual Swautch style/or my style—we got separated from each other. And to tell you the truth, I can't even remember how we finally met up. Perhaps via this BBQ my neighbor and I crashed. Swautch and his friend must have walked pass us en-route to the car.

WOL RaDio cO-hOST

That summer I volunteered as an on-air co-host at a popular AM talk radio station. Not an official internship nor job. I worked the night shift so the day staff never saw nor really met me, so I was able to talk on the radio for several months as an on-air co-host.

aDVENTURES witH SwauTch

Leave it to Swautch to find clever ways to assist me sneaking into events. Movies, clubs and local events and gatherings were low scale and easy to get into. He passed out flyers and tapes to the bouncers and they let us in. Most theaters that have the best movies—at least the ones we like—have thugs and hoodlums as their main customer base. On a weekend night, the employees and security are busy looking for potential fights, they totally overlook a single girl or puny boy. After all, what female goes to the movies on the weekend alone and what can some punk looking, puny little boy do?

Some of the bigger and more prestigious and enjoyable events were the circus festival, black broadcasters gala, and Latino awards. The circus festival, being held at the Kennedy Center, was officially free, fun, and full of performers to network with. There was this hot dog stand where the man decided to leave the cart unattended so we,—the parents, kids, and hungry public—decided to happily help ourselves to some tasty hotdogs and drinks, compliments to the shiftless worker. Afterwards, Swautch and I went to the employee picnic, which offered more food, drinks, and fun. That night, I viewed an excellent play; again, what female would go the theater alone?

Swautch massively exaggerates. He would have people believing he was some big time, huge, million-dollar record producer. Actually, he was an intern at a big record label and thus was supposed to work at this really popular hippie rock festival sponsored by a major radio station. Of course he didn't work but "gave me permission" to work in his place. When the officials found out that I wasn't an intern they freaked saying I was an insurance liability. He got in trouble and actually got mad and tried to blame me for him losing his internship. He even had the nerve not to talk to me for a while, which was fine. I had many things to do and business to take care of anyway!!

I guess he got over his anger when he needed a favor from me, i.e. a ride somewhere. We went to the official Latino awards also at the Kennedy Center. It was a black tie event with an expensive ticket and many famous Latino's like Sheila E, Edward James Olmos, and so forth. Of course we went, ate, listened to music, collected sodas, and drank on the house. We also went to a major function held for black owned broadcasters, which had many famous people like Stevie Wonder, Quincy Jones, and the likes. The event was held in this ritzy hotel. We decided to happily grant Mr. Wonder with our presence in the penthouse suite for his after party. There we ate, drank, and collected more goods. Compliments of alcohol, we did some major networking with the drunken industry buffs as they happily gave out business cards and private numbers. This is something they would never do in sound mind!

LIFE AFTER GRADUATION

After 5 1/2 years of school and almost a decade of time, I finally graduated from Howard. The year and a half of living for free, compliments of my mom, my aunt, and money from Uncle Sam—which I still owe a lot on—has ended. I must change my mode from classes, gym,(and another unsatisfactory attempt to lose weight) and trying to perform; to finding a job to pay my massive pile of bills and finding an abode with a working shower and air condition since my parents refuse to fix theirs.

Sign LANG CLASS

Thanks to all of my volunteering at Gallaudet University's theater department and deaf dance theater rehearsals, I've earned enough volunteer credit for several sign language classes. Finally, I was able to do basic communication. With the exception of 2 or so friends who are completely deaf, most deaf people—like most Latinos that know more than 50 words of English—insist on talking to me in English. They find it easier to speak, no matter how limited their speaking ability, than sign slowly or repeat what they said more than once. Thusly I learned more sign language from my one deaf friend over one weekend, than all of the time I volunteered at Gallaudet.

UNiVErSOuL

This is another one of the million jobs I had. I sold toys and tickets for another circus, the Universoul Circus. This was also a fun job. This is the all black circus. This job was actually held near my apartment in MD.

tHE rENEGADE

While returning from sign language class one day, I saw this wild looking man on the train wearing a hard hat and a shirt with so many holes in it, it could have been one of those male stripper tops where you gently pull and it comes ripping off. A few strings were holding the shirt together. He was cock diesel. I asked what time it was in Spanish. He looked Latino; in fact, he looked like a black Latino mixture of Sylvester Stallone and Bruce Springsteen. Go figure? Well he obviously didn't understand Spanish, he yelled, "Huh?" real loud. I repeated myself and he yelled, "Huh?" again. I asked in English and he wildly told me the time. Perhaps he was drunk. We got off at the same stop. I asked what he did and he replied he supports the arts. I thought Wow! I need some help, money, and support. I asked how he supports the arts and what type and style of art. He replied, "I support the arts by working. I'm an artist and I work to make money to support myself." How hilarious.

We were supposed to hang out on the 4th of July but I had to work at the circus. The number he gave me wasn't a good number either. I left a message the first time but when I called again a lady answered and said she didn't know him. I threw his number away. A week or so later he called and claimed he went to the beach with a friend and a whore and got stranded and arrested. He said he had a horrible time. He said the lady on the phone was his friend's girl who doesn't like him. We went out to this hunky tonk rock and roll club full of bikers. That's when I found out that he was divorced with 2 kids and quite older than me. I already have baggage of my own; I definitely don't need any one else's. Besides, he profusely kept saying how he wanted nothing to do with a relationship, only friendship. When I met him at his apartment complex he was swimming in the shallow fountain meant for decoration. He was wild, funny, and looked like a wild renegade that jumped out of a manhole and fell out of a tree. From then on, I called him Renegade.

BeLieF OUNCiNg mE oUT & aTHSMUS

Another old friend from elementary school got an apartment with me. Like a fool I should have waited until I had a good job but I was hot, needed a shower, and my own place, so I rushed into it. Being broke and underemployed, the deposit and first month's rent came from Uncle Sam's remaining loan to me. The next month's rent came from the few wages from the circus and money from graduation gifts.

She and her friends smoked like dragons and my bronchitis returned from childhood. I had no idea what was wrong. I was short of breath daily and my chest hurt. I went to the hospital. Having no insurance I used Renegades address (which I got wrong) and told them I was homeless (which was almost true). They gave me a chest x-ray and said bronchitis, stay away from smoke.

Well my financial situation got worst—the UniverSoul Circus left town and I was unemployed again. For the 3rd or so time, I did a massive resume fax looking for decent work. Via the want ads, I got an interview for an airlines way out in west hell. The pay was low but benefits great, including cheap trips around the world. Well my roommate was tired of my poverty and needed a sure rental source so she replaced me with someone she knew from her job. Renegade helped me move and I crashed at his abode—transitional housing for orphans (leaving the orphanage) and lunatics leaving the crazy house into normal society.

LIFE IN VIRGINIA

aN aBoDE w/joSE, doN pAuBLO, Julia, heR boYFRienD....

Well after a week or so, I had looked at many rooms near the airport way out in west hell and the surrounding area. One place offered a big room with a semi-private bathroom that I shared with the owner, a driveway, A/C, and was cheaper than some of those other places. Another good thing was that it was near the subway, beltway, civilization, and somewhat close to the airport. They were from Nicaragua and the owner spoke no English, but like the deaf people, all of the other residents spoke some English and thus refused to help me learn Spanish by only speaking Spanish.

There were loads of people living there. There were 2 or 3 people living in the owner's room and over 5 people, plus 3 dogs, living in the basement apartment. Two of the dogs were really cute beagles, one fat and one normal. They were nice and friendly. The 3rd hound was this smelly, slobbering, huge, half beagle half-German shepherd who barked all of the time and bit people. At one point, they even had some fighting cocks in the backyard. I kept hearing a rooster crow in the middle of the day. I assumed it was the Indians across the street. Come to find out, it was the family in the basement who had a cage of cocks in the backyard. The neighbors complained on us and they had to move them elsewhere.

I like animals. My dad's home in the country had many cute nice animals. At different points, there were dogs, cats, chickens, a goat, a pig, and even a pony. Growing up at home I had 3 parakeets named Fefe, who was cute and fat; Chirp, who was cute but puny and became a chicken pluck; and Fluffy who was just as fat and cute. I had several fish including Jaws and Jewel when I was little, and my good friend named Fish who lived 4 years and accompanied me and Fufu—my fat bunny—to college. I even had a newt.

Again via Swautch, another true and complete peasant was sent my way. I called him Eyepatch because he wore one. He was OK looking. He was tall, slim, and supposedly half Lebanese and half Native American. He lived with someone before he bribed me to stay on my floor for $150 for the month. Being broke, I very hesitantly consented. He must have worked in grease on cars or something, because wherever he sat, an oil spot appeared. I had several problems with him. Outside of no more privacy, he decided to service himself on my bed. I opened the door and caught him. I could care less what he did, just don't touch my bed. I have very sensitive skin! I need neither skeet marks nor greasy spoon upon my sheets.

He also made a rack of long distance calls to some trailer park in Waldorf, Md. Of course, he has no money to pay the expensive phone bill. I decided to kick him out my room, not to mention, he never gave me money for the following month. The landlord allowed him to sleep in the stairwell hallway. Eyepatch grumbled and complained every time I turned the light on and walked upstairs to get to my room. I guess I woke him up. What does he expect sleeping in a hallway. Someone said that they saw him roaming around my job grumbling and talking to himself. I never saw that, but I do know he borrowed/stole a bike to pedal to work across the 495 beltway. I must say, Swautch's track record is consistent of serving me the WORSTEST of men! The owner was probably happy when he finally moved out. There were 3 people living in his room; he, his girl, and her son. Once Eyepatch left, his girl's son took his place sleeping in the hall. True refugee style.

CAMP COUNSELOR

Well after getting hired at the airlines and seeing all of the strict rules about being on time and getting sick, and seeing how far it was and how you could only get there by car, I quit after day 2. I soon started being a camp counselor on the weekends for a 2-month period. It was fun although some of the Jr. high aged girls were stuck up. It was a private school and the students went camping in tents, did night hikes—which was fun—canoeing, mountain climbing—that was scary and difficult—and many other fun activities. It even paid better than many jobs I had and it was fun, especially the activities that I had never done before.

ciRUQE AgaIn

Again I got the privilege to work at this circus. This was a different show I got to see. I had the opportunity to even borrow the videos for a few nights. This time, however, this manager was unpleased with my service and work and thusly it ended prematurely.

AirLinEs aGaiN

Back to the airlines I go. This time I stayed several months. As an incentive to not quit, they offer a free trip anywhere in continental US. I wanted to visit San Francisco for free so despite all of the reasons I wanted to leave, I stayed on. Many people left after the first week. The training was as exciting as anesthesia and sedation. I was finally getting offers from my temp agency—which had ignored me for the longest (and the lady that diligently looked for work for me had left) but I had to turn them down thanks to my low wage airline job. The fact that it was actually cheaper to travel as a customer for the lowest fare than stand by with the 90% discount of the highest fare was a major factor in me quitting. I mean, what's the point of working at an airline if you can't travel for free, or next to nothing.

After 2 months of working at the airlines, the temp agency offered me a job paying almost twice as much, working my favorite shift—night, right down the street from my house. It was supposed to be a 3-month assignment too. After careful thought over the weekend, I quit the airline and took the temp job. Unfortunately, the job ended 2 weeks after I started.

7:11

I must say one of my more embarrassing jobs was a part time night shift job at 7/11. It was low paying and embarrassing like working in a drive through window at a fast food joint. I quit in less than a month, and I only worked 3 days a week. It was even across the street from my place. Probably the only thing more embarrassing to me is working in a drive through window or working as that giant coffee cup.

gAS StaTioN aDVENTURES w/fLOYD

Well, I landed another low scale, low paying, easy job. It was overnight and very easy. I got paid to use the computer, watch TV, and talk on the phone. I ran into someone that I met very briefly when I worked at the gym. I'll call him Floyd. He visited the gym only once. I remember his face and twitch. He also lived near me way out in west hell but was fun to talk to. When I got the gas station job, he would come up, buy dinner, and hang out. He seemed not to have to many people to hang out with. Perhaps it was because he lived so far out. He acted scared to leave town and go into the city, or anywhere else. He'd say that he wanted to hang out and would start complaining the second we left Fairfax. He was generous though and paid for things. He would complain and nag whenever someone tried to take him into civilization and the city—even though he would ask to tag along and go. This would get very annoying. Other than that, he really is a nice guy.

He'd visit the station a lot and a few other night owl friends would talk on the phone with me to help pass the time. But even the latest night owl would be asleep by 3am. I still had 4+ more hours to go, and absolutely NOTHING is on network TV during those times, not to mention that I only got 2 channels. So, I easily kept busy with Swautch's prehistoric laptop, my language books, Korg X3 keyboard, and other such things.

wild D'S TriP tO mERTYL bEACH

Well again Wild D and I plan another trip at the spur of the moment. It's Memorial Day weekend, I have to work in 35 hours, and we plan to go to Mertyl Beach, S.C. Floyd lied and said he would go, but like usual, he didn't come through. I begged a co-worker to work in my place, and Wild D and I took to the road. I had just enough for my half of gas and hardly no spending money. We get there from VA in about 10 or so hours, maybe less. Wild D drives like a bat out of hell. We walk around and like Freaknick, all of the southern boys were all over Wild D. Wild D realized it was only due to their slow primitive minds in thinking that high yellow, light skinned girls are pretty, no matter how ugly their face, body, or hair is. This mentality disappeared back in the early 1980's up north in DC and even earlier back in the 1970's up in NY, NJ area.

With no hotel room, we slept in the car and bathed in the bathroom at this restaurant inside this hotel. It was a birdbath; enough to basically clean ourselves, for the bathroom only had one toilet and one sink. The restaurant had a continental breakfast of fruit, juice, and muffins. I partook of the free food. Wild D decided to go to this tasty restaurant. We order the all you can eat, well actually Wild D ordered it, I ordered a coffee and planned to share Wild D's food, after all, it was all you can eat. Well she and the waiter must have got confused because they gave me a plate and stuff and charged me. Of course I had to borrow it from Wild D who complained.

That day we went to the beach where it was Freaknick part 2. The beach was full of black bikers. The white bikers all go to DC and the Vietnam Memorial and the black bikers go to Mertyl Beach. All of the bikers drove around with girls wearing bootie shorts and bounced them up and down on their bike. The way the girls sat on the bike, their entire butt showed as the bike bounced. Again the men were full of camcorders. Wild D met someone she knew and flashed him for $3. A female cop came and said, "You better return that $3's if you don't want to be arrested for prostitution". That was funny; talk about a cheap trick and ho. Of course Wild D was mad and wanted to turn the lady in.

cLASS aT nOVA

I always enjoy learning new languages. I decided to enroll in a class at the local community college (Northern Virginia Community College) and borrow some more money from Uncle Sam so I could start my business. I figured I might find a worthy husband from the large influx of foreigners who take English class, maybe lose weight, and learn a language while I'm at it. I registered for Chinese, dance, and yoga initially. After 4 classes of Chinese, I immediately transferred to

Japanese. It seemed easier because the pronunciation is similar to Spanish and there are words I heard before like sensei and sayonara.

When the loan money came through, for some unknown reason, I had to deposit it in my bank account for a week before I could cash it and pay for my classes. Well in the process of getting ads for this newsletter I was doing for my business and with **absolutely NO help from the shiftless and lying Swautch and Floyd** who both offered their help, I drove to DC alone. I actually had a job interview first and was running too late to take the train. The terrorist meter maids stole my car and held it for ransom. The ransom was over $700 for ignorant parking tickets I shouldn't have received in the first place!! Somehow between owing rent and getting my friend back from the demons, I spent my loan money. Not only could I now not pay for my classes, me applying for the loan was in vain! For I did not use any of the money for its intended purpose, my business. BIND THE DEVILS!!!

aNOTHER tEMP jOB & ChrIsTmas hELP

After 6 months or so, my prestigious and high paying job at the gas station ended because they too fired me. Again I filed for unemployment and again to no success. I got several other temp assignments but I needed something longer than 3 days to a week. I applied for Christmas help at the mall, which is now close to my house. I, however, didn't want to be standing for 8 hours in some dreaded retail store. If the malls and stores are full during the season, then obvious mall customer service needs help too. That was something more on my speed where I could use my outstanding customer service and my little language skills. My theory was correct and she hired me for seasonal help.

2000 N.Y.

I definitely wanted to leave the area for this New Year's holiday, for it was the millennium. I wanted to be in Time Square. Wild D said she would go but her car was broken. I wasn't taking My Feather. Big T claimed he would go but of course changed his mind immediately. Floyd said he would go but like always cancels out. When the time came, I had to convince Floyd to go. I tried alcohol but he refused to get drunk. I convinced him Julie, my housemate whom he stalks and lusts over, invited him to a party and was waiting for him. He agreed to meet her. I convinced him to let me drive but when we headed toward the beltway he freaked. He was ruining all of the plans. I convinced him that it was near and to calm down. I drove into Md. to someone's apartment and said she is over her cousin's house, let's go. He suspected something was up and that I was lying. I filled his car up with gas and headed to Wild D's.

Thank God this was our first time going to Wild D's apartment. I parked somewhere and had to walk to several different buildings before finding hers. The dumb tramp wasn't even ready and took forever to get ready. Floyd was getting anxious and planning to leave me stranded over her house. Thank God he couldn't find his car. When she finally was ready, she asked him if he was ready for the fun trip. He murmured yes. Wild D and Swautch are little and puny but have loud, deep, strong, demanding voices. I believe she scared Floyd. Once headed up 95 north Floyd said, "It's kind of fun being kidnapped by 2 girls."

Unlike Atlanta and the south, open minded, well-rounded men from NY and the Tri-state area liked me. New Yorkers are very diverse and many of them very sexy. Unlike many parts of the US, New Yorkers are from every part of the globe. Now many immigrants live through the US, but usually they are only first generation—and many small towns way out in the hicks and outskirts of the country is still mainly blacks and whites. Most New Yorkers are 5 plus generation American coming from the far reaches of Asia, Latin and South America, Europe, et cetera. And unlike the thoroughbred immigrants and citizens in many parts of the US, those in NY are mixed with a little of everything, like a NY cocktail. You will have someone that's part Chinese, Italian, Jamaican, and Brazilian, with a little drop or Irish, compliments of NY. Even the Jamaicans, Chinese, and Italians living in Jamaica Queens, China Town, or Little Italy look totally different than their countrymen in other parts of the US. Must be compliments of the NY cocktail. I assume that's why they are more tolerant, diverse, and open minded.

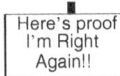
Stupid STANDARDS OF BEAUTY

In practically every city I've been in, when a man would date a black woman, she better be nothing under a Naomi Campbell cover model. Thin with pounds of make-up, fashionable sexy skirts, high heels in the snow, and long hair down to your butt. You better not walk out the house with a T-shirt and jeans on wearing tennis shoes, and forget your make-up and hair. Don't even think about naturals and dreads. New Yorkers happily date full figured natural woman with dreads, pants, and tennis.

A woman doesn't need to wear a micro mini skirt and high heels to be sexy. You can tell if she has a halfway decent body with pants, a long skirt, or jeans on. A 350-pound woman would look just as fat in a micro mini as she does in pants and some anorexic bony woman would look just as sickly in some pants as a skirt. A midget could wear heels and still be short. An ape can put on a pretty wig and pounds of make-up and still look like an ape with make-up. And a pretty woman can go out with no make-up and still look natural and pretty.

I find it interesting and quite irritating what many young men demand from women to consider them pretty. They wouldn't walk out in the ice and snow with shorts and high hill slippery boots on. You see repulsive huge men walking shirtless. And why is a woman considered ugly because she has meat on her or because she is blessed to live another year and thusly aged another year? Men are considered attractive even when they are over 50. A women's beauty is supposedly gone after 30 something. What an insult.

I guess it's the non-matriarchal, very patriarchal way this society was created. A man's success is based on their wealth or status in society, where a woman's success is solely based on beauty. I assume it's the same way a woman's name is based on the man she doesn't have; "Miss", (like me) or the man she married, "Mrs." A man's name is always mister. I'm definitely not some extreme feminist and I would LOVE to be a housewife and stay at home mom; however, this narrow minded, dumb standard of beauty that these idiotic men are so stupid to fall for is an abomination. I actually get more play from foreigners fresh off the boat from Europe and Africa than anywhere in America, except NY! As India Arie so eloquently says, "Am I less than a woman if I don't wear pantyhose?" The answer is definitely NO!

Hmm?

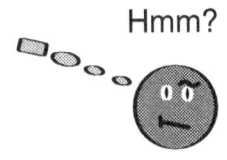

12 hOURS tOO lATE

Well, by the time we made it to New York's Time Square to see the ball, it was soooo crowded we had to go very far away and look at it on TV. People started lining up at 7AM, and we arrived around 10:30pm, way too late for a good spot. En-route to finding a good spot, Wild D and Floyd kept complaining. This cute man was pulling on me and following me. He wasn't allowed to cross the street. Go figure that one out. Wild D and Floyd kept leaving me and not waiting up, so I ended up leaving the first man I ran into. Wild D and Floyd were pathetic; they decided to go sit in the car and sleep instead of at least seeing the ball drop for the new millennium, an historic event I feel. Like losers, they slept through the count down. It almost defeated the purpose for coming to NY. Well I was determined to enjoy myself and see the ball drop, even if it was 7000 miles from Time Square on a giant TV screen.

Well after the ball dropped I made my way to the car, being stopped and pulled by many men. One guy walked with me to the car. Wild D and Floyd were sleeping in the car. They refused to let the man in the car claiming he might rob us. Three of us, one of him. Oh well. We went to find a vacancy in a hotel. Wild D's refused to help drive claiming pregnancy and I had driven the whole way up, getting stopped and ticketed by some pig cop in Jersey. This time Floyd was driving but he was swerving and about to cause an accident because of the massive traffic, people, and confusing roads. I ended up driving again to find a hotel.

While checking in at the front desk, a fancy looking Latin man with very shinny nails was standing there. He was an obvious friend of the pianist Liberace. I asked if he was a designer. I think he spoke 10 words of English. We asked where he was from. He said Southjerz. I asked where was that. Is it near Rome or Cicely? He looked at me strange and repeated Nujerz. Wild D deciphered his words and said he's from New Jersey, South Jersey. We all laughed. He must have just got to Nujerz 2 days ago. Later on, Floyd and I went on the hunt for some drinks, fun, and to get a picture of the ball. After a few drinks and searching all over Time Square, I asked the cops where the ball was. He sarcastically said the apple went to sleep. I have no idea where it was hiding so my lovely photo never came into being.

That night, Wild D insisted on a bed because she was pregnant. I volunteered to sleep on the mattress on the floor. Floyd slept on the bed. The next day, he complained how hard and uncomfortable it was. I sat on the bed and felt how hard it actually was, as hard as a rock! I guess he slept on the box spring. Being up to that point I never bought a complete bed set, I knew very little about a box spring. It looked like a mattress to me. I guess Floyd didn't know anything about box springs either. He said it felt like a rock. I said like the rock of Gibraltar. Wild D said, "Welcome to The Rock, featuring Sean Connery and Nicholas Cage."

That morning the toilet was stopped up. When the plumber/hotel worker/valet parker came to fix it, it was the same man who parked our car when we checked in. He spoke 4 more words than the man from Nujerz. I think this man was from Poland somewhere. He never went home. He asked was Wild D Floyd's wife. We laughed. Floyd profusely shook his head and said no. Wild D said they were married and she was pregnant with his child. It was quite funny.

My thumb was twitching and didn't stop until after breakfast. I refused to drive and we valued our lives so Wild D finally drove. I told her, you can let Floyd drive or me and my thumb drive, in which I refuse anyway, or you can drive. It wasn't a hard decision. Wild D wanted to make it back in 1 piece, she had to drive. We left that afternoon and after doing some window-shopping and eating lunch, Wild D drove back to Va. Floyd called Big T and talked about us like a dog. He called us homeless whores and talked about Wild D's hairy underarms and how she wanted him to pay for everything.

aRENA sTAGE

Once the holiday season was over, I was unemployed again. The classes were over but I got a good opportunity thanks to the Japanese class. Although I didn't learn to speak much Japanese, because the class focused on reading and writing in hiragana and katakana (the Japanese phonetic alphabet) and I missed a lot of classes, the teacher offered a lot of information about Japan. She would post up info when there was a tea ceremony, museum exhibition, cheap airline tickets, and different exchange opportunities. I applied for 2 different exchange programs. Big T, who is an excellent exaggerator, helped me revise my resume and write my essay for this exchange program.

With a revised resume, thanks to Big T, and a more professional work package, I went off again faxing to over 100 different jobs. I got many interviews, but only one company hired me on the spot—well almost on the spot, when I got home—Arena Stage. It was low paying but offered nice benefits including health insurance and free admission to the plays. I saw every play several times and met the cast. It was a nice opportunity to make contacts, not to mention it was in my field—theater.

mORE aDVENTURES WiTh WiLd D & fLOYD

After Wild D gave birth, she invited me and Floyd to meet her child. Floyd was really out of it due to being dumped by some 500-pound internet whore. Although he hated leaving his home, he was willing to go to the other side of the city to hang out with Wild D. He was really depressed and down in the dumps.

He bought a bottle of Thunderbird whiskey and bought some pizza once over Wild D's. Wild D breast-fed her child in front of everyone. I think Floyd was amused at this. He drank the bottle of whiskey straight with the pizza. Wild D went to bed and I went to take a shower. By now he was very drunk. He wanted to call and wake up his mom but couldn't figure out how to use the phone. It was a fancy Mickey Mouse phone with rotary style buttons and Mickey's hand was the way you hung up the phone. He started trying to make a call when I got into the shower. I take long showers. When I finished I heard the beep beep beep beep sound when you have the phone off the hook too long. He was still trying to make the same phone call to his mom.

He soon fell asleep. I was watching Chris Rock on TV when he woke up, stumbled around, and began to unzip his pants. I wasn't sure what he was doing or to expect, so I assumed he needed the toilet. I told him where it was but he obviously couldn't hear me. He kept on so I rushed him out the door so he wouldn't pee on the carpet or me. I thought he would go outside and pee but he decided to do it in the hallway in front of her door. I was scared someone would see him and see me talking to him and arrest both of us for vandalism. He then walked, barefoot still, to the main door and just stood there for 5 or so minutes. I have no idea what he was thinking or trying to do. I quietly walked up behind him and gently took his car keys in case he tried to be slick and leave me or decide to drive and crash his car in some ditch—unless he got arrested first for public drunkenness or drunk driving.

After a few minutes he disappeared. I have no idea where he went. I looked all around for him. I feared he had gotten lost or arrested. He was missing for over an hour. He returned alone, said nothing, and went to sleep. The next day he said he remembered nothing. He didn't believe he peed on the floor and was missing for over an hour. Maybe aliens abducted him because I saw him nowhere and I saw no one else either.

Thanks to Wild D, I overslept and was late to work. I decided to call in but I was too punk to do it myself so I had Wild D do it and make up some poor excuse of how my car broke down way out here and there is no bus or train to get into the city. She told them I'll call when I get into town. That was mostly the truth. I was way out in east hell now, nowhere near any public transportation. My only way back to civilization was Floyd, who had a horrible hang over. I wonder why?!

Of course when I returned to work the next day, they wrote me up for reliability and attendance issues. They were angry that I was too punk to call myself and was too cheap to find a phone card to call from a pay phone, "since I was stranded on the highway with no way back to civilization." After working for 6 months there, I was accepted to the Japanese Exchange and Teaching Programme and moved to Japan.

FINALLY, A GOOD JOB...........IN JAPAN

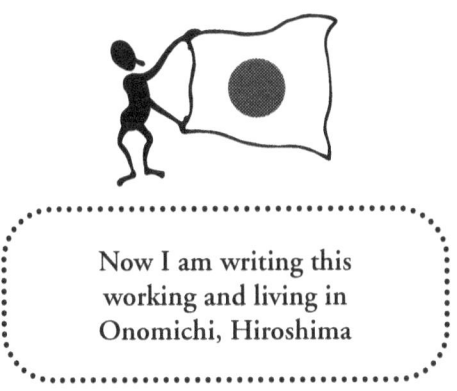

Now I am writing this working and living in Onomichi, Hiroshima

Onomichi, Hiroshima was one of the regions where the atomic bomb was dropped during WWII. Onomichi is an average size town (when compared to a U.S. town). It is mainly a fishing village and a shipbuilding yard. There are some Brazilians living in and next to Onomichi who work in the shipyard. Outside of a few traveling merchant marines just passing through who mostly are Filipino, there are only 4-5 foreigners living here.

Thus far, I'm the first and only black here, and the first mainland American, black, and truly real foreigner they ever met. There is a Scottish, Norwegian, Canadian, and 2 Australian, but the only other non-white and the first foreigner that came from America was a Japanese Hawaiian. Most of the other foreigners came to Japan before and some even did home stays and studied/majored in Japanese in college. I took a Japanese class for 1 semester at NOVA but my language ability is almost non-existent. I am also learning Japanese customs first hand for the first time.

I go to many elementary and Jr. high schools. I talk/show about American culture, holidays, geography, music, and language. Most of the elementary schools have no one who speaks English nor have they met someone as foreign and different as me. Some schools are shocked and surprised at how different I am, and are a bit difficult to teach alone due to the language and cultural difference. Some schools however are great and even if we can't understand a word from each other, they are interested in meeting me and having me teach at their school. Those types of teachers work together very well with me. The students are ALWAYS excited to meet and talk/play with me (even though we don't understand each others language).

I guess it would be the same if a foreigner, or for that matter some big city person went to the deep country. If you fit in, act like them, and don't get out of line, all is fine—even if you are a foreigner. If you go there and don't speak English and don't fit in, you will have a harder time and might feel unwelcome. If a foreigner goes to a big city, it might be easier. There are enough diverse people, to tolerate them. In fact, most folks in a major city are out for themselves so they have absolutely no time to get on your case about you or your differences. You get southern hospitality in the south and mid west and ignored in the northeast. For you will always have people who never left their estates, projects, or trailers and don't intend to, nor are they interested in meeting you. As well as those who are very outgoing and accepting even though they are not necessarily well traveled—such as me, as this is my first time abroad. You also run into people who are very well traveled and know several languages and are as closed minded and intolerant as any bigot.

One thing about Japanese culture is that people are well mannered and always try to be polite. Even if they hate you or are displeased or confused, they will smile and be nice. I think my open mindedness, smile and friendliness has gone a long way to getting me this far!

A JapAneSe SaUna

I hate flying and only flew once when I was 4 from Detroit to DC. That was the first and last time I flew until now. I always take the bus—as you can see—or drive. I was lucky enough to go on ANA airlines. Unlike the other airlines that half of the group went on, ANA had no reported accidents, hijacking, drunk pilots, or problems. It gave me some form of assuredness, not to mention the excitement of the trip, the business class seats, the other excited participants who talked excitedly the entire trip, and the cocktails I drank to relax. When I arrived in Japan it was late July and HOT in DC, but when I stepped out of Tokyo Narita airport … it literally felt like an oven. It was SOOOO HOT and Humid!!! The real temperature felt like it was OVER 100 degrees! It was so hot, it was hard to breathe. Like you only inhaled hot, stuffy air. Horrible if you are jogging, exercising, or even only walking. Unlike most of the other assignments, I had to work everyday. That was a mile plus walk to the job daily in the burning heat. At 8am, it felt like 90 plus degrees! When the boss let us go around 3pm, it had to be around 110 degrees and over 75% humidity! I didn't know Japan could get so hot. Many times I would literally sit around the office until 5:30 just to let the sun set a bit.

When I would leave at 3, I would immediate walk toward the covered street, called a tandori, which was still just as hot, just no sun. I discovered a cute little coffee house call U-U. They had Japanese snacks and hot and iced coffee. It was there that I met one of my best friends while over there, Yuko. She was from Osaka and studied English. I was her English practice and I learned more Japanese from her, and others, than any lesson. I guess worldwide, artists, hippies, and folks who don't get programmed correctly to be a good zombie in society, work at coffee shops. This must be some universal mandate: All hippy, bohemian, artsy fartsy, performers are hereby banned from any corporate professional employment. You are only allowed employment at café's, restaurants, and hippy lounges! She fit that description. She did weaving and other artsy stuff. I would go there everyday and talk, complain about my horrible boss and co-workers, my difficulties, stress, and how hard my job was, and other things folks talk about at bars, coffee shops, and such. On that same street and route, I found other good places to eat and nice people to meet. I met the owners of the Chinese/Japanese diner. Through them, I met Mr. Pita, who was this lovable old guy who reminded me of my dad. He looked a little like him. I also met a Japanese renegade, whom I conveniently titled Japanese Renegade.

Deguchi Sensei(teacher) was the first teacher I met when I moved into my apartment. She helped the girl I replaced leave, and all 3 of us went out for this tasty dish—one of the few Japanese foods I actually liked—okanomiaki. It's like a crepe with fish, cabbage, onions, and other savory spices. It was bold and tasty. I only like Hiroshima style though. Other styles put nasty raw eggs on top. Deguchi Sensei was very helpful, comforting, understanding, and also my friend. She was the one who I called to take me to the hospital after I puked for 2 and half hours in the middle of the night. I thought I was food poisoned, the Dr. said I was very stressed. I'll get to that later too.

Mr. Ue, another teacher, was also very friendly, nice, and understanding. The principal of an elementary school and her daughter—who spoke fluent English—was also very nice and friendly. Her daughter and I went out to several dance clubs and events. She was really nice. Through Yuko, I met Choko and her boyfriend. Choko and her boyfriend worked at this hippie store she owned named Choko Tako. They were all open minded, accepting, and diverse, or well traveled. Choko was also a musician. I bought several hippie pants, jewelry—that my mom actually liked and asked me to buy for a bunch of other people—and other cute clothes. I got my mom a hematite bracelet that helps circulation, and she claims, her arthritis.

Because it was excruciatingly hot when I first arrived, and unlike most participants, I had to work Monday through Friday. I hibernated in my air-conditioned apartment from the time I left work on Friday until it was time to return on

Monday. I made many business calls Friday night, since it was Friday afternoon in America. I actually landed this job about 9 months after I did that 21-day prayer campaign to get a decent paying and enjoyable job to get me out of debt. And it was this job that allowed me to pay on my student loan, my credit cards off, and get out of debt. I even sent money home to my parents and to save. I made enough money to live off of for several months once returning to America, and still have a few dollars left! And anyone knowing me knows that this is a true miracle from God, being that I'm constantly broke.

It was however, during this horribly hot time that most of the international participants hosted parties, sight seen, went to the beaches, got to know each other, and bonded. A rumor started that I was homesick because I hibernated in my room every weekend. My co-worker—as a plea for someone who felt sorry for my "homesickness"—begged me to join them in their beach parties in the sun. Outside of bills and business back home, I truly enjoyed my time to relax in the cool, alone. I still love lofting around my house all day, sleeping until late afternoon, watching documentaries 'til late night, and doing it again the next day. If you must wake up early daily and go to class or work, your time off to sleep, relax, and enjoy lofting in the comfort of your house could make the difference between a breakdown and being able to handle pressure. Once the temperature got cooler, I went out, on my own as usual, venturing around my town and the neighboring town. It was also in the spring, before it became too hot, that I ended up in the hospital from puking 2½ hours. I worked during the week and did things on the weekend, and ended up in the hospital. Proof that I am a delicate human being that needs rest and not some machine meant for pushing to its limits!

I met so many wonderful Japanese, I feel bad not naming or mentioning them all. Many of the school teachers, administrators, and students were so nice and accepting. You don't have to be a world traveler to be open minded, tolerant, and accepting. There are many family and business people who travel and speak many languages that aren't too accepting of people who are different, even from their same town. There are also people like me, who never left their region, that are as open minded, accepting, and warm as a Southern apple pie. I also have the opportunity to learn Japanese, meet many great residents, teachers, principals, students, and neighbors, try many new things and eat many different foods. Many opportunities that I would never have not leaving America and going abroad.

Mt. FuJI

I had various adventures in Japan. One was my trip to Mt. Fuji on Father's Day. I am very glad I went. Firstly, when I asked my Nihonjin (Japanese) friends if they ever went, they all said no. It was similar to tourists going to museums in DC. Locals take many local landmarks and attractions for granted. They all said that they planned to go but just never got around to it. Secondly, it was the first and most difficult Father's Day after returning for my dad. I'll explain that later. Even though Mt. Fuji was extremely difficult, it kept my mind off of life and Fathers Day. In fact, I simply kept thinking about not falling off the mountain and surviving. It's a volcano, an active volcano at that. You walk on complete ash, similar to walking up a steep hill of sand. Every step is only so far. You slide back as much as you go forward. It's hard enough to go up steep hills at such high altitudes, let alone walking on sand.

I walked so slowly, each and every person left me. I was determined to make it at least several miles up. One guy said, "Take you time, and don't die trying to climb. We'll meet you at the next level if you make it." Oh thanks, I appreciate everyone leaving me! If there was a helicopter or donkey to take me to the top, I could easily get down, if nothing else but to slide down the mountain.

Once I made it above cloud level, which looked like you were looking out of a window of a plane, my stupid novelty camera busted open exposing the precious film of me on the mountain. I was SOOO disgusted!! I also realized that I was having major problems climbing further. For every time I stood up, I got dizzy. I disappointedly decided to return to the bus, being that I felt drunk and was too exhausted to walk. Compliments of altitude sickness, every few steps I took made me very out of breath and dizzy. As I struggled to walk down, I decided to slide down on my raincoat from Cape Canaveral, Fl. ruining it with a huge hole where I sat. People felt it was amusing to see me slide. I didn't care!

Come to find out, one athlete passed out near the top, and the others were too scared to climb down once they did get to the top. It's all ice up there and they all felt like they were going to slide off of the mountain. They were all sunburned and crying and some literally kissed the ground once they returned to the bus. We all got to relax at this lovely "onsen" (hot spring) after we bathed and had dinner. This was really good since everyone was super funky and grainy from the volcanic ash.

MoRmonS taUghT mE JapAneSe

I studied Japanese for a semester but as I've said before, the best way for me to learn a language is to be totally immersed. The fishing village was about as remote as you could get so I was luckily forced to speak Japanese since no one in the village spoke English. Unlike the major cities where almost everyone speaks English, no one except the English teachers spoke English here. There were Mormons there "teaching English" as they introduced their religion to hopeful converts.

The Japanese taught us Japanese the same way they taught each other English. The Mormons broke it down to me and taught me Japanese "for an American" if you will. I can't explain their method because I'm not a teacher and never studied TEFOL. They explained Japanese grammar substituting English words in place of Japanese words. Once I understood a grammar concept, I simply placed Japanese over the English and thus, a grammatically correct Japanese sentence. I picked up words just by living there and being exposed to it.

Now losing my American accent is like Schwarzenegger losing his. He became governor of Ca. and still has his festive accent. Compliments of this linguistic course I took, I learned that once you pass a certain age, learning and speaking a foreign language like a native is basically impossible. You switch from learning and being fluent in a new language like a child, to learning it as a second language. Which offers thick accents, bad grammar, and the obvious evidence that you are a flying foreigner in that land. But hopefully at least you can communicate. The way they taught me Japanese was very easy to pick up and understand. I'm sure their method is explained to those who need to teach other teens and adults foreign language, like a TEFOL instructor. The Mormons later also shared their beliefs with me too.

JapAnesE RoAd TriP anD thE YMCA

I took a tap dance class at the YMCA in the next city. It was only once a week and something interesting to do. I always wanted to try tap. It's kind of difficult, for the floor is so slippery with the shoes on. I was always scared that I was going to slip. The teacher had to be over 60 but she was very limber, flexible, and a good inspirations to folks who say that after a certain age you become a fossil. She is an example of a myth dispelled. This is also where I met another friend, Yoichi.

I was allowed to teach African dance at that YMCA. It was funny. I took African dance only a few times here in the states and I was improvising the entire class. In fact, I basically taught Calypso instead of African dance. Thank God no real Africans or Caribbean's were there to embarrass me and call me out on it. Of course, the Japanese seemed to enjoy the class. Perhaps they had no clue what it really was. I guess the same way we Americans eat Americanized ethnic foods not even realizing what it is that we are actually eating.

It was with Yoichi that I took my first Japanese road trip. We went to Kochi, which was on the next island. We had to take this set of long connective bridges called the Seto Inland Bridge(check out this cool site about this set of bridges: http://web-japan.org/atlas/architecture/arc22.html. I believe the sites name is Japan Atlas, which came from the Web Japan site). They connected all of the tiny islands to each other. When we arrived in Kochi we stayed at his friend's house. We went to this village market, to this ninja fair, and up this mountain to see this small ninja castle. There were many steps you had to climb to get to the top of the mountain. Being that I had to climb long steep hills several days a week, I was use to it. They obviously weren't. It took them much longer to get to the top. They were tired and amazingly thought that I was in good shape to climb so well. Go figure! Once at the top we were able to enter the castle for a fee.

> I'm currently writing 3 years later back in the states in a College Park Apartment complex in MD.

We had to take our shoes off compliments of Japanese and Asian culture and use the slippers. In fact, every school, home, apartment, and gym, made you take your street shoes off and wear their slippers. At least they provided ones for you.

I know several Americans that want you to take off your shoes and won't even offer you slippers! As if you want to bump your toe in their fully furnished house! As for me and my American place, I wore my streets shoes all over my apartment. It was only those few occasions when my boss or some visitor was there, that I was inconvenienced to change shoes before entering my abode. I always wear slippers or some form of bedroom shoes. I hate walking barefoot. I even wear slippers around my bedroom. What if I bump my delicate toe on a chair? I just would wait until I sit down in my room or on the couch to rest a bit and then immediately change my shoes. My international roommate from Turkey was startled to see me "rudely" or "filthily" walk around the house with street shoes on. He would change his shoes once he closed the door. Standing up, bags and book bag in hand. Change shoes before walking into the room. Not me. I need at least the comfort of a chair to sit down in for balance, especially if I wore more than some flip flops, which are easy to switch standing.

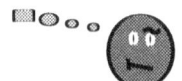

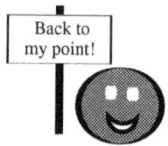

Back to my point!

Well, the steps to this Ninja/Shogun castle were VERY steep and were smaller than a size 6 woman's shoe! Wearing slip on slippers made it scary and dangerous walking up 5 flights of extremely steep stairs. It was almost like a fun house prank or something. The steps barely came out from the wall and I literally climbed them like a ladder.

All of the Japanese and other foreigners laughed and was quite amused by my torment and fear. I could care a less if they and all of their family could climb steep mountains and walls like a goat or bug. I'm 100% human and can only walk on surfaces parallel to the earth, not horizontal. When we finally reached the top, I was too scared to walk outside to see the view. Unlike skyscrapers in America and other places, there was no window, not even a screen or bar, to protect you from falling. It was 5 stories up, on top of a mountain, at the top of the city. You can see everywhere from the view up there. It was so high up; the wind blew the entire time. It wasn't windy walking around the mountain but the top of the castle was quite windy. Why, I don't know. I'm sure some meteorologist, astronaut, or physicist would know. Being that it was so windy and high up, I was terrified to stay out on the balcony. When we finally left, I practically slid down the steps while all of the stupid, nosy, onlookers laughed, took pictures, and was entertained. I was not there to entertain, but to save my life and not fall and break my limbs. MIND YOUR BUSINESS!

After we left, we went to the **Kazura Vine Bridge** which is this scary rope bridge. (Check out my weblog which has a photo of this bridge and many other photos. http://www.bookpreview.blogspot.com) It was this long rope bridge on top of this mountain crossing this rapid river. It was a scary tourist attraction which many folks came to visit and cross. Being that masses of people were crossing it, the bridge constantly swayed and rocked.... .high up on the mountain above the river in mid air. It was so scary crossing it. It kept rocking and I was terrified feeling that it was going to break or swing and plummet me, and everyone else, into the raging river.

Finally, we went to this onsen, which is Japanese for hot springs. It was at the top of the mountain. It was the first time I ever been to an onsen. I know they have hot springs in America but I don't know where they are. I understand that a natural hot spring needs to be near an active volcano. Perhaps they have natural outside hot springs in the Rockies somewhere. I'm sure Hawaii and Washington State has them. I would love to visit Seattle. To hear the music, visit the coffee lounges, go to Vancouver, Canada, and hopefully check out an onsen. They have them all over in Japan.

This onsen was outside on top of a mountain. You can imagine how beautiful and awesome the view was. We had to ride this cable car of sorts up the side of the mountain. The entire ride was filled with beautiful scenic views of the landscape. It was chilly near the top but once you went inside the heated changing room, it was fine. They separate the sexes and provide lockers and even towels. There are different levels of luxury for the onsens. Obviously the more expensive the spa the more luxuries they have. The hot springs were quite hot. I had to let my body adjust to the heat. I think it was supposed to be around 100 degrees. The waters are supposed to be healing or something. The onsen was outside so I sat in this sauna outside at the top of the mountain enjoying the picturesque view of the area. Of course, my camera worked excellent that day too. I hardly got any photos. Besides, it's hard to take photos in a pool. I'm sure there are many waterproof cameras. Since my stupid novelty camera busted at the top of Mt. Fuji, I solely got disposable cameras every since.

WARNING:

If you don't want to read depressing, miserable, bleak things; stop reading here!!

From this point on, <u>life takes a HIDEOUS turn for the WORSE!!!</u>

---

jAPANESE bOSS fROM hELL

Here are parts of a rant and complaint letter I wrote to the regional office pleading for a transfer.

"I think the JET program is an excellent opportunity to come and experience Japan, and I am glad that I am here because I have seen and experienced things that I could not even fathom in America. This is my first time to go abroad and leave the US and of course my first time to Japan. I am experiencing Japanese life, culture, and language first hand. The JET programs offers foreigners one of the best exchange opportunities around, however your placement is the luck of the draw—and I always have bad luck. My problem is my placement.

Unfortunately, as Inoue Sensei stated on several occasions, "Now that you are in Onomichi, we (some narrow-minded teachers and schools) expect you to act and be like a certified Japanese teacher." This was told to me my 2nd month teaching and 3rd month in Japan.

My supervisor, Mr. Kazoe Inoue, needs a thorough training in tolerance, cross-cultural understanding, and diversity. An AET—Assistant English Teacher—is supposed to team teach with a Japanese English teacher in a Jr. High or High school. The office where I was placed focuses mostly on elementary schools, which is great to expose them to different cultures and English at an early age. However, this requires the AET to have basic Japanese ability. On top of this, the AET is expected to have basic Japanese etiquette and teaching ability. These are some excellent requirements and they are perfectly valid. The problem is that JET's are not required to be fluent in Japanese or have prior teaching experience before leaving America—or their home country. I assume that's the reasons JET's apply for this job, to LEARN Nihongo, Japanese culture, customs, and history. (Nihongo means Japanese)

Bruce (the second AET from Scotland who also gives me a very hard time and dislikes America) warned me to "Eat the kyushoku's (nasty school lunch) and fit in as much as possible. It would make everyone's life—especially yours—much easier here." It is impossible for me, an American, to go to Britain and assimilate into British culture and become British in less than 6 months. If nothing else, my accent will give me away, and Britain is a western country like the US. I wonder how they expect a foreigner (from a country totally different in every way) to "become Japanese" in 3 months?!?!

I find it astonishing that I'm having such a difficult time and not even invited back! It is—according to many people—quite unusual in Japan to display such an unfair attitude towards someone they must be around. It was said that to "keep the peace", Nihonjins(Japanese), would not show such attitudes towards someone they must work or live with for a long amount of time. This is, perhaps, the reason he tried so hard to get me to quit. My supervisor tries to make work almost impossible for me. As Deguchi Sensei stated, **"No matter what I do, he will have a problem with it. Even if he requested me to do it!"**

I find it extremely stressful and very unacceptable of his treatment and blame towards me. He said in various ways and on various times that I should/can go home. Once when I was asking Bruce why he goes to half of the number of schools I go to, Inoue jumped in and said I replaced Keri's schools and if "I don't like it I can leave!" Bruce said, "They just have to get used to you." That is very ridiculous almost to the point of being insulting. Why would a host family/school/job, et cetera, request a foreigner from somewhere that they "have to get used to"? It is just like someone applying to go abroad and is not ready to leave their home nor interested in the country are they asking to go to. This makes absolutely no sense. They requested an English speaking exchange person but want them to "become Japanese as soon as possible"

This treatment, because my stroke order for writing Japanese is wrong, or that I am not exhibiting proper Japanese manners and etiquette when teaching 2nd graders because I "moved the chair the wrong way" is unfair and ridiculous. Or as he and Bruce arguable question, what is my problem for not wanting to happily eat school lunch? He even complained about my ability to ride a bike, which I am still wondering why he mentioned that in the first place. He complained that "I am unable to get around alone because I can't read Japanese," another lie. I go to Fukuyama weekly, Hiroshima, and everywhere else alone. I never ask for anything being that "they bend over backwards whenever they help me" according to Bruce.

This treatment is unfair and tremendously stressful. I am even experiencing physical symptoms. I've had insomnia since Oct. and take sleeping pills for it. I usually get it at the beginning of the week, in particular when I go to the board of education or to certain unwelcoming schools. Other nights I sleep fine. I never had insomnia to this extent in the USA. I also started getting mild headaches, slight dizziness, and indigestion. If it is from spicy food or alcohol then I don't question it, but those symptoms would come out of nowhere. The Dr. and a friend both agree it is work related stress.

I don't want to take up too much of your time and apologize for taking up this much. I, however, do want to put this in writing with the hope that something will change. I really want to stay on the JET Program, it appears to be one of the best programs. I really, however, don't want to continue to work in such an unfair, unhealthy, and extremely stressful environment. I really enjoy the students, and most of the schools and people in the office. It is my boss and a few situations that make working almost hazardous."

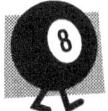 Of course, what can you expect with my luck! As I mentioned earlier, 98% of the things I want, get, or get into almost ALWAYS change for the worst! I know EXACTLY what I want and never regret choosing a situation, job, school, etc. It is almost always the job, guy, or what have you that changes like a demon possessed for the worst. I am not coming to work drunk, being nasty, or breaking all of the rules. My boss and Scottish co-worker just don't like Americans nor obviously someone as foreign and unJapanese as me. Despite my horrible boss, Scottish co-worker, and a few small schools with mean teachers that weren't used to foreigners; my experience in Japan was quite a learning and exciting experience. It was also quite a stressful one too, but a pastor said how the devil can switch things up in the night and you end up with something TOTALLY different than what you started with. This obviously is the case with

98% of everything I try to get or do. Japan was quite an adventure and learning experience. One that I'd never conceive of if I didn't take the job. Besides, how would I have met all of the really nice people I did meet and see the really exciting places that I have never seen before?

LikE AnY RespEctaBle ForEignEr

Once my program was over, like any respectable foreigner, I went traveling. The day I moved out from my apartment, the staff came to help me clean it. I snuck away with Deguchi Sensei, had lunch, and took the bus from Onomichi to Kyoto. It was the first place I visited. I saw the huge, beautiful train station/mall. I stayed overnight there. I next went to Nara, stayed in a youth hostel, and saw Dai Butsua, that's the giant Buddha you see in pictures. To get to the Buddha, you must go through this beautiful park with very hungry fish, turtles, and deer. They literally walk or swim up to you for you to feed them. The deer would start nibbling on your items if you only fed them once. They are eternally hungry. They are cute but intimidating. The fish, they're stuck in the lake so they're no danger to me, and the turtles are slow. The deer, they were intimidating!

I then went to Iga Ueno, which is where ninja village is located. I was expecting a little more in ninja village. It is one notch bigger and better than Onomichi. They had a cool ninja funhouse with trap doors and all. There was also a ninja museum and display show. That was about it in this town. I wanted to see ninjas appear in a puff of smoke, or fly across the air, or some other Crouching Tiger Hidden Dragon type of stunt.

When I left there, I went to Korea via boat. I really hate flying. The only time I flew was when I flew to and from America. The Japanese boat going was nice. I took the bus to Seoul. I went to a spa to get a body scrub and facial. My skin was soft and creamy once they were done. Afterwards, I went to this indoor park named Lotte World I found by accident. I stayed at the Go Gook Hotel. It was OK. I prefer hostels. They had a men's club downstairs. Hearing the music, I nosily went to see what was going on. They stopped me at the elevator. They showed me this expensive price list with $10 sodas and subtly explained that for about $100 I would get a nice room with wine, snacks, and cigars. I asked what else comes with it. They said that a girl would talk and dance and you get snacks and soda. I think for $100+, you get a 15-minute f@#k.

This also was my first time to try Korean food, and to my surprise, I loved it! I don't like Japanese or Chinese food. The Japanese food was either bland, sweet, slimy, raw, or yucky. I never did, and still don't, like Chinese food. I always order American dishes at carry outs and restaurants. I actually was surprised when I had some very delicious, savory Korean food. It was bold, spicy, savory, and very delicious. I would love to go to a Korean restaurant for a date. I actually like Korean food better than any other Asian food that I have tasted thus far. They even have this tasty, sweet, pancake type snack called ho docks or something.

The traffic back from Seoul to the port in Pusan, Korea was horrible! I literally missed my boat. I had to stay at another slut hotel. The room was cheap and near the port. I then noticed that it was mostly men, and a lot of them walked around in underclothes and underwear. I saw a rack of Korean porno then I saw what must have been some hookers. How lovely! To top it off, the boat back was a Korean one. It was smelly, rocked a lot, dirty, and some got seasick on it. I was even infected with a sty on my delicate eye. It was such a potent germ, that a month after I returned to America, I went to the doctor to try to cut it off. It dried up and shrunk into a hard bump. It finally disappeared.

All of my travels through Japan and Korea were alone. I, of course, knew enough Japanese to get around and survive by that point. I have unfortunately since forgotten most of it due to the fact that I have no one to practice with. I, however, knew absolutely no Korean except two words, good morning and thanks. Unlike big cities in Japan, the only folks who spoke English in Seoul were other foreigners. I figured, if I can travel to a foreign land, alone, knowing absolutely none of the language, then I should be able to go to any English-speaking place in the world!

ME GOING HOME 4 DADDY

As I write this here, there is over a 3-year hiatus from
my chronicles in Japan until now.

The entire world has changed. Many people died, several earthquakes happened, an avalanche, 9/11, death of Sadam Hussein. Even a whoring cat returning with kittens and an infestation of fleas for the entire basement cat population—and before this, my mom hated cats. Even through all of my trials, tribulations, and turmoil I kept writing and journalizing my activities. This section, no doubt is the HARDEST section to write about. Sometimes, many times, it's easier to not think about tragic things than to keep remembering the past. This book, however, is way overdue, so I must keep on writing and finish this already.

When I got the message at 12 noon from Nagai Chu gakko(Jr high) from the vice principal that I had a call from home, I knew immediately something was really wrong. DC is 12 hours behind us and it was still 12 something Sunday morning—basically the middle of the night in Maryland. My family mostly consists of older women who are definitely not night people. I feared the worst and hoped for the best. I mean come on; anybody with an ounce of sense would know something horrible happened. What possible reason would your family call you at work and ask you to call home in the middle of the night unless it's some great tragedy. Deguchi Sensei drove me home and I was anxious and tense the entire ride. I called home and my mom asked me to sit down. Knowing it was a tragedy, her telling me to sit proved it. I immediately asked who died. "Who died?!?!" My mom kept sobbing and repeating my name. "Was it Granny?!" "No," she said. "Daddy?!?!" "Ah huh." I just screamed, cursed, and yelled s#@t, damn, why, why, why?!?!?! I mean, why does everyone else not only get to have a fair and decent life, a prosperous and rewarding job, get to get married, let their dad give them away, and have a family, and I can't even have a dad anymore?!?! This is a STRAIGHT UP abomination!! This life I have and the cards I seem to have been dealt is EXTREMELY unfair, unlucky, and full of crap!!

What kind of karma crap is this?!?! It's funny because I prayed practically every night thanking God for His gift for this extremely stressful and unfair job working for Satan and A'holes, family, friends, and such, forgive me for my sins, asking for

76

weight loss, and a family reunion style wedding where daddy would give me away. Obvious answers and positive results again won't arrive!! I gained every pound I lost (and I didn't even lose that much!) plus 20 more once returning to this horrible country and still see absolutely no man of worth at all!!!!!

Satan could at least tricked me and sent me some guy that will soon become horrible after he marries me, buys a house, and impregnates me! Obviously, he's busy keeping a poor girl miserably single and broke, which is extremely stupid and pointless, instead of doing something of worth and intelligence like that!

There is absolutely NO reason for me to keep doing this prayer thing when all I get is curses and the complete opposite of what I ask for. I asked for blessing and health for my family my first semester of college, and my mom fainted and needed a brain operation because of a tumor. I BEG for a man and marriage and successfully remained miserable, single, and broke. Wow, this prayer crap really works and offers great results. I think I'll keep on praying so every part of my life will be damned, miserable, and shot to hell.

Well, compliments of luck, fate, misery, and the curses of hell and earth combined, I must return home for my dad, who I didn't even get to see again and say goodbye to. Oh, and how nice to steal him 3 days from his 66 birthday. What a wonderful birthday gift for the whole family! I called him a few days prior to see if he received my package from Japan. Unlike my mom who didn't send my Christmas gifts until 1 month late. I told him to wait for his birthday to open it. I wish I let him open it earlier. It's just like the dollhouse mom made for KiKi, and Re made her wait until Christmas. Of course she cried and conveniently the place flooded and the dollhouse was ruined. KiKi never even got to play with it.

Well he conveniently didn't get to open my present—nor any other—either. And instead of us having a birthday bar BQ that Saturday, we had his funeral instead. Now what kind of karma crap is this?!?! I used that month's check to fly home and Bruce, the A' hole Scott, was surprised that I returned to Japan. The only reason I did was to finish what I said I would, and hope to find another job. Not to mention, to try and clear my mind.

I didn't get to come home Christmas—daddy told me to stay and save my money, and Moas never bought that RT plain ticket. He must not want that green card all that bad, oh well. Because I didn't go home for Christmas, I pack as much stuff as I could carry under and on the flight. Carrying the heavy bags from the bus to the subway and then to the airport shuttle was impossible. I had to find other foreigners to help me carry the luggage. The Japanese wouldn't help me. Tokyo folks are like DC and NY people, they won't help you unless you fall and collapse on their lap. At least the airport had rolling carts to easily carry my luggage. It took me 12 hours to go from Onomichi to Tokyo—which was an overnight bus ride, and several hours to go from downtown Tokyo to Narita airport—which is where I struggled getting foreigners to help me with my luggage. It is a 13-hour non-stop flight from Tokyo to Washington Dulles.

Everywhere I looked and saw cute little Japanese men with chubby cheeks reminding me of Daddy. Every time I tried to lay back and sleep, mom's phone conversation rang in my head, over and over again. My mom first put my aunt on the phone to talk then she got back on the phone. All I kept asking was why. How?! He wasn't sick. He exercised way more than my mom. Then I asked a very big question, where is his body?!?! Where is it?! Is he in the hospital?! At least if he's in the hospital I can see him. It offers a chance that he might make it. It may be a slim chance, but it's still a chance. My mom numbly said the morgue. Damn, no living being stays in the morgue!

I arrived 15-20 pounds lighter, locks in my hair, and my sinus problem allegedly cleared. Now I didn't think so until after a week in this God forsaken crappy town. The DC area is so low class swamp like that people from Brooklyn claim that after living their entire life in smog, they develop allergy's here, in DC. That trip and those 2 weeks being home because for daddy was the hardest things I ever had to do. I wasn't that close with the other foreigners but got to know the Japanese. Because I felt close to my Japanese friend and knew they were sincere not just appeasing for pity's sake, I confided in them and they helped me. The Mormons who were there "teaching English to the Japanese" helped in a microscopic bit too. Outside of teaching me Japanese, they happily told me about their religion, which is very interesting, and consoled me to what minuscule degree it could.

To be honest, 2 American friends back home—Big T whose grandma passed and Belief whose dad passed in Dec.—and my close Japanese friends were the only ones that effectively consoled me. My other friends back home were as comforting as this keyboard I'm typing on—and I hate typing! I never saw such inconsiderate, non-caring jerks! That slut Wild D asked if I wanted to go to NY and how much money did my dad leave me—none of your damn business and NO! Swautch wanted to go to the club everyday. I had to kidnap him the day before the funeral and then he left to go to his brother's graduation. At least he did spend the night and tried to take my mind off of it. He also rode in the limo with me. Big T wasn't even going to go; he had a "job interview." Floyd bull-crapped about some funeral in Florida. When I called him the following day, he amazingly returned to Va. without anyone even knowing that he left.

That's almost as amazing as when Floyd went with me to this international gathering once, and of course, he was ready to go home after 1 hour. He offered to take this girl who lived near me, home. She was the sexy guest from Rwanda. Since he was so ready to go, I discretely went around trying to find myself a ride, I wasn't ready to go. He loudly told me he'd give me a ride home in front of everyone. I guess he didn't want to look anti social and unfriendly. The girl found another ride home. This guy offered me a ride home so I told Floyd I had a ride so he didn't have to wait. We were planning to go to some club. Floyd told all of us he had to go. His response to why (I was alertly listing because I wanted to know his p#ss poor excuse too) was that he had an emergency.... with his grandfather. It was after midnight.

The guy said, "An emergency? With your grandfather? Now?"

Floyd: "Yes, I have an emergency now."

Of course I believed him. When he found out I was going out to the club instead of going home and be miserable and board like him, he quickly changed plans.

Floyd: "You're going to the club? With the sexy guest? Well I'll go too."

Me: "Floyd, I'm already going with this guy. Besides, I thought you had an emergency with your grandfather."

Floyd: "I did."

Me: "Well how are you now able to go the club?"

Floyd: "I took care of the problem."

Me: "How?"

Floyd: "I just called my grandfather."

And like his Florida trip that no one knew he went on, or that he even left the house; he magically made a phone call without even picking up his cell or dialing the phone number, let alone talking into it. True magic!

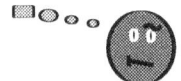

I must say that through all of the foreigners I met, the open minded Japanese, the well traveled diverse Japanese, or the Japanese from a big city like Osaka, were the nicest and most comforting during this ordeal. The foreigners all made friends and clicked up the first month. Because I lived in a very small fishing village that many Japanese never heard of, I ended up meeting other friendly Japanese who were outgoing and nice to me. With the exception of my Japanese friends, co-workers, and the Japanese embassy in DC, no one else knew of my tragedy. I wouldn't expect the other foreigners to be that comforting.

That gremlin Bruce and my imp boss tried to be nice and comforting to me. I guess I was supposed to forget about how much of a demonically inspired, true and complete A'hole and jerk they were; nor how they treated and talked to me every other time. Unlike my current roommate and Vic (I'll get to them later), I'm a very private person. I don't go and tell people all of my business—despite what others may think. I also don't want someone to be cordial and nice to me for pity's sake. **That in itself is an insult!!** My roommate, Vic, Bruce, and my boss would talk down to me and about me to others. I know this because I hear it from all 4 of them. They would talk in front of me or within hearing distance. Perhaps my boss and Bruce felt my Japanese wasn't good enough to understand, but they were quite wrong! I knew and understood way more Japanese than they realized. Besides, one can always tell when you're talking positively or negatively about them.

DREAMS OF DADDY

I've had various dreams of daddy. Starting with the day he crossed over to the land of the ancestors. After I did my "hap hazard" prayer for the night thanking God for that awfully stressful job working with Satan and my family and praying for my marriage, a family reunion style wedding, and weight loss, I fell asleep. I dreamt of someone visiting my room. I dreamt of me sleeping in my bed in my room, and someone/something went into my dirty clothes and put on my short black dress and started dancing around in it. I was a bit disturbed because even though it was a dream, it seemed very real and I know in reality clothes don't walk around by themselves. On top of that, it was only my dress. There was no body appearing in it—unless it was the invisible man or something. It kept dancing around me until I told it to stop. I said stop, then it stopped and collapsed on the floor into a normal piece of fabric. I then felt bad for the dress. I mean, if it was happy dancing around and it wasn't really bothering me, then I guess it should be ok to keep dancing. So I said it was OK to get up and dance. It did and it danced around again. Then of course I got a bit disturbed at seeing an invisible person dance in my dress so again I told it to stop. Finally after seeing it laying on the floor, I said, "You can get up now." I thought it was interesting how it seemed to listen to me. It only danced when I said it was ok; otherwise it would just lie there on the floor.

Now I guess you're wondering how this pertains to my dad. I wonder too. After my dress danced around in my dream I finally woke up. I don't remember if it was my alarm or what. I felt unusual after that weird dream. How often do you dream of yourself laying in bed trying to sleep and being awaken by some article of your clothing dancing around your room. Most dreams are more elaborate and interesting. Taking place in far away locations and doing amazing things. Not just lying in your bed sleeping being disturbed by dancing clothes. In fact, this dream is the beginning of me having dreams like this—as you will read—where I am actually dreaming of me laying in my bed or something and some weird activity is going on around me. These types of dreams are extremely convincing and realistic, it's just I wake up from them. Being that this was the first time this type of dream occurred, I thought it was odd—and I still think they are odd. Even though I saw no one inside my dress, I definitely know it was a ghost or something. I mean, what else can explain a piece of clothing coming to life. That disturbed me. Why would something come visit me? And why would it wear my dress?

After I realized what happened, I called my mom back later on that day. I discovered she found Daddy around 6pm Sunday. She concluded that he died of a stroke or heart attack between 4:30 to 6pm. When I calculated the time difference, 5pm Sunday in DC is about 5am Monday in Japan. That's about the time I had the dream. On top of that, I actually wore that exact dress home. It wasn't dirty in the hamper, but clean and waiting to be worn. I wore it—without thinking—because it was easier to use the bathroom on the train and plane (unlike guys who can just whip it out and call it a day). In retrospect, I realized it was the dancing dress in my dream, which I dreamt Japanese time when he died in America. Perhaps after he died, he decided to visit me. I was sleep and perhaps he didn't know how to appear in my dreams just yet so he simply played around my room dancing in my dress—which I actually ended up wearing home. So yes, this silly dream of a dancing dress seems to have a direct correlation to my dad, via what I wore home that fateful day and the time of my father's death.

Right after I returned to Japan, I had another dream. I dreamt that I was at my parents' home all alone. For some reason I was a bit uneasy being alone, as if someone or something was there. I was in my bedroom and my parent's door was closed. I began to smell daddy's cologne and the door opened. Of course I was startled but then I was immediately happy to see him. I yelled, "DADDY!" as I did when I was a kid. He came out looking a bit younger with some sort of scarf on his head. There was some sort of red spot on it, as if he was bleeding from the head. He came out mumbling his usual mumble grumble and then sat on the top step. Very unusual for my dad, I never known him to wear a scarf nor sit on our steps. Then he said in a very annoyed and anxious voice, "Don't wait 'til the last minute for nothing, I mean nothing!" I guess I was supposedly back in film class and I had an assignment due. I contested that I had not waited 'til the last minute. He argued a bit and kept saying don't wait 'til the last minute for nothing. I told my mom this. She said that he probably told you that because he never got around to leaving a will for his estate.

I just remembered having another weird dream while I was still in Japan. I dreamt it was right after his death—in which it actually was in real life—and mom and I were trying to arrange the rooms and stuff. Somehow he was still around, but it was in the past, before his death. In the first scenario and past, life was perfectly well and wonderful with him around. It just, for some reason or another, did not feel quite right. So he went to a different past and it still did not feel quite right. Still, he changed it to another past, but it still did not feel quite right. He kept changing different things like the year, paint, or some other little thing. No matter how much things would change, it never quite felt right. Somehow, in the back of my mind, I knew he wasn't supposed to be here, regardless of how much I would love for him to be alive. Every time he tried to change something, he asked how it felt, and as always, it never quite felt right. Finally, he said, "You must either pick and settle with a past, or deal with the now time and present." I guess, as hard, unwilling, and unfortunate life and the events panned out to be, I finally decided to settle for the present. For no matter how many times, scenes, and scenario's he created in the past, it just never felt quite right. It always felt unsettling and not right.

This next dream was also extremely vivid, almost to the point of being real, if you would. I dropped Renegade off at work near Union Station at the crack of dawn. He would stay at my parent's home or I'd stay at his mom's A/C condo and sleep in the loft, and take him to work in the morning. I even drove my dad's car; mine was still down the country with my aunt. I was not only tired as hell—he had to be there by 7am—it was rush hour traffic. I would park and rest near Union Station until traffic subsided. Sometimes I'd sleep there 'til noon.

Well this time while I took my usual nap, Daddy appeared in my dream. What makes it so real was that (again like the first dream with the black dress) I dreamt I was sleeping in his car exactly like I was sleeping in reality. He walked up to the window and woke me up. I was surprised to see him. I said, "Hi". Of course he looked normal like in most of my dreams. He smiled and said, "I have a message for you at 12:30." He then left and I woke up. Now how real is that?! I wondered what message it was. That was before Sept. 11. In fact, it was still probably in late August. I dreaded what the message was. Was it a car accident, death, 12:30 a.m. or p.m.? Of course I purposely waited to drive home until 1pm. Since nothing happened at the p.m. side, I knew it was on the a.m. side. When night fell, I was extremely nervous. Was he going to appear and visit me? What? What dreadful thing is about to happen? For some reason, I automatically figured it was something bad. Everything that ever seems to happen in my life is unfortunate and bad. I tried to stay awake well pass midnight, looking around the house fearing what would jump out of the wall or something. Mom was sleeping upstairs as I watched music videos.

When I finally went to bed, I dreamt of him introducing me to a bunch of people. That was very much his nature, introducing me to family. I met a bunch of people, including his mom who I never really knew. She died when I was 3. They all, however, looked young and all about the same age. I guess it's like that Bible verse somewhere that when you get resurrected, your body gets restored to its best condition—or I don't know, something along those lines. I really didn't recognize that many people except my uncle. Grandma, however, did look like I expected her to look at a younger age, just like the rest of my aunts. I even saw Belief's dad. I asked daddy and the rest of them if they believed in ghosts now. Somehow they never really answered that question. Mom said maybe he meant Dec. 30, a date not a time.

After time passed, 9/11 occurred and a bunch of other things. I wondered if the end of the world was coming. Will it be Dec. 30? Well, New Years Eve came and left. I was now staying in College Park, Md. I began to have anxiety attacks due to various problems, issues, and things in my unfortunate life. I talked to this metaphysics lady who said I was a young spirit not yet recycled in reincarnation. She thought my dreams were special and nice and I had absolutely no reason to worry. What was wrong with me?! Well time went on then I had another dream.

This dream was a weird one with Daddy and my matriarchal grandpa—who is always laughing and smiling at me in each and every dream he appears. I don't remember much except I must have been over Granny's in her basement for some reason. Daddy and my grandpa appeared but it was in the form of a moving photo or flat screen TV show of some sort. On top of that, the image appeared in the form of a moving tattoo. I don't remember much conversation, if they spoke at all. I think my uncle was even in a photo or wall painting smiling. Perhaps that was a different dream, I don't know.

Well, my ringing cell phone awakened me from that dream. Usually, I have my ringer off when I'm sleep, and I rarely answer my phone if it does wake me up. For some reason, my cell rang and I even answered it. It was my mom and when she realized that I was sleeping, she said that she called just to say that she loved me. Well, OK. When I checked the time, it said 12:30pm!

Seems like people over there in the spirit realm enjoy appearing in photos and movies instead of other ways. You always see in haunted houses, movies, and even Harry Potter's Hogwarts School, ghosts in moving photos. Speaking of dreaming of the dearly departed, I had dreams of Belief's dad—as I mentioned above, a cameo from Big T's grandma, and even Renegade's mom. Of course I never told anyone because it was only a dream—with no message in it. Besides, who would waste time listening to my dreams or even believe me?

I had another odd dream that I was performing on American Idol or something. Zombies were trying to get me. I guess they were the everyday corporate Americans and judgmental, small-minded, people that I constantly deal with, I don't know. Daddy, grandpa—smiling as usual, and other relatives and friends cheered me on and were proud of me. Daddy also congratulated me for graduating from college in another dream, even though I already graduated from college. The last dream I had was one that I was half sleep and he appear to me but his image was not so clear. His face was shadowed in and he did not appeared in his usual form. I felt that I was half sleep when he walked up to my bed, talked goo goo talk to me, and them touched my hand with chin stubble. I was a bit startled. I even felt the stubble on my hand after I woke up.

Here is a letter I wrote Daddy after Sept. 11th and some of the dreams. My aunt suggested I write him a letter en-route to the funeral polar. On top of that, many people write letters and leave gifts and offerings to their loved ones, God, and even Santa, so this is not some foreign dumb idea. I still write him when I have time. And I left it right on his grave with the flowers or gift.

Tuesday, October 02, 2001

Dear Daddy;

Hello, How are you? Genki?(Japanese for how are you) I hope so. I wish you were here. Mom is coping a bit more. Floyd and Big T insist on calling me on my expensive cell phone, of course never wanting nothing. Renegade, as you probably already know, cleared out the basement in one day so the waterproof men could come. I got My Friend(car) from Aunt Sally, thanks. I told her about my dream and 12:30. She told mom. Do you mean Dec. 30? I of course got your last dream about seeking shelter and protection from the bomb?

Here is a copy of my certificate of completion from the JET Program. Was that you looking through the screen smiling when crazy Meow Meow kept harassing me? I'm trying to build me a home and "bomb shelter" before the world ends. How is everyone over there, where ever over there is? The Mormons keep coming pass. I guess I can visit their church and see the video. What do you think of the Mormons now that you are over there? Where is over there? Do you know the outcome of this ridiculous war turmoil everyone is going through? This is ridiculous! Just when I'm ready to travel, this must happen. I will build me a house, finally put a bathroom in our basement and make that into a room, and travel the world before hell freezes over and the world ends.

Well I'll talk/write to you later.

Lots of Love Always,
Me

`I ♥ Lory`

While driving on the beltway to go to VA I saw this unusual message. You know the kind that people place on bridges and fences by highways and major roads. Many schools make messages with colorful paper or cups for a football game. After 9/11 everyone placed "God bless America" messages on fences, doors, bridges, over passes, et cetera. Well I saw this sign on a highway overpass saying

`I ♥ Lory`. Even though that's not how you spell my name that is how you pronounce it. I usually tell people Lory because people seem to have a hard time spelling it the correct way, _Lourye_. It's French and inspired by my aunt's name. I deliberately tell people to spell it _Lory_ to distinguish **me and my name** from another Lori. Now I would have simply ignored it if it said `I ♥ Lori`. Every Lori I ever met spells her name that way. That's the common way to spell it. I would assume it was meant for someone else. If I saw `I ♥ Lourye` I probably would have skid off of the road. All of my life, I NEVER had a secret admirer or some friendly message in some unusual and unique form. (Perhaps before this world ends, I would actually meet a romantic man with flowers and sweet secret messages. Unfortunately, I won't hold my breath). Since it said `I ♥ Lory` I noticed it and even went back later to find the sign. Perhaps it had some note attached to it or something. I was unsuccessful at every attempt to locate it.

A week or so later, a friend named Myro and I went to Pa. to see this spectacular musical, compliments of Floyd and my roommate. En-route back, she started remembering her bad E trip and then started talking about spirituality, God, and the unusual things that happened to her. We talked the entire night in front of her house. Her roommate Nancy, who started Myro going to church, came out to go to work. She joined our conversation about Christianity and spirituality, all which Myro was completely new in. Myro didn't even recognize the antichrist in the play. Nancy invited us to follow her to work and continue our spiritual conversation. As we drove on to her job, I passed my sign!!! I started honking and we stopped to look at it. It was made from red plastic cups stuffed between the holes of the fence. I noticed the bridge was a few blocks from where my dad is laid to rest. What an interesting coincidence!

I thought this was a very lovely surprise. I took a photo of it, but of course, like every other curse upon me, the camera completely disappeared. It vanished into thin air. I developed a roll of film that I thought contained this photo as well as some other **extremely important** photos. None of the pictures on that roll, except one, came out. A freak accident? A curse released from the pit of hell? A screw up

86

by the photo guy? He claims that even if he did open the disposable camera and expose light to it, something should still come out. The only explanation is that some supernatural curse from hell and earth combined is upon me and tries to ruin absolutely everything I have and do!!

ATTACK ON MY CAR

There seems to be a million attempts to not only harass and attack EACH and EVERY area of my life, but there's even a constant attack on my dear and lovely friend—my car that is. Seems like every time she sits like the lovely and dear auto she is, some idiot harasses her. It's seems kind of like the attack on America in 2001, only it's an attack on "My Friend". And if it's not my dainty Feather, it's the previous old Nissan that I drove. Driving in DC alone is enough to be hell on a car, or any wheeled vehicle—even a skateboard, compliments of the millions of pot holes, speed bumps, traffic circles/triangles/and squiggly lines that infest the streets. On top of all of that, DC has the most confusing roads on earth. The streets are filled with yuppie government workers, lunatics, and killing machines known as cabs, all speeding 70+ miles in traffic trying to hit me.

My first car was a Nissan which had many problems—car and otherwise. It was first stolen/towed by the terrorist organization known as DC traffic enforcement. It was kidnapped while quietly being parked overnight in Wild D's ghetto neighborhood. It was also in an accident by some African—who had NO insurance; when I was trying to politely drive home from some wannabe jazz café that never even hired me.

I bought a car in Florida being that their public transportation is great, as long as it's your own. Otherwise they have absolutely NO public transportation, forcing everyone to get a car. I still have that car and unlike the Nissan, she's the most reliable friend I have, and so dear and lovely. When I first returned from Florida, I went to this DC club where they enjoy towing cars for fun. Welcome back to Washington! Also on the same dear and delicate car was theft of my duffel bag and cell phone in front of Howard Univ. gym. My window had a microscopic crack, enough for gutter rat thieves to steal from. She was also attacked on New Years Eve, also at Howard Univ. Some hood rat thief broke her window and then found that I had absolutely nothing to steal, so they left me with glass all over my car and my lovely selection of music on my seat. Serves you right you gutter rat thief, hope you cut your hand!!

As I mentioned earlier in this book, this homeless drag queen stole food, wine, a radio, and My Friend. I told the very efficient cops who didn't find her. They wouldn't even dust for prints and obviously didn't update their computer the following year. Over a year after I found her, some cop who had nothing else to do, stops me while I'm lost in Laurel and reports it found. She also incurred an accident by this reject ex DC cop who hung out at fat girl strip clubs via his USS tanker thug mobile.

The D C government may not be able to find stolen cars, or any other useful activity but they sure as hell know how to issue tickets, boot cars and then steal/tow them. My Friend was nicely minding her business in DC when they decided to kidnap her. After booting her, they held her for ransom at $750. Solely because she's My Friend, and only form of transportation, I rescued her.

My current residence is not only extremely shiftless in regards to management, the greedy, terrorists steal as many cars daily as possible, including my delicate Feather. Twice they tried to steal her. Once, while I was unloading this heavy desk, the A'hole hitched her up. I came out just in time. They then demanded $75 cash as ransom. They also towed her because the tags were allegedly dead. They also towed Myro's sister car, my friend's car, and attempted to steal Floyds's car. They started towing at 8:00pm and we arrived back at 8:01pm. They were inspecting his car ready to rig it up. Obviously doing nothing during the day except being a public menace and harassing innocent residents!

When I returned from Japan, I went to make an appointment at this wannabe dentist in this filthy building next to PG Plaza Subway. He charged me for an exam without even cleaning or doing much to my teeth. Of course, I immediately complained to my insurance company and told on him, then immediately changed to another dentist who actually had a respectable office. When I initially went to schedule my appointment at that filthy rat building, another swarm of terrorists towed my car.

Also, right after the one week black out, she was in another accident. **I saw this "scam" on 20/20 about insurance fraud.** Some crook, who actually worked for the same insurance company I was with, stopped suddenly on a rainy day, and the lady behind me slammed into me. My Friend was sandwiched between the cars and injured on both ends. And finally, I can prove that I drove everywhere I said via parking tickets from every city my car has been in. And like any respectable hippie, of course all unpaid!

On a post note, as I try to proofread to FINALLY FINISH this book, I recently bought a used car at a local auction. My Friend, also known as Feather, is tired of driving a million miles a week. My church alone is over 25 miles away since I moved. Struggling, she drove the 5 millions miles and just barely made it to church. Unfortunately, she wouldn't start afterwards. I left her there in the parking lot. I pray for her safety and repair as well as this new (used) car I just got. Less than a week after I bought him, another band of terrorists towed him from out of this lot while he was minding his business trying to sleep. When I finally took Feather to rescue him, they charged me over $150. To this day—over a month later—they have YET showed me the photograph of his alleged illegal parking space. There obviously are a few good and useful towing companies who help you when you are stranded and come to rescue your car. Of course, this good quality service is only compliments of my mom's AARP roadside membership. Other insurance companies have extremely poor quality service, operators, towing, and everything else. The best thing they offer is a complaint section. I guess you must be a senior citizen to get fair and decent service!

And for several months over the summer I had to use public transportation due to my newly bought car being in transition. Not broke, just in transition—I won't claim any additional bad luck on him. Well, due to my million-dollar surplus and wonderful non-existence helpmate; my financially struggling, poor-little-mom had to bail me out. She helped pay to fix my car—fearing me walking from the bus stop at night in my "prestigious" neighborhood. Well during this time, I realized something. There are few guarantees in life, very few. Taxes, death, and the J bus continuously being late. Being that this bus only ran once an hour, it was always a delight to have to wait that much longer for this retarded bus.

ANTICS W/RENEGADE WHO BECAME KONG

I officially renamed Renegade "Kong" once seeing how much of an ape he could be, such as; throwing tantrums, breaking items, yelling and screaming in public, among many other gorilla like antics. Kong's mom was selling her condo and moving to the country. I wanted/needed a spacious place to stay on my own and to store my stuff. Mom wanted me and Kong to move in with her. Kong asked if he moved in, where would she put all of her stuff which is a very good point. There is no room for me and my stuff, where in the world would Kong fit his junk? My stuff I had from my last place was already in storage since I returned from Japan. My mom has a really cozy country cottage style house full of what knots. I started to look for a place on my own and for myself, but—despite what Kong and many others think—I was trying to be considerate and look for something for the both of us. He tells me how nice Baltimore is. I give him the benefit of the doubt, the only thing I know about Baltimore is the Inner Harbor. As my roommate said, me being slum on my cards and not noticing and realizing things, I overlooked the many signs and wonders and foolishly moved in with him.

Renegade and his mom started packing up their condo a week before they had to move. He actually waited until the day before to pack. I had to get a u-haul and his mom had to call his job to say how he was sick so he could get off work (he did have a cold). They spent the entire day rushing and packing."

We move to north Baltimore in the pit of the ghetto. When we arrived in Baltimore, we were greeted by a heroin march. The addicts asked to help in exchange for money. One stole my food stamps.

The place was so lovely. It was shot to hell and old. We had this tiny little mouse. I'm not scared of mice, I am, however, afraid of rats. There were many huge rats living in the alley behind us. The back yard and trashcans were like Rat Disney Land. Being that I can't tell a mouse from a baby rat, I wanted a cat, immediately. After all, what makes you think that one of those huge, infested rats didn't give birth and the baby decided to visit our place? Ms. Cutie's brother came to live with us. Ms. Cutie is mom's sophisticated, adorable, fat cat. She's a very intelligent super fat that's white with black spots. Ms. Cutie was supposed to move up to Baltimore, but mom—who initially wanted to evict her and put her out—kidnapped her and wanted to keep her.

Unlike Ms. Cutie, who we got as a baby kitten, her brother was big. He was scared and used to living in the rural trailer park area. This urban ghetto was very scary for him. He would hide in the kitchen until we all went to sleep. Then, he'd sneak out, eat, crap, and hide again. Even though he was very anti-social, it worked; the mouse/baby rat was gone. For some reason, Kong thought the cat ran away every week. He would then throw out the dirt box/kitty litter and the next day the cat would crap on his clothes or the floor. Of course Kong was mad at this.

After going through this several times, he decided to find this cat. He searched and found the cat squished up inside the corner of the stove. Go figure, how a huge cat squeezes into a tiny space. He was amused and decided to entertain himself by planting firecrackers inside the gas stove to scare the cat out. Of course, I ran in the room in case the entire kitchen exploded. I should have run outside. I tried to stop him, but of course, he NEVER listens to me. And off went the firecrackers and out came the cat. The angels must have been working that day too; the house is still in one piece.

Kong also would get mad a lot. One of his main problems was his lack of anger management and realism. He'd throw temper tantrums all of the time. He'd brake bottles and throw them out the window. He'd yell and scream on our balcony cursing about everyone. He even broke our banister off. Of course it was my fault for complaining and making him go nuts to break the banister in the first place. Turns out he hurt his side when he fell off the steps like King Kong. Our slumlord found out via the wannabe cops below us who filed a vandalism report on him. Our slumlord of course complained and asks us to pay for the banister. He, however, had a problem with fixing the toilet in the basement that backed up sewage onto the basement floor weekly. I finally called the city on him so he finally had it fixed. He even had the nerve—like my current ghetto lord here—to not want us to have cats to scare away the rats that live <u>on his property</u>.

Next, Kong's sister moved in. He would complain about her and say how much of a thief she was. *Of course she wasn't one anymore when it was time for her to move in.* I really didn't know her so I could only go by what I heard. I should have used some intellect and kept my laptop, radio, and other valuables at home or get a lock—that slum lord wasn't able to fix—on my door. Soon afterwards, her boyfriend moved in. Of course, no one had any money. Not long after that, between her, her man, Robocop downstairs, the addicts, and who knows, my laptop was conveniently stolen from my bedroom. It was definitely an inside job. I mean, how would anyone know exactly where it was.

Another Kong associate was the Professor of Funk. His place was so fresh and lovely. He called and hired Kong to clean it. When I arrived to the dirty, slum apartment building to pick up Kong, you could almost smell the fragrance from the street. Of course, the entire block stunk. The Professor of Funk lived in a one bedroom with 2 big full-grown dogs, a rack of cats, and he was old and senile. There was cat, dog, and human crap all over the entire house. It was on the floor, the couch, on the dog-spit-chewed-up furniture, just everywhere. The crap hardened into decorations and sat conveniently throughout the apartment. It was cat, dog, and human food everywhere. I asked where was the nurse that was supposed to be taking care of him. Kong said, "Yea yea. She's dead in the closet." If she was, it wouldn't be any surprise. I never in my entire life smelt anything so disgusting. I actually had to run out after a few minutes. It smelt like **solid RAW AMMONIA** with a hint (or 5000 hints) of disgusting funk. It was so filthy and dirty, I only saw 2 roaches—and they both died on the kitchen counter trying to escape out the window. Kong was cleaning under his box spring and, "meow, meow, meow" there was a litter of kittens living inside the box spring.

Soon after the Prof. died, we rescued the animals that didn't jump out the window to escape. First it was Fuzzy, Meow Meow, and the Runt, and then, there was the arrival of Fat. Fat is a super sized Siamese cat. Fat's brother, who was bigger than her, must have also jumped out the window to freedom. She was pregnant but had an infection of filth and was oozing when I was driving her home to mom. Mom took her to the vet assuming she was giving birth. Her kittens died inside her from her filth infection. Mom kept Fat but Fat is very jealous and spoiled. She began to fight Ms. Cutie so mom evicted her and I took Fat back to Baltimore.

Nina, the Professor's ex wife, moved in with us too. Kong was pleased, he had someone to cook, clean, sex, smoke, and drink with. I was actually jealous—even though he claimed she was gay—so I accidentally tossed her shoes in the trash. They unfortunately found them. After a while, I had nothing against her. He was a mess and I didn't want him after some time, I just hoped in the beginning something would work out. I was VERY desperate. I was so desperate, I told Kong on a trip to Baltimore, "I am desperate and at my wits end. I am so desperate, I'm willing to settle even for you." He burst out laughing and sarcastically said, "Yeeeaaaa." I do know it doesn't matter if you are desperate, down and out, drunk, homeless, sleep, or even in sound mind for some men. As long as there is an option for sex, everything else can come later. Are you too ugly, old, or something? Don't worry about that, just close your eyes or put this bag over your head and let's get to work. Maybe I'm too much a prude, but I do have a minimum level of standards. If a guy tells me I'm only a quick act of convenience and lets get busy before he gets back in his right mind, I'd be very insulted and wouldn't want him at all.

EveN KonG's TirEd oF mE

On top of that, he'd complain about me every chance he got, to everyone he knew, everyone I knew, and even complete strangers. He would say I'm lazy, fat, self centered, inconsiderate, stingy, and stupid. Perhaps I have some—or many—amounts of these traits, but I do give myself way more credit than that. I know

I'm an outrageous mess, but I do give myself way more credit than 98% of these men I deal with give me. They obviously get tired of me quick, then take me for granted. No one is perfect and I do have many good, charming, positive traits—which got me this far in life—along with the bad. If I was SOOO horrible, why did I meet so many people that are willing to hang with me, deal with me, and so on? He obviously was tired of me also, and thusly took me for granted too.

The only difference between him and Vic (who I'll get to later) was that Vic didn't have too many friends, girl friends, or family members to complain on me about. Most of his family never met or knew me. Most of my family never met him and the few friends and family members that did meet him offered mix feelings. Some were cordial, friendly, or indifferent to him. Others disliked and distanced themselves from him. Kong, on the other hand, amazingly had a magic and charm upon him to convert my family to liking him. My friends were either indifferent, cordial and friendly, or thought he was a maniac. My family still speaks cordially and kindly of Kong to this day. He is usually a hilariously funny and kind person. It's just when you are around him and close to him for a longer period of time, his tantrums, vandalism, inability, and insanity breaks in.

I still am quite desperate, but not that desperate. Even though Kong now had 2 girls living with him, as well as his sister, he wished to be a pimp and would find and bring home crack whores. Nina, the Professor of Funk's ex-wife, was irate about this so she stole a rack of his CD's and left. I can't say I feel sorry for him; he shouldn't have brought home a bunch of thieving crack whores in the first place. What do you expect when addicts surround you? That hurt him the most; he LOVED his music. He was quite obsessive about his music. Because of this, he tossed her 30" TV out the window and busted it on the ground.

Even though at one point we had 5 people living with us, they—including me—were all broke. Kong was the only one bringing home any amount of money each month, and that was unemployment. My substitute-teaching job paid little. Thusly, we had a cycle of late bills, cut off notices, and disconnected phones. Being that the main reason I moved to Baltimore was to establish my music, writings, art, and finish what I started, I was never going to progress in this environment. I had a fax but no phone line due to the excellent disconnected phone service. I had a laptop with internet and all of my work on it, but not anymore compliments of the New Year's thief! I had a million ideas and also a million and one headaches, distractions, and insanity going on around me. I could not focus, progress, and finish a thing. I started plotting how to get out of the lease and move. Kong and his sister claimed they were both moving, I guess it never worked out for them, who knows. I sure as hell got up out of that mad house. The official icing on my madhouse cake was when Kong tossed a crate at me for some rice I burnt. He also threw a chair at his sister for drying her sweaters, jeans, and clothes in the clothes dryer. Well, time to go!

THE ESCAPE

My transition from leaving the mad house was this bus trip to San Francisco. Of course, that was an adventure in itself. My mom—and grandmother and aunt—are Kong's biggest advocate. I was considerate, even though few people seem to notice it—and didn't tell everyone the stuff he did and so forth. I lied telling him I was moving back home but a mutual friend told him where I was going. I lied and told my mom I was only moving my stuff there for safety and to deter theft. Even though she asked for Fat, my Siamese cat, she complained when I dropped Fat off to baby-sit for several weeks, having no one else to watch her. Kong called and tattle-taled on me.

En route to San Francisco on the Greyhound, I met the chicken bone man who had snot on his face like a toddler. He kept tying to steal my pillow while I was laying on it. I was about to curse him out. Then he started playing with chicken bones laughing while pushing them under my seat with his umbrella. Perhaps it was some form of homeless voodoo. When I got to Iowa, some toothless guy sitting in Greyhound said, "Welcome to the armpit of America!" Also some guy, who must have took some drugs, got on the bus in the Midwest. His eyes bucked open the entire time and he talked a lot saying he just escaped prison and ended up getting kicked off the bus in the middle of nowhere. Reno was a surprising disappointment. Everything was closed except some hotel/casino full of addicts and homeless people. We—some other passengers and I—almost missed the bus dealing with this worthless casino. Some homeless crack head tried to steal my money.

I stayed in San Francisco for a week with Yoichi from Japan. On the way back this Bulgarian guy was going to Chicago via Utah—where I went to the Mormon museum. He caught my bus instead of another Chicago bound bus going a different route. Every time we stopped, which was a lot of times, he asked the driver which bus should he catch to Chicago. It was quite funny, but not as funny as the quote made when we finally arrived. It was cold as ice up north, even though it was May. He said, "I'm going to froze."

The trip took a final turn for the worst after leaving Chicago. I sat on some p#ss!!! The lazy, shiftless, employees did absolutely NOTHING about it. On top of that, the heat then stopped working on the bus and I did "froze." In Cleveland, some A'hole baggage guy lied that he was a manager, refused to let me get my bags, and told me if I didn't like it, fly next time. I'm writing a formal letter of complaint to corporate regarding this dreadfully repulsive treatment and their disgusting customer service!!! By the way, that was the LAST trip I took on Greyhound!

95

MovInG ouT oF thE maD HousE

When I got back from San Francisco, I conveniently moved into my new apartment. I found it by the grace of God. I wanted and thought of this place when I was scheming and planning my escape from Witch Mountain, AKA Baltimore's madhouse. Of course, the apartment had a 100-person waiting list. They closed it for the spring and weren't going to open it again until the fall. I looked at several places. They were all inhabited by a bunch of pre-yuppie stuck-ups. Every apartment was supposedly taken. I went to the university off campus housing board and saw one last ad for the building I wanted. I checked it out and it was jacked up, filthy, junky, and shot to hell, but it was Berkley Apts. I said I wanted it and wrote a post-dated check to hold it for me. I was even allowed to move some stuff in before I left for California.

I even slipped through the cracks of Maryland's application fee. I applied for government aid and admission to several universities. I applied on line for several universities but never paid the application fee. Some schools won't even process the application until you pay. Thank God, MD will process it and expect you to pay when you drop off your transcripts. Somehow, they "lost" my application or something. I gave them a copy of my transcripts and they somehow found it. In the commotion of it all, I somehow slipped through the cracks of paying for my application. It may only be $20, but every penny counts.

My roommates Filthy and Linda were super hippie, green peace, bong smoking, keg drinking, drug users. They were cool, just filthy as hell. Floyd had to help me clean the apartment. There was lipstick all over the mirror. The closet doors were down and being used as tables for cards and beer pong. The window screens were on the floor and being used as a plant stand. There were over 50 holes in the walls throughout the apartment. And the place was full of Filthy's junk, trash, and food.

Compliments of the grace of God, I even slipped through the cracks of getting on the lease with Filthy. The management was good, shiftless, and ghetto. The landlord hardly worked and her secretary had long nails, kids, and a Bar B Q in the office. Because, to my convenience, they didn't do their job thoroughly, I got on the lease, without even a credit or background check. The background check, I'd pass, the credit one, I'm not sure. On top of that, I was able to slip through cracks again by securing the apartment when thousands were waiting.

fEATHER u-hauL

While living with Filthy, Kong called my mom supposedly "looking for me." I disregarded his few calls, but because his sister called several other occasions, I decided to finally return the call. She claimed they were getting evicted. I figured she was lying and just being shady not wanting to hold my desk and two or three other items I left due to lack of space and help transporting it out. Even though I never got a chance to get a van, I decided to drive My Feather up there to move my desk since they are supposedly getting evicted. I went up there the following evening. They had cable, HBO, working phone service, and absolutely nothing is packed—even though that could be a track record. I had to manually unscrew the desk with Kong's screwdriver. I appeased him as much as possible. The only thing he complained about, outside a few grunts regarding the landlord and supposed eviction, was his boom box that his cup of pure vodka fell on because I accidentally moved the table when I got up. I told him his money was at my mom's to appease him and that the landlord would surely listen to him.

His sister's boyfriend helped me carry my desk as Kong's patience ran thin. He started complaining about me leaving my three items—which included my desk kept in his sister's room—in Baltimore. He threw my items down the steps. On one occasion, while her boyfriend was walking down the steps with a piece of my desk, Kong tossed another section of my plywood pulp desk down the steps barely missing him and me. My desk was ripped and I had to get the drunken janitor at Berkley Apts. to fix it. While loading the last things in my car and talking to his sister about how they can possibly be getting evicted if cable is still on, Meow Meow was crying. Kong kindly tossed the kitten out the 2nd floor bathroom window because he was crying. Thank God for 9 lives; he definitely used up several living with Kong.

kONg's mOvE

A week or so after this dreadful incident, I was preparing to go to Hershey Park with my family. My mom blew up my cell telling me to come home, someone is here to see me. I knew my little cousin was coming over so what's the rush? I finally got my clothes gathered to wash them at home. My mom greets me at the door. I go downstairs to wash my clothes when I hear the washing machine on. I wonder whose male looking clothes are these. The last person on my mind is Kong. I mean, he's in Baltimore supposedly getting evicted, why would he be here? I go upstairs to get my mail as I wait for that load to finish and I see Kong using the phone. Surprised, I mumble hi and go directly to my room. He talks to me from the other room asking about Floyd and other mutual friends as if nothing happened and everything is fine. The perfect sign of insanity. I offered vague and quick answers to questions.

After I check my mail I proceed to go downstairs when I mention his clothes. I need to wash so he needs to get his stuff out of the wash—my motive for reminding him of his clothes. As he loads the dryer and I load the wash, he asks about where I live and what I'm doing, and offers me his Kong-like plans. I vaguely listen and ask about his sister and their alleged eviction. He tells me how he needs a moving van, which is why he's down here. They have U-Hall stores in Baltimore, why is he down here? Secondly, he has no license nor does his sister. At least his sister can drive. Why is he down here trying to get a van, instead of the Baltimore U-Haul with a licensed driver? As I wait for my clothes to wash and his to dry (approximately an hour) mom tells me how he injured his foot on the job—a usual, and he's getting evicted—something I already know. He came for the $300 you owe him. What?! First of all, that is just money I promised him to appease him. I never planned to pay for squat. I had many of my personal items (such as my car, water pitcher, laptop, teapot, and such) damaged via rough treatment, destroyed via vandalism, or even stolen. Secondly, it was my security deposit lost to the slumlord compliments of their eviction.

My mom actually expected me to help him move and get a van for him. Kong had difficulty calling and making a van reservation? As soon as I put my first load in the dryer and the other load to wash, I left. Mom asked me where I was going and told me, as if I didn't know, that Kong was upstairs on the phone. I said OK, I'd be right back, and drove off. After calling several friends and blowing off steam, I returned hours later. My aunt was there trying to give me a guilt trip. I half listened and tried to tell them what they wanted to hear and stayed inside avoiding him and them as much as possible. I talked with my 10-year-old cousin and told her and her friend that he was crazy. Her friend tried to be funny and ask him if he was crazy. He responded he didn't know under his voice, frustrated that I didn't want to deal with him.

sHaME oN yoU loRy

When he was ready to go, my mom and aunt actually tried to get me to take him to the Greyhound or somewhere. I asked to drive her car because I didn't want him in my car. He's rough and breaks too many things, and my car is very delicate. My mom, who was insulted at me for trying to drive him home in her car, offered to take him instead. My aunt, after a shame on you lecture that stuck as long as liquid water on plastic, decided to take him home. The next time I saw him was at his mom's funeral where I basically agreed to help him get his stuff out of the woods where his mom lived. In exchange, he would help me move to another apartment upstairs. It was during that time that he playfully tried to bang down my bedroom door when I was getting dressed, thus waking up and startling my roommates. He also decided to break the Venetian blinds off the window because he had to stay at my apartment instead of his tent in Baltimore.

WARNING:

If you feel that you may have read enough—thanks for your patronage and support! 😀

IT DOESN'T GET ANY BRIGHTER, HAPPIER, OR SWEETER FROM HERE!

Basically BITTER RAMBLINGS & RANTS 'til the end!

Not exactly for the overly sensitive, uptight, politically correct, and/or faint at heart, and

!!! YOU GOT YOUR WARNING!!!

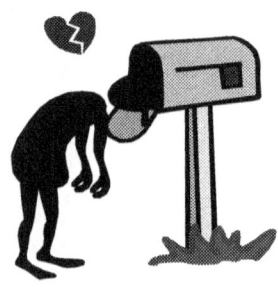

THE WORST, THE WORSTER, & THE WORSTEST!!

I got this word from Myro's ex-boyfriend. She is the one who introduced me to the church I currently go to. He is a straight up comedian, a wannabe Dave Chappelle. Like Kong, he would make up and say funny things. He would tell stories using his amusing style, and this was one of them. Like how his friend's old car, which was a certified citrus lemon, broke down in the middle of a major rode during rush hour.... "and that was just.... just the worstest." I liked that word so much, I still use it today. It is a perfect word and way to describe the horrible pile of men that unfortunately keep appearing in my oh so lovely life.

While I was in Japan, my mom didn't send my Christmas gifts off until January. It was the most wonderful, cozy, and warm Christmas I ever had. I felt like banging my head into a brick wall over how nice it was. Every foreigner went back home or traveled with their friends. All my friends were working Japanese who didn't celebrate Christmas, it's just another day. And unlike America where they have toys for tots, and such, to help the poor and homeless feel welcome— the Japanese who don't celebrate Christmas, made Christmas feel like a **typical American Valentines Day**. Wonderful for all of those freaking couples out there. I guess single people don't exist!!

There is ABSOLUTELY NOTHING for the single except misery and loneliness on Valentines Day. Where's the Hearts for Singles campaign or some other caring and thoughtful attempt on helping the lonely female who needs a Valentine more than anyone on earth. For those darn couples have each other every other day so even if he forgets or does nothing, she can yell at him and get something the next day. He was there before and he'll most likely be there after. The only thing singles have is a slap mockery, snub of the nose, and a smack dab in your face reality check that you are not only lonely, you are single and gets absolutely nothing!

My wonderful dad gave me something every year and every now and then, a male friend would give me something. My mom gives me something sometimes. And the only thing these slugs of the male specie give me is abandonment way before Valentines Day so I'd spend another Valentines alone, lonely, and with no one. Of course, these same slugs give me nothing on my birthday either. They make sure to run, hide, and melt away—like a slug with salt on it—way before Valentines and my birthday. It's the most important day for a female, just like the Super Bowl and basketball play offs are for you males. Of course you can't expect the average man to even remember this.

A (very) feW gooD meN

1. The 1st nice American boyfriend I had.

Before I can complain about ALL men outside of Europe, Africa, and New York City, I must marvel, praise, and give credit where credit is due. The first guy who officially claimed the title as boyfriend was this black American guy in DC. I was a grade and year older than him and met him at People's Drug, aka CVS. We met and dated over the summer. He either worked there or went there a lot. I was in 9th grade and he must have been in 8th. He was a really great, wonderful guy. We would talk all night on the phone and he never once tried to molest me. He was very respectful and enjoyable to be around. The saying girls mature faster than boys must really be evident. Outside the fact that we went to different schools—he went to an all male Catholic school, and I went to a super ghetto public school—I was also somewhat embarrassed of him because he rode his bike to meet me and that seemed so child-like. I guess in high school, I hoped for an older guy, I mean gentleman, with a car—not an adolescent on a bike. Other than that, he was one of the nicest guys I dated. We gradually stopped calling each other once school started, however we stayed friends. I even introduced him to my cousin and they dated a bit.

2. Majid and toilet.

Myro was astounded that in her eyes, I never had an official relationship, in particular one that was longer than a few months. She asked if there was EVER a guy or relationship I had that wasn't pure crap. I thought hard about it for a bit then replied Majid. Outside of the guy above on the bike, Majid is no doubt, the best guy I dated to this point. He was from Morocco. I'm attracted to north and east Africans. Unlike East Africans who only marry their own, the rest of Africa would date and marry anyone, and they also like thick black Americans. I saw Majid shopping one day with JV. He worked in a trendy male retail store in downtown, DC. We eyed each other as I left the store.

101

In fact, it was after JV and I left that store that we went to this Asian wig store where I called myself window shopping. The Asian owner said, "You want try on?" Of course I replied, sure. We tried on the wig then she told me the price. I said I was just looking at that time. She replied, "If you no buy, we close now." I was insulted, how dare you, I can't window shop without you putting me out?! As we both left, JV gagged laughing, as if it was a comedy show.

Some time later I went back to his shop pretending to look around. We spoke a bit and somehow exchanged numbers. I called him and he called me. Unlike many stupid Americans who have these **foolish games** in regards to calling and spending time with each other—"Oh, she's pressed because she called me.... .," foreigners usually never play those games. You should be honored that someone DID call you and give you the time of day, instead of judging and looking down at them. We called each other almost everyday, if not everyday. He never seemed to get tired of me calling and I loved to hear from him.

We saw each other almost every day too. I would meet him after he got off of work and spend the evening with him. Many times we simply would go to some bar with his co-workers and hang out. Other times we would go out. We went to the museum, the Inner Harbor in Baltimore, a picnic, and various parks in Maryland. He drove and even had a car—note to peasants who actually think women want to drive you around.

I'd rather ride the subway together than drive and chauffeur someone—man or woman—around in my delicate Feather. Like the exquisite lady that I am, deserving of royalty, I enjoy being driven around. Swautch even called me "Queen of Sheba." His car wasn't that luxurious, which I could care less about; I just enjoyed cruising the city with him. That's chivalry and romantic, at least to me. Majid and I even went to Trax, and I always said that I wouldn't want to go to a club with a guy. What if I want to dance and meet another guy while there? However, I really enjoyed myself with him. I didn't even desire dancing with other men, even though there were many other cute guys there. Majid even was the one who introduced me to a mango. He was very romantic and wonderful!

When Myro and I talked of it, her boyfriend—a typical guy—was disgusted by our desire of romance. He (like many guys who could care less about that dreaded Valentines Day) think only of themselves. This is why women are never satisfied, sexually and otherwise. Many guys think of romance as some mushy female deed or something annoying. Roses, boat rides at the lake, picnics, candle light dinners, or holding hands walking on the beach or in the park are wonderfully romantic but annoying to many guys. In fact, when I lived with the Nicaraguan family in Va., the 16 year old who was in and out of jail said he wouldn't be caught DEAD inside a museum. Shocked, I wondered why. I guess he feels why go to some stupid museum when I can go back to jail. And the professional, educated guys that do like romance are SOOOO programmed and zombified; they only date trophies! You must be a top model, size skeleton, dime piece over 5'5" for them to even give you their number. Otherwise, they only want some quick head in exchange for a soda and a blunt. And most guys who seem to deal with a woman like me would rather call romance movies and carry out, or "at my place or yours," so they can molest you via some perverted sexual act they enjoy. To me, and many females, romance has nothing to do with sex! In fact, the only romantic part of sex is the sensual part that annoys most guys. They simply want to get down to business and not participate in annoying hugs, soft touches, conversation, and cuddles.

Women, at least I, enjoy gentle touches and dry soft gentle kisses—not wet sloppy licks. Romance is subtle. Gentle rubs along her back, playing and talking into her hair to tickle her scalp with your breath, not pulling the hair. Obvious some women like it quick and rough, but even women made music agreeing with me. "I want a man with a slow hand. I want a man with an easy touch. I want somebody who will understand, not come and go in a heaping rush" or something along those lines. Compare that to the typical R&B song or any other pop song by some guy supposedly singing to a girl.

Perhaps the reason he was so romantic, didn't take me for granted, and was nice, was because he was older. I guess outside of a foreigner, you must find someone much older to appreciate you, not worry about those stupid dating games, and show you romance. Majid was a bit older than me, by around 12 years. Big T rudely claimed he saw him on Good Morning America. I asked what he was talking about. He claimed he saw them recognize him for his birthday along with all of the other dinosaurs that turned 95 years old or older.

He lived with one other African in a one bedroom. I guess his roommate slept on the porch. I remember the first time we did it was a story in itself. He told his roommate to leave so he went into the back porch to give us privacy. We played my Enigma tape—which he kept—and we had sex. In the beginning, it was sex as usual—meaning that the man mainly gets the pleasure—and suddenly I actually begin to enjoy it. This was astounding being that this never happens. Sex with a guy and pleasure for me? That was a first—and unfortunate last.

Well we both seemed to be enjoying it, then I felt this warm sensation go in me. "What was that?!" He simply smiled. Not knowing what happened I repeated it then got up and saw the busted condom. Freaking out about disease and pregnancy, I ran to the bathroom wondering what to do. Perhaps if I soak myself, the semen will exit…. hopefully. I looked in their extremely filthy and dirty bathroom and said I didn't want to touch the tip of my delicate toe in his bathtub, let alone my private. The toilet…. no good! Well here's the sink. I thought, perhaps I can soak it in here. I filled up the sink with water and sat on it to soak my private. I sat for less than a minute before "BAM" the sink fell off the wall. "Oh my God, what happened," as water fell everywhere. Majid rushed to the bathroom and simply said, "You effed up now," in his accent.

Like most foreigners, he had a second job. He also worked near UDC (Univ. of the District of Columbia). I sat in his car and waited while he worked for 3 hours. I basically fell asleep and the corrupt meter maids, who have nothing else to do—like stopping crimes and murders—gave me a ticket while I was still in the car. What type of crap is that? When he found out, he argued at me. I told him I'd dispute it for him. They refused to grant me asylum regarding this stupid ticket that I unfairly got while I was in the car. So he was upset that he had to pay it. I told him to forget about it, I never pay any of my parking tickets. He preferred to pay his. He let me use his car once and when I met him, we went to the park to talk. When he went to turn it on, it wouldn't start. Now this had nothing to do with me. I drove the car perfectly fine. He was in the driver's seat and it was then that it wouldn't start. He blamed me of course.

Majid and his roommate moved from that place to an efficiency for the both of them, typical refugee style shelter. The new place was full or roaches. I went there once and roaches crawled on me wherever I sat. I ended up standing in the hall because the roaches kept harassing me. I guess between the sink, no privacy due to his new living arrangements, and his car, he became tired of me.

3.   Spike Lee DJ.

I met this DJ who reminded me of Spike Lee. He of course was from NYC. He was a cool guy. I'd chill at his house and we'd listen to music. He never tried to molest nor rape me. He had no car but we'd go on dates on the metro. I met him one July 4th while I was chilling downtown alone after work, while everyone was picnicking. We both worked downtown at tourist attractions. I worked at Tourmobile and he worked in food concession at one of the monuments. He was a nice guy. I locked my keys in my car once over his house and panicked. He calmed me and said he'd get them out. Obviously he did. I don't remember much else. We never had sex and he respected me as a lady. So I definitely put him in the GOOD GUY category.

anD ThiS iS tHE lAST oF thE gOoD gUYS....

4.   Moas & green card

When I met Moas, who's also from N. Africa, he spoke 15 words of English. He wasn't that impressive. He worked washing cars, probably under the table, and tried to molest me when he would visit. He even felt me up and tried to get some in a public phone booth outside. Years later, when he spoke much better

104

English, he offered me $5000 for marriage. Being super broke and not realizing what all I had to do, I hesitantly agreed. He said I could even move in with him. When I first met him he lived in an efficiency with 3 or 4 roommates. He then—like the Jefferson's—moved on up to a 1 bedroom with 7 people. I guess 3 or more slept in the bedroom, 3 slept in the living room, and there was a mattress in the kitchen. He claimed they used a mattress for a table to eat on. Of course you do. Surely I'd move in to get gang raped by the horde of horny Tunisians and sleep in the spacious and luxurious closet or bathroom.

He claimed all I had to do was say, "I do," at the court. He paid for my pedicure, some shoes and clothes and offered me money. After we left the court he gave me less than $1000. I asked where the rest of the money was. He said that I'd get it once he got his papers. Every several months he'd call needing something; tax forms, a signature, a possible interview, and it seemed to go on and on. I even asked Floyd to pretend he was my fiancé to scare him off. That stopped him for a good long while.

I soon moved to Japan and forgot about him. He called and left several messages on my voice mail regarding some interview with INS. I told him if he bought me a Round Trip ticket on ANA airlines, I'd call it even. I guess he never got the money. How else is he expecting me to go to America for his green card? When I returned for daddy, he called and I finally spoke to him. He said his father died also while he was here. Surely no one would lie about that. He was dating and wanted to marry his newborn baby's mother. Thank God, hallelujah, finally, he's off my back and on another, and this time, it's hopefully for real. I won't say he's that bad, but he's definitely not in the good guy category simply for molesting me constantly. That's definitely a turn off.

5. Ami the Jew

Another worsest Swautch tried to set me up with is Ami the Jew from Is-rye-yell (Israel). Of course Swautch was trying to be funny. He spoke about as much English as Moas, around 16 words. He worked as a hired hand in furniture delivery. Swautch worked as a salesman in the same store. Ami called me a lot but I was solely being cordial to him. I was in no way interested in him. I guess I was reluctant from my preconceived phobias about Jews bombing things up and fighting all of the time—not as if they fight here—among other media centered fears. I was not interested in being blown up, in warfare or for financial problems. I stood him up on several occasions.

He finally came to see me at work. I see why Swautch tried to be funny, he looked like a jacked up Nicholas Cage who fell off a train, dragged on the ground, and swung from a tree. And I don't find Nicholas Cage attractive at all. He said that his grandfather was from Africa. He is basically a North African

Safaric Jew and N. Africans are usually attractive. His face was horrible but he showed chivalry. He bought me dinner while I was at work then he massage my back and played in my hair without trying to rape me. Of course, he's neither American nor Americanized yet. I guess Moas slipped through the cracks. Perhaps he was in America long enough to know you can molest the "typical American female whore" instantly but not here long enough to speak English.

I can definitely say Ami dispelled the myth of the stereotypical cheap and greedy Jew. He spent loads of money on me and showed me plenty of chivalry. He drove his roommate's car. He would not be anything I would call attractive. He solely had a nice body. I guess if you lift furniture daily, you would be cut too. After spending a fair amount of money on me, I gave him sex. He gave me the keys to his place and came home for lunch and sex and went back to work. He wasn't that much of an affectionate man anymore; and after the first few weeks, the language barrier kicked in and his chivalry kicked out. Soon, he said his father ordered him home for marriage. I guess sowing his royal male oats, as Semi did in "Coming to America", ended. He had a brother who started a respectable business in NY and married a lovely Jewish woman. "You came to the US and became a lowly hired hand, date fat blacks, and smoke weed until your bottom lip is bleeding and cracked. You're an embarrassment to the Jewish race." And that was the end of that one.

6. Worthless, leftover, Boston Market peasant

I met this less than moderate looking peasant while I was getting an oil change. He started a conversation, and I figured he was a half way decent guy. We exchanged numbers. This peasant would call me and say nothing on the phone. You know the kind you must hold all of the conversation with and the only thing they can do is answer questions with a yes or no and repeat the same battery of 2 or 3 questions to you. "What are you doing?" and "Are you coming out?"

Well, this peasant claimed he was a computer engineer and programmer just laid off. When we finally met up, I showed him some specs off my dinosaur of a computer because I wanted to buy a voice processor. He looked blankly at it, then looked at it again. Shocked, I asked if he understood it and what software program I should get. He stared at it some more and handed it back to me. He mumbled something, which I guess meant he knew jack squat on computers and just lied about it. Being that he looked stupid with it, he changed the subject. We went to Boston Market and he waited in the car while I went and spent my money on my food. I figured the least he could do is treat me since he slithered out of helping me check out software at a computer store. Obvious, his lack of knowledge prevented him from helping me select good software. After buying my food, he had an (imaginary) "emergency" with his mom. He dropped me back home afterwards. What a waste!! I could have stayed home, kept relaxing, and made my own food—for free. Since, in reality, he knew just as much about computers as a tampon, I had absolutely no reason to waste my time with him. To top things off, I used my check card at the market and went over by 10 cents. The A' hole bank charged me $30 overdraft fee for that stupid transaction.

7.   Big time producer

Another worthy man Swautch introduced me to was Vani. Vani told me he was a "prominent" producer and DJ, and had a studio in Maryland not too far from my lowly income job. I mentioned this story earlier in the book. After playing some beats and eating, he offered me the option of crashing there for the few hours I had until I needed to be at work near his place. Being the naive and stupid female I was, I fell asleep with all of my clothes on as he made beats. The female, who I assumed was his girlfriend, left. I awoke to something hitting my butt. I turned and saw his thing slapping me. I asked, "May I help you?" He simply smiled. Obviously I'm not going to get too much of a good sleep here without something entering or slapping upon me. Fearing some sort of ultimatum or threat via the flesh killing dogs if I refused services, I faked a call to my friend saying I was leaving to meet her for her sudden emergency. I got my coat and got the heck out of there.

He later had the nerve to tell Swautch that I was scared of his thing. What crap. I'm not scared of anything from a respectable guy that I'VE KNOWN FOR MORE THAN 2 HOURS! And hell no will I offer services or screw some guy, no matter how cute he is, after 10 minutes. Vani was quite attractive. I guess like someone told me, never lay in bed with a guy if you don't want sex from him. I guess, so true. It must be the anatomical nature of man.

8.   Danny and the homeless slut

The same year I met Swautch, I met this nice looking New YoRician. He was very nice and respectful. Unlike most guys, he never pushed himself up on me. He would rub my back and we would play around but he never disrespected me. I could even lay in the same bed as him and not have him molest me in the middle of the night. It got to the point that he ended up never doing anything with me. I even told him how much I wanted it. I guess I needed to molest him, in which I am too shy for.

There are many aggressive women who would molest and rape a guy in 5 minutes. I am too shy and thusly lose out on many subtle and decent men. Being that this homeless whore stayed over my house a lot, she jumped in where I left off. He left me for this homeless slut living in a shelter for girls who are wards of the state. Of course, she and he hid from me when I went hunting them down after I discovered what was going on. He reappeared when I returned from my Disney intern. He came to my job and tried to hang out with me again. I was disgusted. Not only did he lie to Swautch that I sex teased him (which was an abominable lie; I told him specifically how horney I was. Perhaps he was scared of sex) it was an utmost insult to my intelligence for him to leave me for some homeless tramp that I initially befriended.

9. Sexy Mustafa from mosque

When my cousin became a Muslim and she was about to marry her first husband, I went to the mosque with her one day. That was my first time there, and it must have been dating season. My desire for foreign men is constant and it was there and then that I learned Africans and Europeans are WAY more open minded about dating diverse women than many Americans. I even went there 2 weeks ago, and several times this past December searching for a mate. I am desperate and disappointed. I only met a 5' Mexican. All of the sexy camels fresh off of the boat were not out searching. America must have returned them after 9/11. There were only a bunch of cab drivers.

Mom and Myro both asked why would I settle for some guy who only wanted marriage for a green card instead of love. First of all, love and marriage must have gone out of business in America circa 1965 since most marriages end within 5 or so years in the first place! Unlike the older generation who prided themselves on family and marriage, people now marry out of convenience, money, lust, status, a trophy to brag and boast about, and every other stupid, superficial reason to marry someone. If it was *REALLY* FOR LOVE, then when his money leaves, she gets sick, she gets fat, old, and wrinkled, or you grow tired of him—you would stick it out and stay. Obviously for better or worse, richer or poorer, sickness and in health are just parts of the ceremony along with the beautiful gown, wedding cake, limo, and cheesy sounding band or DJ with absolutely no skills whatsoever. Seems like to me, Americans pride themselves on divorce. You have pre-nuptial agreements, many divorce lawyers, and many spouses ditching their significant other for a younger, sexier, more exciting trophy as he sits and listens to the next, sad, country song. You couldn't convince me of love until **AFTER** I SEE IT FOR MYSELF!! Not until after I actually/allegedly meet a man (who isn't forced to be nice and loving due to lack of looks, him about to die, being retarded, etc.) that I am FINALLY CONVINCED REALLY LOVES ME FOR ME, will I **EVER** believe in this myth called love!!!

At least foreigners not only believe in chivalry and taking care of their woman, they also believe in marriage. Love, who knows, who cares! But they do take care of their responsibility. Even if it's a marriage of convenience or business, we both get something out of it. I get a house, chivalry, sex, and a child with a sexy, sane, immigrant and he gets a green card. I still have my standards, however. He must be physically attractive, **SANE**, wholesome, show chivalry, drive, and not be a peasant scrub or thug. Even if he decides to leave afterwards—which of course, I hope not—at least I have a home, child, and money since they aren't like those dead-beat dads who refuse to pay child support and take care of their responsibility. Foreigners do take care of their responsibility. At least until they get tainted and become Americanized.

Well this sexy African named Mustafa introduced himself to me. I was pleased to meet him also. We went out several times at the Univ. of DC, which is where I assume he was studying English or something. After the 2nd or 3rd date, however, he asked for marriage. Even being only 19 and horrible at picking up clues and signs, I realized that this is extremely odd. I've known you for 2 weeks and you want marriage? I knew absolutely nothing about green cards. I wondered and asked why so sudden and soon, you've only known me for 2 weeks. He explained that you first get married, I guess ASAP in Islam, and then you get to know each other. Disappointing, that one didn't work out. He was very nice and respectful too. I guess you have to be. How else are you going to hitch someone ASAP unless you kiss up to them and be on your best behavior?

10. Another African for Marriage

There was this nice looking but extremely tall Nigerian who I met when I came home from Japan for Daddy. We went out and I took Big T as cock block. He was very nice and we went to this nice coffee lounge then back to his place. He then decided to molest me while Big T and his cousin watched TV. He spoke of marriage and how once I marry him, it would only be me and him, no one else like my friends, his friends, Big T, his cousin, nothing. I decided to give him my number in Japan, besides, who'd actually call me way over there—except Floyd? Well he did, and a lot. He would always called just as I would finally fall off to sleep, then argue at me for not calling him back at the exact time he told me to. He was very bossy, possessive, and quite annoying after a bit. After a week or so of me dealing with him waking me up and then fussing at me for not calling him back, I cursed him out and told him never to call me again. He then tattled to Big T on me. Big T called and asked what happened. I told him and Big T laughed. Last I heard, he needed a green card and marriage ASAP before being deported. I think he made arrangements with this weed head lesbian—unlimited weed and 40's for marriage. I don't quite know what ever became of that situation. Oh well.

I'm desperate and want marriage, but not that bad. I DEFINITELY don't want no Ike Turner.

11. Burger King Moroccan

I met this sexy Moroccan when he came to UMES for a soccer game. He went to UDC also. Note—UDC is for Africans fresh off the boat like NOVA (N. Va. Comm. College) is for Asians fresh to American soil. He worked as a manager at Burger King. I would call him a lot and tried to make arrangements to go out on a date. I would visit his job, with his West African asst. manager, and collect free food. He would take me in the back, feel me up, and try to have sex in his office, which anyone could pass and had absolutely no privacy. He never took me out, but came over my parent's house one night after work. He most likely lied about taking me to Denny's or somewhere, but of course when he arrived at my parents house, he didn't take me anywhere. Like the typical Americanized camel he was, he wanted sex at my parents' house. When I refused, that was the last of this lovely one.

12. Bullet

Here is a true jerk. He is Turkish and I met him at a super stuck up Americanized camel club. The only reason I would even go there was because it was free and I'd hang out there until the club I really wanted to go to was up and jumping. I would meet all types of jerks and A'holes there. The nicest ones were definitely the ones fresh off the boat. This jerk taught me a good lesson though. People do not respect the black American, as anyone with 2 brain cells would know. They—including other black Americans, Korean storeowners, whites, et cetera—do considerably respect Africans a thousand times more.

After calling each other and going out on various dates, he would always return to his Ethiopian or Brazilian ex. Once he asked where I was from after seeing my African dress/top. I told him the truth. Disappointed, he asked if my mom or dad was from Africa. After saying no, he asked about my grand mom, grandpa, aunt, uncle, cousin, fish, dog, cat, anyone. After being honest and saying no, he disappointedly asked if anyone in my family was from Jamaica, Haiti, South America, Ghana, anywhere but here. Curious and wondering why, I honestly and naïvely said no. "Oh … you mean you're only American? Humph." Well I learned from that mistake. Finally, after a year of me wasting time hoping for a relationship, he explained that we were too different. I was too short and American. Americans are just too different from him. He said that he once went out with a white American, and it really didn't work out. He said this after he dealt with me for almost a year. Why waste my time in the first place?!

Come to find out—and to put his jerk icing on this insane cake—he has absolutely NO reason to talk. He offered me use of his fax in his house one day—which he started complaining about once I was done. Seeing a family photo I asked who the blond white lady was, being that he took after his dark dad. He unenthusiastically explained that she was his mom, who was American!!!! How dare you not like Americans when you are half American! I could see if he was all camel but he's half what he hates.

I complain about American men because they are TOO programmed. However, I praise and talk so wonderfully about New Yorkers. I would (and have) date a man regardless of race, religion, language, and the like, if I could just find a nice one. I guess he hates what runs in his veins, America. As for me, I will use my American privilege and enter as many countries with Carte Blanc status as much as possible. This may be one unfair, unjust, brainwashed, full of zombie country, but there are many countries a WHOLE LOT WORSE then here. And I sure will travel and take advantage of my American privilege as much as possible. And if I actually find an attractive and nice American who amazingly isn't from NYC, then I'll marry him ASAP. Of course, with my luck, the end of the world would be right around the corner.

13. New Orleans guy 2 screw in truck,

Before meeting the toothless hillbilly in New Orleans, I met this dude at some community college while I was waiting for my lovely "friend" to finish class. For some reason, no man takes me serious—except fresh off the boat foreigners. As that lovely friend—who allowed me to stay at the Covenant house for runaways—said, "I'm a black version of a dumb blond." So lovely and dear, I am as intimidating as a little rabbit.

Well, the dude and I spoke for several minutes in the parking lot. I was basically walking around the campus. He was standing in front of his pick-up. After chatting for several minutes, he offered me the opportunity to climb into the back of his truck. Go figure. Shocked, I asked why would he even ask me such a thing. He replied, similar to Bolivian who wasn't in his right mind after church, "I figured you wanted to." Shocked and amazed how guys see me, I kept prying and asking upon his assumption about me. I really want to know and understand what it is about me, and other women, which make guys, either fall to their knees in worship and obedience, or feel them up and molest them. Obviously he was tired of answering me and kindly apologized and left.

14. Korean I wanna try a black girl

There was also this Korean American, most likely with a family being that he had a baby seat in the back of his car. I worked at the gas station then. He would come to the station every morning. After a few visits offering small chats about life, et cetera, he decided to try his hand and luck. Around the 3rd or 4th visit, he asked to use the bathroom. He was a respectful customer, so sure. Of course he decided to feel me up saying he wanted to try a black girl. I played my usual, not now, hard to get roll. Unfortunately, this became routine. I soon dreaded his visit because every time, he'd come after I'd open the doors for the morning and if the customers left the store, he'd start a feeling. I tried to push him off onto my friend or what have you. Like any respectable pervert, "Bring your friend so we ALL could have some fun." Every attempt backfired. After all, he wasn't asking for a commitment—which is the reason I profoundly said no—he just wanted to screw and try a black girl. "Why don't you try a dancer or prostitute?" "I want to try you." Thank you angels. I guess after constant turn downs and me avoiding him by not unlocking the door until after I saw him, offering poor excuses of why I couldn't let him in, he finally gave up and soon stopped coming all together.

15. Amid Ishmael, "if u calling me back …"

Now Amid Ishmael is a really nice guy fresh off the Turkish boat. Outside the fact that he was ugly as hell, he would be someone nice to deal with and a good guy. His English was equal to Ami the Jew, approximately 24 words. He was someone I met via Wild D's trickery toward us. He saw Wild D dance, and obviously after tipping, must have gotten "her phone number." I knew nothing of him. He starts calling me out of the blue leaving all sorts of entertaining refugee messages. "Hello, this is Amid Ishmael. I calling for Lory. I call 202-225-5555 but I no find she. She be Lory. If she calling me back, I will be glad." Now how entertaining is that. I saved that message along with a few crazy one's from Hyattsville, and played it for everyone.

I never ask how someone looks because they lie. When you get an image in you head, they look absolutely nothing like you figured. They usually look worse. I also figured I met him in my travels and never called him and/or lost his number, which happens a lot. When we finally met up, I realized I had never seen this hideous creature before. He did have a fax machine that I hoped to use, which was the main reason for meeting up with him. After giving me many excuses of why I couldn't take his machine home to use, he asked where did we meet. I had no idea, and asked how did he get my number. He described Wild D's club. I immediately knew Wild D gave him my number and name lying like I was her. I immediate call Wild D as she laughs; saying she thought I would like him, he's super foreign.

16. Wallied

I met Wallied sitting on the steps of his apartment complex. Like Snoop Dogg, he was fall-out drop-dead gorgeous. He was tall, slim, and extremely sexy—probably one of the sexiest guys I dealt with—and a walking whore. Like most foreigners from his region of the world, N. Africa, he worked at pizza delivery and also needed a green card. He, unfortunately, has been here too long and was tainted. He knew English, had a car, and an efficiency apartment with only 1 or 2 roommates. I would call him all the time and show up unexpectedly because his A'hole roommate would always lie for him. They lied that he was never home. He would stay out in MD with the "French faggot" as Floyd called it. I agreed. Once I called his job and some hood rat answered. "Who are you to him because I'm his girlfriend?" He had a nerve to get mad at me, saying, "You're giving me crazy." It's not my fault you're a walking whore and don't know how to handle all of your women. If you want to be a pimp, you first need to know how not to get caught! Of course, I would still be tempted at taking him. A man that sexy is hard to say no to. Of course I wouldn't trust him further than I can spit and would not make it a point to be faithful to a walking whore.

mEN oF iLL rEPUTE

17. Mothug,

While living in Fairfax, Virginia, I met this thug peasant without a car, with a Popeye's chicken job, and not much else. I wasted a little time dealing with him, less than 2 weeks. While dealing with him, of course like all guys, he put his best foot forward. He had a phone but I remember seeing and dealing with him while I was at Kinko's taking care of my business. I gave him a ride home one day after we talked a bit. He lived with his aunt or someone. He invited me in and I went in for a few minutes. It wasn't long after he showed me his place that he was all over me. He kept trying to rip off my clothes. I kept every bit of my difficult to strip jeans on and kept pushing him off. He kept smelling like strong chicken grease.

I must be a super prude, but I don't want sex, even from an attractive guy going down on me, that I'm not comfortable with. How can I, or anyone, get comfortable with some whore they have only known a few days, let alone that he's trying to molest you? Of course, molestation and rape are perfect ways to show your friendship, care, and get to know a person. Why didn't I think of that?

Well the next time I ran into him I was with Floyd. We called him Mothug because he looked and wore his hair like someone from the group Bone Thugs in Harmony. I was with Floyd and Mothug asked for a ride home; the peasant that he was with no car. He invited us inside. I felt OK since I was with Floyd. We went in and chilled a bit. He had just finished work and had a bucket of chicken. He offered us some. I ate some and drank some soda. Mothug ate the chicken too, so I actually thought nothing of it. Floyd tried to be slick and leave while I was still there. Mothug was very pleased about this as Floyd smiled. He left and of course, Mothug starts molesting me the instant he leaves. I must have parked near his house because I faked some usual excuse of why I had to leave and went to my car. He lived near the plaza where I parked and he and Floyd worked. When I got back to Floyd, I cursed him out for trying to be slick and leaving me with that grease monkey. You smell like pure chicken grease every time you exit his place. Floyd was very amused at the situation and even said that he didn't want any chicken, he probably skeet on it. Yuck!

18. To strip in my car

Another four-star man of ill repute is this pervert that singled me out. I was with Myro leaving her sisters house. I was extremely tired and a bit hungry. I stopped in a decent neighborhood at a seafood carry out. While I waited for my food, up drives this Latino in a typical thug car, some long caddy. He spoke very respectably and we exchanged numbers. After I got my food, he walked me to my car and we spoke a bit more. He said he was from LA, it was his birthday and that he was dancer. I figured he meant hip-hop or something. He explained that he was a stripper. He then invited me into his car. I may be dense, but I'm not that stupid—finally. After he realized I wasn't getting in his car, he asked to follow us to a safer and better place to park to talk more.

I drove down the street and parked in a decent populated area with other cars and people. He got out of his car and went on Myro's side and kept talking about his dancing skills and asked to get inside "because it's cold out here" as he simultaneously opened the door and hopped in the back seat. Mind you, Myro was sitting there and obviously did not lock her door and I do have a tiny delicate car, and he wasn't that small. He quickly slipped into the back seat. While there he kept saying it was his birthday and that he wanted to perform for us. I'm sure you may know exactly what he wanted but I kept wondering how are you going to dance and strip in my tiny little car. I couldn't figure what he was trying to do, even though I know it was something sexual. Of course, Myro knew exactly what he was going to do. Before she could say anything, BOING. The next thing we know, his thing was flying around. He then asks us to watch him as he performs and jerk off. The nerve! Obviously he isn't concerned about nosy neighbors or other cars driving around, especially being that it was broad daylight. I mean, isn't it against the law to expose yourself in public? And I don't have tinted windows at all. Then he requested us to join in and participate wondering why aren't we getting into this.

I don't know what type of women live in this country, and maybe I'm just SOOO old fashioned and prude like to understand and enjoy this disgusting sexual pervasion, but does romance, respect, and decency still exist?!?!?! What is it about me to attract the WORSTEST stock of the male species?!?!? I gather my usual fake excuse to squeeze out another retart predicament via some man. We tell him we're running late and someone is waiting for us. I promised to call him later, of course throwing his number out instantly.

I have another conversation with Myro about why A' holes always run to me and try to molest me while they beg for marriage from her. I'm sure with the instance of rape and molestation in this country and the world, that it happens to more people than me. And I know in this day and age, "something is wrong with you" if you're single and not having sex in middle school. That's what it was like when I was in middle school, so I know it's much worse now. I was a loser and nerd because I wasn't having sex or playing around by 14. I believe there were **WAY** more virgins and students who never kissed or did foreplay than me. But no one wanted to admit that they were inexperienced and hadn't had sex yet. If you did admit it, there was something wrong with you. You were some sort of religious fanatic or just too ugly and disgusting for anyone to date and have sex with in the first place. Basically, if you were alone and a virgin, you were—in a nutshell—inexperienced, ugly, and unscrewable. Welcome to the new age where it's a curse to be single and a virgin!!! Wow, we really have progressed! You should be able to meet a guy and go out with him in his car without him feeling you up. You shouldn't be looked upon as an oddity and a freak of nature because you don't enjoy some guy jerking off in front of you. Myro agrees; we must be a minority of many women who would like to get to know guys before being felt up.

angelS werE dEFINATELLY waTchIng!!

19. Amin, the 25-year-old pedophile

While I was in 10th grade and 15 years old, I met this 25 year old pedophile Jew who lurked around my high school. I met him from another 10th grader who gave me his number. I believe she dealt with him also. We spoke over the phone for several weeks and he asked to be my boyfriend after the 3rd or 4th conversation. Even being a 15-year-old naive virgin who lacked awareness, I felt it was odd for someone to ask to be with me, sight unseen. What type of person asks for a relationship, sight unseen, after only a few phone or e-mail conversations? There is something wrong with them if they do. When we finally met up—like every other Americanized camel—instead of us going to the movies or somewhere, he drove around the back of the mall molesting me. I lied that I had to go to work and jumped out of the car. He yelled for me to never call his perverted, pedophile @ss again, and drove off. Later I saw he busted my neighbor, also in high school, in exchange for a new pair of tennis shoes.

20.   The Refugee Rapist

Here's another lovely A' hole that the angels were definitely with me on. This jerk from El Salvador or somewhere worked at Nations Bank and I saw him when I went there. We spoke a bit and exchanged numbers. We met at some coffee house or something and we talked. I believe I followed him in my car expecting to go somewhere. I can't remember where he offered to go, but it definitely wasn't his place. Of course, we somehow end up at his place. He, like all the rest of them, beg me to come in because my mom, kid, or someone is home (a cock block). Or I have to make an emergency phone call or turn of off my gas, or get my coat, or what have you. I'm going to be only a few minutes but I don't like people staying in my car when I'm not here, or it's very dangerous out here, or I really would like to show you my place. So many reasons to get you out of their car and into their place.

I drove, but for some unknown, stupid, retarded reason I go inside anyway. He shows me his place, and I stand after he offers me to sit—of course, on his bed. After a few minutes of him making himself busy, he starts to feel me up and kiss me. He pulls me on the bed and obvious plans to have sex regardless. I guess it was very wise for me to drive, at least I'm not stuck out here with Mr. Rapist. I ask to go to the bathroom as he tries to get on top of me. "I have to use the bathroom for a second." I guess he expected me to freshen myself up or something. I went to the bathroom to figure out what to say to leave. "Oh, I left my?? in the car, I really need it. I'll be right back," and walked the hell out. When I got to my car he was behind me asking what was wrong. I quickly locked my door and started my car saying I forgot something at school. He asked if I was coming back. Of course. I would love for you to force yourself upon me while I'm lying in your bed and you're on top. Wait right there. I started to call the cops, but what would I say. This guy tried to rape me by climbing on top of me and feeling me up. That's not enough and they'd say, why were you over there in the first place. This is, I'm sure, why most women never tell about their rape, especially if it's a date rape. It's always their fault, why were you there in the first place. And then it's his word against yours.

21. Dulles Afghan

While looking for an airline job way out 100 miles from civilization at Washington Dulles International Airport, I met this sexy Afghan. He worked in the officer's lounge. Don't ask how I got into there, I must have started talking to this black bartender who was formally a stewardess. We spoke of jobs and she told me of the benefits of airline work. He must have also worked at the bar. After doing my usual (hanging out in places that some feel I'm not meant to be) I spoke with the Afghan. I ate, drank, talked, and soon it was time for him to go. He was sexy and offered me a ride. Being that I did not drive my car way out there and took some bus from the closest metro a million miles away, I stupidly accepted his ride.

Of course, he did not take me home or to any train station. We somehow bypassed any route to my car and ended up at his place. After talking for a while and realizing I was stuck there for the night, I went in his apartment. Of course, he begs for sex and feels me up. After turning him down a million times, he finally stops and we watch TV the rest of the night. Of course, I got no sleep fearing something entering a bodily opening. The next day he drove me to the metro, 24 hours after he originally offered, while barely speaking to me. I guess he was disappointed in his quest for tricking me for sex. Oh well, suits you right!

I definitely have angels working over time for me, as much crap as I get myself into. I could have been raped, kidnapped, or even killed as many times I was tricked or swindled into some retarded situation. I always said that I used up all of my good luck on the angels getting me out of retarded situations that I'm only left with bad luck for everything else in my life. They say God protects babies, the elderly, and the retarded. I wonder where I fall in. Anyway, thanks be to God and each and every angel and heavenly host looking out for me. And props for a job WELL DONE!! Because, I now realize how I'm an SUCH A MESS!

22. Capitol Plaza Indian, and other molesters

The angels bailed me out again. While in 9th or maybe 10th grade, I went to see this Indian who worked this taco stand at the local mall. He would flirt and he was cute and gave me tacos occasionally. Once, he invited me behind the counter. I saw nothing wrong with this, after all, it's a counter in the food court at a mall. What could possibly happen? Everyone could see us. I went back to make me a free taco when he grabbed me and pulled me off to the side—a side that I didn't know existed cause I never saw it—and felt me up. Of course I snuck out from him, made my taco in the public eye, and lied about why I had to leave. Disappointed, he asked if I was returning. Of course I lied and told him to wait. He waited as I left with my food. Of course, I never went back.

23. Angels hard at work again

Another nice occasion when the angels had to work was when I was spending the weekend at TW's house near Ocean City. Above her apartment was this decent looking dude/rapist. He invited me up after being very polite outside. He said he lived with his mom. Stupidly, I went upstairs. After all, what could he do with his mom home and TW downstairs. Of course, no one was home except him feeling me up and wanting sex. I asked for some water cause I was dying of thirst. He consented and went to the kitchen to get me some juice. I immediately left.

24. Another lovely guy

Another lovely guy is this Indian who lied and said that he would take me out to dinner and a movie after calling me on the phone a bit. Like every other pervert, they never say over the phone that they are some molesting pervert who's going to feel me up and molest me. They all LIE like they are decent, respectable, men. I do get many guys who tell me up front what they want and what they are all about. I don't mention them here because we never gave each other the time of day. They told me upfront what they wanted. I'm sure millions of women would enjoy and respond to such propositions very well. However, if a guy told me off the break all he wanted was sex, no matter how sexy he is, I wouldn't be interested. I want a relationship, not some molesting pervert with uncontrolled hands or one night stands! They would tell me what they like done to them and ask what I like to do on our fist conversation. After changing the subject, I quickly get off the phone. Realizing that I wasn't an easy screw, they never called again, and of course, I never called them back either. These guys I mention here are the perverts that lie. They waste their time and mine.

Well, this camel was a mechanic at this shop and gave My Feather a tune up and oil change. He claimed he was very rich and went on cruises all over the world. He had several houses and women threw themselves upon him. He was nice looking but I wasn't going to give him sex. Of course we never made it to the restaurant and he decided to feel me up in his car. After annoying and harassing him to take me somewhere decent, he dropped me off at my car and lied that he had to be home. Another lovely molesting A' hole and lair

25. Another lovely pervert I met through Swautch.

Swautch called me somehow from this perverts phone. Seeing the number on the caller ID, I called the pervert looking for Swautch. He told me Swautch went to the store and he'd return in 5 minutes. We struck up a conversation. He had an accent and was very friendly, polite, and intelligent so I happily talked to him. Obviously this is where my dumbness and naiveté kicked in. I guess it's no problem talking with someone over the phone, just not meeting up with them. However since he knew Swautch I saw no problem. He lied that he was a diplomat and had millions of dollars. This is obviously a very popular lie, along with "I'm a computer programmer", "I actually have a car, it's just in the shop now", and the biggest lie, "I love going to museums, theaters, and such" and then they NEVER take you. He told me he was 30 and he was going to an embassy gala. He invited me to the gala and I met him at the mall. I bypassed him because this man appeared to be 30 square (that's 30 x 30). Perhaps he was only 58 but he was definitely not 30! We definitely never went to the embassy either. We went to Georgetown and I had to beg him to get me something to eat at this gyro place. He lied that he had to turn off his stove at home and drove me straight to his home way out in the suburbs. Of course, he at once felt me up. I finally got in touch with Swautch and cursed him out for tricking me with this perverted fossil. I told him my boyfriend was on his way to meet me so he immediately drove me back to the mall. While driving, he felt me up while he explained to me that he was impotent and needed me to jerk him off to get hard. What a nasty old pervert.

26. Another lovely camel

Another lovely Americanized camel was this guy I met at a club. He, of course, was a millionaire and made over $7000 a month. He did drive a fancy red BMW but he lived in a room for rent and worked two remedial jobs. He said that he worked for the French embassy—even though he was Moroccan—and he did security clearances. He also said he had a typical camel job, a waiter in an Italian café. As usual, he was going to take me to a coffee shop. It was snowing and I insisted that he come over on a nicer day. He insisted on seeing me that night. My roommate knew off the break it was a booty call. Like an idiot, I actually expected to go the coffee lounge. We of course, went to a parking lot so he could feel me up. After complaining about going to the lounge, he asked if I actually wanted to go. Hello you idiot, you did say that was where we were going to go—not to this lot to feel me up. He explained that he was going to sleep, he was fasting, and he couldn't drink coffee or tea. I guess eating and drinking is forbidden but whoring and fornication is perfectly all right. Incredible! Well he dropped me off disappointed after I didn't put out and I of course was extremely disgusted. Obviously no nice men anywhere! The next day someone called me from a Hallal meat market saying they had the wrong number. Perhaps it was him on his second job. He did tell me he had to work that day; he just didn't say it was at a meat market.

27. The Bolivian Christian pervert

Another wonderful pervert was this very stuck up Americanized Bolivian I met at a church. I went to this international gathering which hosted many snobbish Americans and very Americanized stuck up foreigners from Fairfax, VA. Anyone who knows anything can verify that Fairfax County is the headquarters of stuck up men and women. Well, the host promoted this huge affluent church in Fairfax explaining how many professional singles are there, so of course I went. The first time only the usher spoke to me. After complaining to him, the host begged me to give it another try. So I went again and actually ran into him.

He introduced me to several stuck up yuppies then he ditched me. What a lovely, Christian host. Invite someone to your church, then ditch your visitor to hang with your stuck up friends. I complained to this other lady who agreed with me. She invited me to this café where I again ran into Mr. Host. He gave some poor excuse of why he ditched me and invited me to sit with them. The lady who invited me left so I went to sit with the stuck up bunch. I sat across Bolivian at the table. Bolivian did construction work so I spoke to him about some work. The café was closing so he walked me to my car and we spoke for another 40 or so minutes outside. He invited me to this 24-hour coffee house so I went to continue our conversation. Being that there are several 24-hour cafes in the Washington area, I thought nothing of it. I followed him and we parked in this hotel parking lot and he asked me to get in his car to carpool there. He was very professional the entire time and never once flirted or even showed any remote interest in me so I saw absolutely nothing wrong with it. After all, we just left church.

Glory hallelujah, the Lord is with him. He started to subtly feel me up and asked for sex while, "he wasn't in his right mind." We went to this lovely invisible coffee bar in the dark woods and I asked to return to my car. I then asked where did this come from. "You looked like you wanted me." Oh, I guess this is a look that only some guys know. I asked why wouldn't he take me out on a respectable date. He said that I wasn't his type. Oh how lovely, I love to be degraded after church by someone who doesn't find me worthy enough to date in public but able to bust up in while he isn't in his right mind. I couldn't be more honored! He, and many others, are genuine hypocrites—in EVERY sense of the word!!

For if you find someone decent enough to screw and they are compatible and nice people, then why are they not worthy enough to not date? Are you that much of a stupid, programmed person. You can only date someone your peers or friends would be impressed with or jealous of. Obvious, having a mind of your own is something unheard of. For me, as some claim that I am so picky, I will date and befriend anyone. Unfortunately I seem to attract the most wrought iron complete A'holes from across the earth.

I can see if the person is physically repulsive and makes you cringe, even with a wonderful personality. Be cordial and friendly with them, yet, DON'T lead them on. If, however, you actually have some form of attraction towards them, even if it's bare minimal, then what's wrong with pursuing the relationship for more than a tease and quick screw?!

Now I know programmed idiots only want a sexy broad, more so who can impress their friends and peers, and tout as a status symbol. But I'm sure there have to be some members of the male species that live outside of NYC that may not be fall out drop dead sexy, but at least have some level of attraction, and not be a wrought iron idiot. America is very big. Surely there have to be men that exist that aren't hideous looking and are forced to be nice. Surely in this huge country, there are some nice looking men who are actually not stuck up, arrogant, superficial, whores. Now before you go and claim yourself as one, ask yourself this:

- Do you lead women on who you never plan to date, and if so, why?
- Are there women who you would have sex with but not want to take out and spend time with?
- If you can't stand being around her, why do you screw her and most likely date her?
- If she has a wonderful, charming, personality and sex with her is possible, then why won't you spend time with her and date her?

To me, maybe because I am a woman, these are common sense questions. I don't care how sexy a guy is, if he's argumentative or very mean, or all he wants is sex, I'm not interested. And visa versa, if the guy has a wonderful personality but physically makes me cringe, I would happily be his friend and hang out with him but I would NEVER lead him on nor peruse a relationship with him.

And for you "liars" who say looks are not important. How does you spouse or mate look? Are they repulsive to you? Even if they would not be what you would ever call attractive—like me with Ami the Jew and Hyattsville, as you will read—there must be some level of chemistry. Perhaps their smile, walk and mannerisms, even just the way they dress and suave personality. It's something about them that turns you on, or you would literally feel like you're being affectionate with a trashcan.

Looks can be very superficial if your only motive is to impress others or a trophy, regardless of their personality. And for you who say looks aren't important and are really shallow; how can someone's voice, walk, style of dress, or suave mannerisms be less shallow? To me it's even more!! What if they get a cold and lose their voice? There are really nice people with speech impediments. And suaveness and walk can only get you so far. What if they're on crutches or have a limp? And what if they are a really nice, attractive, super geek? Would you run from them? You can take a sexy model, throw on homeless ragged clothes, and mess his hair up and he'd still have his sexy bone structure, frame, and features. And you can take an ape and put on the nicest clothes and cologne and he'd still be an ape. What's the difference?

As for me, I can care less how someone dresses, where he works, lives, his educational level, where he's from, or even if he speaks much English. As long as he's nice, subtle, and can control his hands, SANE, decent looking, somewhat romantic, isn't abusive, an obvious walking whore, pervert, nor peasant, I'll happily date him. It seems like I'm asking sooooo much from fate or whomever, to find a guy I have chemistry with who actually likes me, wants to be with me, and is not a lunatic. It seems like I'd either get a sexy, attractive, shallow, superficial lunatic or whore or a really nice guy with a great personality who is hard on the eyes. I guess in this extremely superficial society, they are forced to be nice. Which is why NYC, Europe, and Africa is so much better when it comes to a mate!

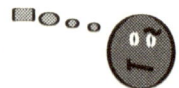

28. Another Holy Bolivian Pervert

I somehow met another super holy Bolivian Christian at the SAME stuck-up church, and of course, he was a bonafied pervert too! I was doing another one of those 1-month prayer campaigns; similar to the one I did to get a job and ended up in Japan a year later. Well I did this one for, of course, a husband, as well as 14 other things—including health for some family members, finances, and help for my church. Well I had VERY detailed requests for what I wanted, including and especially in a husband. As I said, I KNOW EXACTLY WHAT I WANT and I NEVER have problems making quick decisions. Well approximately 24 hours after the last day of this 30-day fast and prayer campaign—all of which I failed miserably on in regards to following—I met Mr. Pervert. Perhaps I actually have to follow it 100% for it to turn out successful. Which is why I never waste time even trying to fast, I'll cheat within the first 24 hours! Whether it's a food fast, a fast from certain music or activity, or even a fast for me TO DO something everyday, I'll cheat within the first 24 hours.

Anyway, the very next day following the end of this fast and prayer campaign I cheated my way through, I went to that same stuck-up church in Va. While there with a few people I just met, Mr. Pervert walked up. Like a Monet painting (as in the movie Clueless), he was definitely the most attractive of our small little group—but that's not really saying much. We went out to eat and to get to know each other. I fake some excuse to ask for everyone's number, including his. I had another poor excuse for calling him the following week. I called him about a ride to church that following day and we ended up hanging out with Myro that night. We went to this really nice play and went to a club since Myro's friend refused to let guys over to his BarBQ—whatever that was about. I love dancing and obviously Mr. Monet enjoyed seeing me dance. We went out that following Monday to the movies.

In the time talking to him, he seemed to be the answer to most of my very specific prayer requests for a husband in regards to occupation, being a perfect gentleman driving and cruising around the District, claiming to enjoy traveling, even going so far as to pick me up and drop me off at my front door! Men, do you even realize how amazing that is to females?!?! Well at least to me and a few females I know. Most guys either don't have a car, and some pathetically don't even know how to drive or even have a license. When a woman has to be the one driving and picking up a man, it is completely amazing to find a man who not only has access to a car, but will actually pick a woman up at her door!! That is like chauffeured limo service!! To me that's better than a bouquet of flowers!! And to not only meet her and pick her up at her door so she doesn't have to drive to meet you anywhere and lose her parking spot or walk to the subway (which is all perfectly fine, especially being blessed to live walking distance to a metro) but to ACTUALLY TAKE HER WHERE YOU CLAIMED TO TAKE HER and not to some alley to molest her!! To me that's a miracle and on the grounds of marriage!! At least to me that is!!

Of course this couldn't last too long however. Mr. Monet told me how spiritual he was which seemed really impressive and decent. He even told me how he apparently gave away all of his goods to God and the poor so he could focus totally on God. To me that seems like the most wholesome type of man! Now perhaps you can see right through this but he DID put on a very good front. Unfortunately by the end of the night he needed to use my bathroom, and I had no cock block that night. He decided to try his holy hand at sex afterwards—after only our second date! Well after I finally pushed him off, he went home.

He did call and apologize after I grilled him on how he could claim he is soooo holy and stuff then feel me up. He tried to blame me and my dancing as seducing him, tempting him, and leading him on. Now perhaps that is sinful and wrong to dance, enjoy yourself, get exercise, and have a good time, but EVERYONE dances like that. If you're not used to seeing women and couples dance Salsa, belly dance, house and club dance (and house and club dance isn't even some seductive type of dance) then that just means you haven't been out to any bars lately—like within the past 20 to 30 years. Now maybe that was some sinful horrible thing, and I did take his point, but obviously he did understand feeling me up in my place was completely inapposite too, thus he apologized.

The fact that he tried his hand at sex is not the main reason he's here. As one lady says, that's just a man showing you that he's still a man. The fact that he hardly ever called me, claimed every weekend to meet me and then stand me up with some stupid excuse, and stood me up when my car broke is the reason he is here. I know people are busy. Heck, I'm one of the most insanely busy people I know on earth. If you're super busy, don't lie like you're going to meet me then not show up. At least say you'll try, or that you would like to, but you're just way too busy. Now maybe I'm being like the typical needy, irrational woman, but he did say he'd try every time instead of just saying that he'll make a date when he actually does have time. Obviously after his holy hand at sex fell through on me, he had to think of more ways to convert Christians to sex after their 2nd date. The thing about it is that when he did seemingly have time he always spent it with his sister and her kids. He also complained about how tired and exhausted he was. I truly believed him so I asked why he spent so much of his spare time with his sister's kids instead of sleeping. He really never gave me any good answer.

The main reason that he is here and the reason he's Mr. Pervert is how he stood me up when my car broke and his holy act the last time he visited. The very next and final time he visited my place was for dinner and to chill and finally "get a good night rest" since his group house was in constant chaos with no electricity. After dinner I offered him my bed and I was going to sleep on the couch. We, however, were watching TV in my room simply because that is the only TV in my place. He decided to lay in my bed and begged me to lay beside him. After I flat out refused, he tried to act like he was into the film and falling asleep. He then pops out of nowhere and told me he was ready to give me my back massage. Now I thought this was weird popping out of nowhere. He then got my baby oil from the bathroom and begged me to strip and lay on the floor. Annoyed that I emphatically refused, he then tried to give me this unsuccessful guilt trip. He said how all of his other female friend let him rub oil on them naked (seems like I heard this one before), how he really wasn't going to try anything (of course you won't), and why I will stay single since I have major trust issues and won't let men feel me up and rub oil on me shirtless. And of course he definitely wasn't going to try anything. He tried to make me give in saying how I'm so odd, all of the females trust him and want him to massage them, and how I had some major trust issues with straight men.

I'm very sure he is exactly right. I'm very shy and reserved as you can read. I also won't put out until I feel comfortable around a guy. And it definitely would only be with a man who shows and has good self-control, and is able to sit near me and be around me without him molesting me. I truly trust a man I am able to lay next to and have him ONLY play in my hair and hold me, not lick, grope, and molest me. A man that has excellent self control to not start feeling me up within the first 5 seconds.

Unfortunately, according to Mr. Pervert and Belief, those type of men are all gay. They said if a guy doesn't try and feel you up he is gay. I don't totally believe that. Myro, this American born Indian friend, and a few other females I know will have guys acting like they're in 5th grade being COMPLETELY reserved, obedient, and wholesome. Perhaps they are too scared to feel them up fearing that they will dump them or curse them out. But I do know that men exist that have self control. I met a few myself. Danny had EXCELLENT self-control. In fact too excellent, we never had sex. I really don't know what to do. Seems like the only men who respect me and don't try to molest me are men who don't want me, are hard on the eyes, or according to Belief and Pervert, are gay.

Finally, when my car broke down not too far from his job, he claimed that he would come out and help once he got off of work. My car breaking down is not some mushy lets spend quality time together. That is quite a bit more of an emergency over "quality time." Well he claimed he would come and help me, but once he got off of work, he "accidentally" lost his cell and of course, never answered nor called me on my cell because he forgot my number. In fact, when I finally did get back in touch with him several days later, he claimed that he just got reunited with his phone. I asked did he get my million messages and rants left on his voice mail. He claimed he didn't have a chance to hear them. Of course I believe you. I later found out by a mutual friend—who knew nothing about our antics—that he had at least one kid, if not more, by the girl he used to date for 5 years. Obviously his "sister's kids." Another mutual friend told me Mr. Holy hasn't been back to their church SINCE THE DAY I MET HIM. That would have been several months by that point! Well, I guess his holiness has been paying off—or wearing off one!

TRILOGY OF INSANITY

29. Vic

Vic is the last in my trilogy of insane Americans. He said he was Gods gift to women, a state of the art software writer and computer engineer, a mathematician, a very religious and piteous person, a master car mechanic, and an Einstein genius. Unfortunately, every claim fell through. First and foremost, he's off in the head and insane. He was this nice looking shuttle bus driver who was fired for some stupid reason. Obviously, this shuttle bus job has an extremely high turnover rate. I saw him in the computer lab speaking of dropping daisy cutters (bombs) on campus. Columbine High, are you there? He also spoke of guns, shooting animals, and Sadam Hussein, while he played this cheesy retart looking shooting video game. Then he started singing church songs. I solely asked him to sign my form so my student group could get off the ground, and like every crazy person I know, he started talking to me. I'm not certain, but from various documentaries and shows I've seen, I believe he is Paranoid Schizophrenic.

I'm very sociable and we talked all night. He was nice looking and I was, and still am, quite desperate and lonely so I enjoyed his insane conversation. Like every other guy, he said he likes to travel and go to museums. He said he was going to pack and drive to Montana or somewhere and camp out. He invited me to church that afternoon and I obliged. Somehow that morning he followed me home. He embarrassed me and told Myro's boyfriend (my roommate at that current time) he had no friends and that I was his only friend. What?!

The first time he met my mom I was solely going home to do laundry and he embarrassed me again. He told my mom he took me to church and that we were not having sex. Of course, my mom only came downstairs to show me where something was and she barely said hi to him. For some reason, my mom didn't see this as insane. The very next time he came over we both sat in mom's bedroom looking at the kittens. The Runt went whoring around and had 2 babies. They were under mom's bed. Unfortunately Fuzzy—the Runt's cutest and friendliest sister—died about a month before the Runt had kittens. While looking at the kittens, I sat in the chair he was sitting in. I guess I didn't think and wasn't too hospitable. I should have allowed him to sit in the chair while I sat on the bed. Instead I sat in the chair and he sat on the floor. I didn't think of this because I was about to go downstairs. When I left he could have sat back in the chair or left also. When I came back to mom's room, he embarrassingly was stretched out all over the floor taking a nap.

126

Now to me, as bad as I am on my cards, this is a major sign that something is wrong. This and the blowing up the campus while singing church songs. Of course my mom, who said absolutely nothing for several months about it, thought it was very rude. I asked several people, never revealing whom the person was, and each one of them said insane. One said what drugs was he on. The other gave this comical look and said to call St. Elizabeth asylum at once. The other 2 were very reserved and didn't want to prejudge. After prying one said it was 40% rude and 60% crazy. The other wouldn't say, but later said that he sounds like someone who would fall asleep in a barn.

Now my mom and I got in a big debate over this. I specifically asked what was the drawing line between rude and insane. Obviously, sleeping or sitting on your bed is very rude unless you insist that he do so. But when does it become insane? Is it when he sleeps under your bed with the cats? On top of the dresser? What about sleeping on the kitchen or bathroom floor? Surely sleeping on the roof or in the gutter is insane. And speaking of that, he said how he was sleepwalking one night and ended up on the roof of his house. I asked if his parents ever tried to take him to counseling. He said he refused to go. That means yes. An enormous tell tell sign that someone is insane is if you call them crazy and they get very defensive and offended. People call me and millions of others crazy all the time. No one seems to get defensive and ready to fight or curse you out. For if they do, watch out, most likely they are.

Somehow his boasting and bragging fell through also. He put a car engine together all by himself. He supposedly has numerous certificates in breaks, mufflers, et cetera; however, he wasn't able to do a tune up. I thought that was mechanics 101. He also owned this computer and needed a safe place to store it. Me not having one, I offered my room. He later said that I could keep it. Vic boasts about how he knows soooo much about computers and he built this dinosaur from scratch. Another friend helped me—sight unseen via the phone—speed up this fossil. Vic said, "How dare you go behind my back and get someone else to work on *MY* computer. From now on, you are to call me with anything," or something along those lines. So I did. And he—building this computer from scratch and being an expert in all forms of engineering—successfully kicked the internet off the computer. Of course it was something that I did wrong. Every time after that when he came over to "fix the computer" he ended up accidentally playing video games. Perhaps that's the way to remodel this dinosaur of a computer—ancient video games. Compliments of his high level of computer skills, this computer hasn't had the internet since 2003.

He's also very religious. Extremely religious and piteous. It's just no one else knows it. He stopped going to the church because he got into some argument.

He would read the Bible while he drank a beer, then talk about how some woman wants him, touched his butt, or asks my roommate if she stuffs her bra. Perhaps he was reading Song of Solomon's sex poems or something. Of course he's God's gift to women. But when I said this in front of another woman, he had to clarify himself. He's not God's gift to women, just God's gift to Burger King women—where he worked in the drive through. This must be why he's single and deals with me; a desperate, lonely, female only in the 55 percentile of decency and beauty (as he puts it). The only other woman he has is this crack whore who dumped him.

Now with Vic being a Top Model containing high levels of sexiness and being God's gift to women; you would imagine that the pickings are enormous—unlike me where I feel forced to travel to Africa, Europe, NY, or even to the Caribbean to find a decent suitor due to the extremely slim pickings I have in DC. Somehow even with him being God's gift to women, he was unsuccessful with getting a girl. In fact, he even confessed to me that the last time he got laid was with this toothless prostitute who was over 40 that he found in front of a crack hotel. You would think with him being in the upper 90% on the scales of beauty (as he puts it), he would have women lined up to pay him, or at least have sex mutually for free. For some reason, the only woman he could find was some old, toothless, crack whore to give him head for $10. Maybe he was doing a charitable deed helping give money and sexual opportunities to the underserved? Well perhaps he got his money's worth, guys always yell, "No teeth!"

The main reason he is the worstest, outside of his arrogance and immense bragging about how smart, hard working, sexy, handsome, skilled, and talented he is; is how negative he was to me. He explained how lazy, unorganized, and untalented I was. I was a shiftless, frivolous, flake. I need to give up this flaky hope and dream and get a reasonable job as a cashier at Shoppers or somewhere. I was so way out of my league with him and every other man I was interested in. I was too short, fat, and non attractive in my face, hair, and such, for the men I was interested in. The only reason NY men would talk to me is because they have absolutely no ideals and standards. That I need to lower my standards and find a nice, short, fat, American (not foreign because they are too different than me) guy in my league. The idea I had on promoting non-traditional beauty and talent is stupid. "Who would want to date a midget or look at some fat lady dance. And everyone knows deaf people can dance." They do? I didn't know that when I first ran into then at the club, and I'm very well rounded. "There is a reason society, TV, and the magazines show what they do." I'm sure there is. Well, what's that reason? Brainwashing? Zombie manufacturing? Cloned American dummies? It sure as hell aint reality!!

He said that if my talents in music, writings, and art were any good that I'd be famous by now. If I were any good, I wouldn't be so discrete and would let everyone hear my work. Obviously he has never noticed that the ones who brag usually need to—to inflate their skills and ability. If you are really good, rich, smart, or what have you, it's self evident, no bragging is needed. Usually the best ones are the most reserved. Didn't you ever hear the one with the biggest mouth usually can't fight. It's the quiet ones who surprisingly kick butt. Obviously his boasting paid off. He dropped out of school with only one or two classes left to graduate. Of course, that was my fault too. I made him stay up late several times and thus he had to drop out of college. **What?** He works in his dad's shop near Baltimore. Perhaps he's improving his already high level of automotive skills.

A post note on him

After he was going to hang out with his co-workers on that horrible Valentines Day and give me my sole card some days later, I was ready to drop him. As I said earlier, Valentines Day is HELL for lonely singles. There is ABSOLUTELY NOTHING for us!!! Being that he was like the typical guy and planned to hang out with the boys was IT for me! That was the final straw of me washing my hands of him. My current international sub leased roommate brought me more stuff for that horrible day. And he's not dating me nor is he any more obligated than my dad or brother. He gave me a teddy bear, candy, and heart picture frame. I gave him a card and CD (I already had). I wasn't sure if he'd remember and get me anything. Besides, it's a girl's holiday. I'm not getting a guy jack until after I see what they gave me. And as for Vic, I quickly made him a card once I received mine. That was one of the last times we hung out, Feb. 14, 2003. He'd call or come pass—always unexpected and unannounced—and I wouldn't answer. When I did reluctantly run into him, I'd make up some excuse to ditch and leave.

Like with any habit or addiction, you have to wing yourself off of it. For friends or couples (especially for those desperate, lonely ones out there) you do suffer from "I wish I had someone and wasn't alone, why didn't I wait until I actually found a replacement before we separated" withdrawal systems. But like with everything else, with distance, avoidance, and time, you slowly wing yourself off of that person too. As for me, after a month or so, I was SO OVER him. I wanted ABSOLUTELY NOTHING to do with him.

After a while, he'd call because he urgently needed to get to his computer. He needed these dire, important, files. He "found" my disc. He called me over my mom's saying he found my disc and he wanted to come over to get stuff off of his computer and return my disc. That's funny, I never knew it was missing. It must have somehow jumped out of my drawer and into his pocket and accidentally walked out of my door with him. Then it must have hid to lay dormant inside his room for the perfect opportunity to appear (like conveniently finding Sadam Hussein). Perhaps as a last resort to contact me. Of course, by that time I had already moved up stairs and there was no way I wanted him to know where I lived. The most unusual thing is that whenever I did see him, he never once brought up his computer. Hum, I wonder why?

The last time I spoke to him was Christmas 2003. I called him to be cordial and nice and to see what the heck he needed with his computer. I was trying to make arrangements for him to get his computer back once and for all since he so desperately needed some files. This dinosaur is very slow and old. I could use Swautch's prehistoric laptop he gave me for word processing just as well. It takes up less space and neither one of them have the internet. I could use the free, high-speed T1 lines on campus for internet access. And since both can't do too many things outside of word processing, I was willing to return it. I am eagerly awaiting a laptop from somewhere.

I find it funny. As many message he left with me about this important file, he not once mentioned it on Christmas. Maybe he forgot? Perhaps it was all a bunch of bull and just another reason to come over and revel in my woes in the first place. After all, with all of the looks, talents, women, skills, and intelligence he has, he must still have only one friend—me. I purposely called him from over Kong's house so he would get Kong's number, not my home number, on his caller ID. I also had an official reason to get off of the phone with him. He, among others, thought Kong and I were an item. Surely he wouldn't disrespect Kong's home and call again for me. Also, with the exception of my cell, this cuts off all ties to me from him. He doesn't know where I live, my new phone number, and the only contact he has is Kong's number and my cell granting him no success for contacting me.

30. Hyattsville

Hyattsville is a book in itself. He is the first in the trilogy of insane Americans, and rightfully so. If you wonder who the second and last ones are, take a guess. Kong, of course, is the next one, and as I just mentioned, Vic is the final lunatic I dealt with. Outside of lying about travel, museums, close relationships, and such, Hyattsville was the only one who actually told me he was screwed up. I met him at a rave I drove Swautch to. Swautch introduced me to his attractive, muscular, friend. I guess I talked the dude's ear off so he quickly passed me on to Hyattsville. Hyattsville was a decent looking guy, nothing that I would call sexy at that time, but he was definitely someone whose personality grew on me and all of his pluses were exaggerated and his minuses became cute.

I never thought Chinese looking squinting eyes or very Native American features were that sexy. He also had a gray birthmark streaked in his head like Frankenstein and white spots on his eyes. He would not be anything off the break I would say was too sexy, however, he had an extremely arousing body. He was cut, solid, and full of veins. I am very aroused by veins. He also had thick eyebrows and a long Roman nose. And when he did comb and braid his hair, the black girls also thought he was sexy. He, however, was into whites. He's Caribbean and adopted by a white family and raised here. He had all of the classic attractions and feelings that a minority growing up in a white environment— school, neighborhood, family, etc.—would have. Even though the other whites would date anyone, the minorities only want to date whites and they also have self-image issues about not being white.

I still can't blame his insanity or self esteem issues on drugs. His mom was scary and reminded me of the witch from McBeth. She was old, withered, white, and gray. She was rude, crude, and scared any human near her. Don't dare call the house. Her scratchy, cigarette smitten, manly voice would curse you out for calling on her phone for Hyattsville. She was crazy and he either drove her mad or she drove him mad. Nonetheless, they both were off in the head. The dad was the only one normal looking and acting in the public eye.

Hyattsville and I would talk about everything and he always thanked me profusely when I called. Interesting enough, he knew Eyepatch, another peasant scrub Swautch introduced me to. On one of our first phone conversations, Hyattsville's hag of a mom was yelling in the background, perhaps because he was talking to a human on the phone. He told me he punched the wall down because his hag wouldn't give him his money. Why did she hold your money? Are you too irresponsible to hold your own money? When I finally met up with him, I totally forgot about that conversation. After all, I figured he was exaggerating. When I saw him, I thought he chewed and gnawed on his hands. I asked if he was chewing on his hands. He smirked and commented how ugly they were and how he hates ugly looking things. Things seem to have gone crazy from there.

The reason I actually thought he was nibbling on his hands in the first place was because I worked with someone like that at the Smithsonian National Gallery of Art—another job I had. I worked the Van Gogh exhibit with her and various other internationals and college students. She was this intelligent, articulate, chick from some private college in NY who would bite her hands. I've seen people suck their thumb and even their fingers. I've seen many folks bite their nails, but never their hands. She would very discretely nibble on her hands. The only reason I figured it out was because it was dark and puffy where she would nibble. I finally subtlety asked her why she did it. Her answer was, "You're so mean." I'm not exactly sure what that means except I should mind my business and pretend that I don't see her biting her hands. Outside of that, she was perfectly normal and extremely intelligent.

Well so far she is the only person I've ever met who does that, Hyattsville decided to ruin his hands tearing down a wall. Note to ~~greedy~~ corporate developers and folks who need rehab work. Forget about picking up day labors at 7'11; find Hyattsville, Filthy and his addict friends, Kong, and some drunk frat boys. They'll do any demolition job for some pizza and beer. Just drop them off, blast the music, and yell GO FOR IT!! Within a few hours to a day, your property should be gutted. Give them their tax deductible receipt for their volunteer services and thank them for a job well done. You can really be generous and offer a few cigarettes, some weed, and E pills. Note: make sure to have a well trained building engineer so you won't end up with a collapsed building with you all inside—that won't be good. PS, look out for the cops before you and everyone else is arrested!

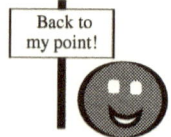

Well anyway, outside of Hyattsville's major mood swings almost border-lining a split personality, I don't know the exact condition he had, perhaps bi-polar or paranoid schizophrenic. When he was chill—usually while on weed—he was very chill and great to be around. When he was happy, he was really enjoyable and fun to be around. Most of the time he was paranoid and angry at something, and perhaps a bit dangerous to be around. One moment he was a pastor, preaching and asking—quite embarrassing and loudly in public—was I saved and who was saved. The very next day he was annoyed because I should have been gave him head. Which one is it?

We also never went to the museum nor on road trips with his car. When he got his car, he had no time for me. Then he got into an accident and lost it. Suits him right, and he still owes me a ride in his car!! Whenever we did go out, once the high left, he was really paranoid and uneasy being away from home. Sometimes he was overjoyed to see me and other times he acted like I was a thorn in his eye. It was then when he told me he was messed up. I thought he meant drunk, high, or gotten beat up. He basically said in ghetto terms, he was crazy. The ONLY one who actually admitted he was off. He even bragged to me about how strong and bad he was. He explained how he was trying to sell drugs (perhaps his mom's medication) and his mom called the hospital because he took her medicine. When the hospital came he jumped out the 2nd floor window and jumped the fence. He said it took 4 men to tackle him and strap him down. He said he was still paying that hospital bill.

It was after that that I would only call him every month or so. In between, I dealt with Ami the Jew, Wallied, Mothug, and a few other peasants. The following year Hyattsville offered to put his big, thug system in my little feather. Of course, I was down since my half broke radio hardly worked thanks to Floyd who completely broke my tape deck with his clumsy finger. I had 1 and a half working speakers, and a broken tape player. Hyattsville threw my radio in the trash, deeming it worthless, after he put his system in. Knowing nothing about electronics, I still wanted to keep my radio but he wouldn't let me get it and tossed it in the trash. The catch was he wanted equal access to my car in exchange for the system. Such as, a ride to court for getting arrested for smoking weed. Actually, the folks at the courthouse knew him. He cursed me out for trying to keep the system when he thought he was going to jail for breaking probation. I, of course, wanted the system and figured it was the least I could get out of this haphazard relationship. After avoiding him and never returning it, he showed up at my job about ready to blow up. I had to leave work and go all the way home with him just so he could drive around in my car, calm down, and inevitable, allow me to keep the radio anyway.

Later on, he allegedly was kicked out of his house for weed. I know it was more than that. He was a weed head. Why all of the sudden you're evicted when you smoked weed daily before? He went to a Christian men's rehab in N.C. for weed. I was told there is no such thing. People told me you go to rehab for hard drugs, heroin, crack, etc., not weed. I got a call in the middle of the day asking me to come and pick him up. This is what he said happened: He allegedly was kicked out of the rehab for reading the Bible. He then had to walk 40 miles at night in the woods being guided by ghost lights. He sold his ring to get on the bus. And here is the best part, are you ready? He saw Jesus Christ when he got off the bus. I asked what did Jesus look like. He said Jesus was in the form of a homeless man. Of course, Jesus needed some food, money, and clothes.

I happily let him move into my room, even though we never had sex nor did he hold and caress me the entire time. Perhaps this is not a guy thing. Several females explained how their boyfriends would lay while they went down on them, then straight to sex. I know men are not into foreplay unless they are nasty perverts, like R Kelly, but what's wrong with holding hands, playing in her hair, caressing her back, gentle touches, and romance? Surely, some wholesome, non-perverted, guy exists who is gentle, caressing, and romantic. Naturally, ALL men claim they are. Of course, the truth is self-evident. Hyattsville was no exception.

The only time we had sex was on my car. He rented a hotel once and was mad at me because I don't like giving head. I guess I'm that obsolete model Chris Rock spoke about. I hate going down and I can't even make pretend. He obviously was so disgusted at my lack of interest, enthusiasm, and disgust; he told me to turn around and went straight into sex. Then he was mad because it wouldn't stay in. Like it's my fault. I was surprised, disgusted, and of course, still horny. The second and only real time we successfully had sex, was a booty call to his home. When I got there, he told me to get on top of my car and he actually was able to keep it in this time. Of course I was still horny afterward. That was actually the last time I had sex, if you even call it that. The only romantic and gentle guy was Majid, who was 12 years older than me, and African.

To be honest, the only thing I got out of Hyattsville staying with me was arguments and stress. I hate needles but I needed to give blood for this job in Japan. I was so mad at him. I complained to the nurse about him so much that I amazingly didn't even feel the needle. Wow! That's either mind over matter, or me really being mad and stressed out. I don't know.

This one incident is actually when my blind, stupidness, whose is as dense as a brick, was finally disturbed. He was late returning my car to pick me up from work. Perhaps he was selling drugs, who knows. When he arrived I instantly started to argue. We both argued and yelled. He was good at arguing. He went from yelling and arguing with his face beet red, to instantly in a snap, "Aaaah, you feel better now?" All is well, no more arguing, red face, nothing. "Want some pizza, I'm hungry." Now I'm not sure, but I think that's kind of crazy. How can someone go from irate to calm in an instant? I was slightly uneasy with that one.

Later, he was looking for work and everyone gave him the run around. He walked into fast food joints with an attitude, and of course, everyone looked at him. He angrily balked how he'd really give the yuppies something to look at. Columbine High, are you listening? I was slightly disturbed so I called the hotline on him. Why did it sound like his mom answering the phone? And why did the city officials know him by name? They referred me to Fairfax hospital, which was near me. They actually thought that he was going to willingly go to the hospital. Why, I don't know. I told them to surprise him at my place. A nurse called the next morning; while he was still allegedly sleep. He must have crazy house radar. While she was making sure he was there before she dispatched the van out to my place, he caught on and started cursing me out. He called me crazy, a fatal attraction, possessive, and what have you. He packed his 3 trash bags, went to Hyattsville, MD, and took his thug system out of my car and to the pond shop. In all of his turmoil, he forgot his cell and a few other items. I was going to keep his cell.

He called and was so cordial to me happily talking about how he finally got his new place. Since returning to DC from the rehab and seeing Jesus, he kept showing and telling me about this place near his home. He obviously wanted to meet me to get his cell phone. I showed up and wanted to be nosy and see the inside. He was persistent with not letting me go in. I complained, "How dare you. I let you stay with me for several weeks and drive my car and you refuse to let me in. I need to use the bathroom, let me in!"

As I complained, some man—perhaps a counselor—came out and asked what was wrong. Puzzled over what was going on and who he was, perhaps the landlord or some cop, I told him I was dropping off Hyattsville stuff. The man said I could place Hyattsville's stuff in that door then he turned and they both walked the opposite way down the street. When I went to open the door it said **Guide Psychological Center**. Well, well. It must not be an apartment after all. He was staying in some transitional home near his mammy and lied and claimed that it was this lovely apartment he was applying for and hoping to get. In fact, that was when I first heard of Guide, so when I found out Kong stayed there, I knew exactly what it was, all thanks to Hyattsville. Like I said, Hyattsville is the first in the trilogy of insane Americans, and rightfully so. He is a book in and of itself. He is the first of my trilogy of insanity, and the reason that I look toward NY, Europe, and Africa

LefTovEr uSeleSs peAsanTs

These peasants are so insignificant and low on the evolution chain, that they only get these few sentences. PJ was this attractive juvenile delinquent from high school. He also was a public high school drop out. He disrespected his mom, (by cursing her out for getting caught skipping school and trying to have sex in their house) passed gas on my windshield, was in and out of jail, and very rude. I sent him a beautiful card with a ketchup filled tampon. I should have used real blood.

Then there was the 3-eyelash A'hole that I mentioned above that stood me up for my prom. To top things off, this worthless peasant has eyelashes that naturally clumped together in groups of threes. As I said earlier, I did make it to 2 other proms at WAY better schools—and nether one of my other prom dates had eyelashes clumped together in clusters of three or four!

And there's this peasant named Crocodile who lived in the section 8 homes near my current residence. Crocodile is a low class weed head with no money nor car and goes door to door begging for money and rides. He's attractive but there are still other members of the male specie living on earth for me to deal with. There was also this Iranian peasant I met at the MVA one year. He was there trying to get some ID and spoke 13 words of English. We exchanged numbers. He'd call and not understand a thing I would say. "Hello, what are you doing?"

"I'm watching TV."

"I don't understand. What are you doing?"

"I'm making a sandwich."

"I don't understand. What are you doing?"

"I'm talking on the phone."

"I don't understand. Are you coming out?"

Now what the heck is that all about? Why do you even call if you don't understand? And why do you keep asking the same questions? After going through this a bit, I decided to go out with him. I drove my Nissan and picked him up at his apartment. I went straight to the gas station to fill my tank. We went pass a friends place that wasn't home then I dropped him back at his place. He said, "Wait a minute!" I guess even with limited English, he wanted more than gas and go. He also promised to pay off all of my credit card bills if I married him—obviously for a green card.

Through my niceness of not cursing them and a few others out—like this compulsive lying dummy named Aaron and this sexy New YoRician with rotten teeth who was straight up insane—they kept coming around until they finally got the picture. I guess you must yell, curse, hit, and spit on some guys for them to get the picture.

Wallied's rotten tooth roommate

And last, but not least, is Wallied's rotten tooth roommate who spoke no English. He was from N. Africa also and quite sexy until he smiled. He worked at a fashionable clothing store in Georgetown. He dressed like a model and was tall, slim, dark, and handsome. I really don't know what happened to his teeth, they were all orange, brown, black, chipped, cracked, or gone. Surely he had some whole, complete, yellow teeth left but he had so many black and brown ones it was hard to count. Wanting Wallied, I dealt with him assuming and hoping to find Wallied. He took me to their place, where Wallied was of course not, and started feeling me up. The fact that he kept trying to kiss me with that disgusting mouth was such a turn off, I politely kept moving away to wait for Wallied. Wallied never showed, perhaps he was having sex elsewhere. Once I realized that, I told rotten teeth I had to go. Perhaps he can get some false teeth to place in that mouth of his. Well, I guess it doesn't matter. He'd probably be deported soon anyway and those teeth are perfectly fine where he is from.

GOD DOESN'T TEASE?!?!?

In regards to God, blessings, problems, and curses, I went to this 3-day church anniversary this past week. The speaker said that if there is a specific blockage, obstacle, hindrance, or "No" to you in regards to obtaining your purpose, then you are looking in exactly the right place. Later he also said that God doesn't tease us. I would like some more info on that one since there are many basic everyday things that everyone else on earth seems to have—except me. One of those major things is a partner or relationship with someone that they at least like and are attracted to somewhat. I NEVER, NEVER, EVER seem to be able to attract a man—whom I'm attracted toward—to be interested in me for more than a friend or sex. Isn't that a tease? Let everyone else in front of my face, have someone for them, and let me be habitually single.

The speaker even said that if there is a specific illness, door closed, or problem personally specific to you, that means that the devil and demons are working overtime on you—or something along those lines. His wife, for example, got a prophetic word one year about being cured of an illness. Neither she nor her husband understood it until a year later. Almost a year to the day later the problem arose. She was diagnosed with a rare throat cancer. A kind only Asians get and she was a black American. They even wanted to cut her face to remove it. She was a singer and speaker and this was a perfect and specific way to hinder her success in achieving her purpose. She amazingly went into remission within two of the seven weeks of her scheduled chemo.

You may wonder how this relates to men. Well, in regards to physical bodily problems, I seemed to have acquired a condition that usually only white women with small, narrow hips get much later in life after having many kids. I am quite black, have massively wide hips, and don't even have the luxury to have raw sex with a spouse; let alone giving birth to a tribe! The archaic solution in barbaric medicine is a hysterectomy. I heard via this acupuncturist, some patient got some alternative treatment using some screen mesh inside her. An easier and non-evasive form is to do these Kelvin exercises to strengthen my uterus. The crappy icing on this dreadful cake—which I guess personalizes it via the bowels of hell and earth—is that this exercise is not only supposed to strengthen your pelvic after a rack of kids—none of which I have, but also make sex more enjoyable for you. What?! I need absolutely **NOTHING** to help me!! I need a relationship with someone I'm attracted to who's interested and affectionate towards me, or something to CALM me DOWN!!! I had raging hormones since 12, if not earlier. I

137

obviously have too much testosterone via my annoying beard, which won't go away. To top things off, a friend said I had big child baring hips and one room-mate always spoke (and with much glee) how I look like I'm 5 months pregnant.

Oh how lovely. I have problems that pregnant women of 5+ months get and women who gave birth to a village get. And the WORST thing about this, and the icing on this dreadful cake is that I'm habitually single, alone, in heat, and my biological clock is ticking—ticking—ticking away in this God awful place of no suitors! The only decent place in continental US, Alaska, and Hawaii is NYC, and thanks to Swautch, I never lived there. As Myro's ex-boyfriend would say, **this is just the WORSTEST!!!!** And I desperately stay single, alone, and celibate as I look for this imaginary, fake, non existence, never arriving mate I'm attracted to, who will actually like me and want a real relationship. Like a prude, I stay miserable, lonely, and single waiting for Mr. Right—where ever in NYC, Europe, or Africa he is. Because he sure as hell aint here!!!!

I ♥ NY

NY guys are so much more diverse and open minded compared to the rest of continental US. The only other place with such open mindedness is Europe and Africa. New York and Western Europe had such a flux of diverse foreigners in a small area, they were forced to tolerate and get along with each other or blow the entire place up. They both had diversity and foreigners for over 100 years whereas everywhere else in America is just getting introduced to diversity.

LA, Miami, and other cities known for their diversity may have had foreigners upon their soil for a while, but the area is more spread out so people are not forced to live and intermingle with each other. Miami has many Cubans, but how many African, Mexican, or Chinese neighborhoods are within walking distance? LA and San Francisco have many ethnic neighborhoods but you definitely need a car to get to them. People are not forced to live in such close proximity.

NY has so many people living so close to each other. China Town is near Little Italy, which is near Spanish Harlem, which isn't too far from Jamaica Queens. Also, unlike many other cities, the subway in New York is one of the oldest—if not the oldest in the country, and it's supposed to run all night. It's easy without a car, to get around to all of the different neighborhoods. If not by foot, by train. LA and Miami have limited to no subway and horrible public transportation compared to New York.

More Proof I'm Right!

Many people try to prove me wrong and dispute me, but they never succeed. In fact, I remember as a child around 8 or so, on my first trip to New York, I saw something unusual. Outside of all the weird people, I noticed interracial dating between races I never saw in DC, and I was only a kid. Myro, my mom, (and I'm sure even you the reader seeing all of the crap I get into) will admit how slum I am on my cards and how hard it is for me to notice things. As a kid (who shouldn't be paying attention to interracial dating patterns) I noticed black ladies with non-black and non-white guys. This was unusual to me because I had never seen that before in DC. I've seen black men and white men with every race of woman. And, of course, white women with every race of guy on earth. I however, never remember seeing black women, or other minority women, with other diverse races.

If I'm that bad at noticing things—and I even noticed something that I shouldn't even be paying attention to as a kid—then I must be on to something. Why as a kid would I even care about who dates whom? At that age, I was only concerned about the boys in my class. In fact, I think I still had crushes on Rambo, the Tin Man, and the boy from the Jungle Book. Surely if I'm thinking about them, I shouldn't be worried or even notice adult dating habits. It must have been **SO noticeable** and different that I remember pulling my mom and pointing them out. The same way I noticed the lady's super long nails who sat behind me at the Radio City Music Hall production of Peter Pan. I kept pointing them out to my mom too.

FLOYD AND FAT—THE FAT PUSSYCAT

Floyd requested to meet a fat pussy. I laughed loudly. At the same time, Wild D wanted us to go with her to Colorado. Realizing how Floyd only went to NY with us because we allegedly kidnapped him, I knew he wouldn't go. Filthy, however did not exactly want to watch Fat for the week. He barely fed and watched her other times and mom was still annoyed about when I dropped Fat off to go to San Francisco. Since Floyd wants to meet a fat pussy, I have just the one for him! She's adorable, sweet, purrs, has a big tail, very affectionate, enjoys snuggling, and seafood. She's a great girl to meet. Of course, Floyd was excited to meet her. He planned a trip to a nice restaurant and a movie for them.

When Wild D and I arrived, I saw Floyd taking out his trash. I told him the fat pussy is here, come and meet her. He was hesitant and not interested anymore. Filthy annoyingly told him—as if it was any of his business to tell in the first place—that I was only bringing my pussycat. Well I dropped Fat off at his apartment with his roommate, the newly arrived roommate's mom, her huge dog, and white cat. Neither roommate nor Floyd seemed willing nor pleased to watch Fat. Wild D and I told them how they should be pleased to watch my lovely and dear cat. She's not only a fat pussy, but her travel cage matches the white cat. We left Fat there and headed for Co.

Being that Wild D was rushing me, I forgot my ATM card, not as if I had much money anyway. I tried to get food with food stamps at a gas station. Wild D has a nerve to act as if that is really stupid. They sell food so why can't I buy it with food stamps? Of course she has me drive through Pittsburgh after she drove like a mad man through the mountains. Of course, with her going to sleep, she was as much help with direction as Fat's kitty litter. We obviously took a wrong turn somewhere and ended up north somewhere in Ohio instead of southern Ohio. She was taking her child to Denver to stay with her sister and mom for the summer while she went to Egypt. We finally found our way south as I continuously search for a Bank of America.

The stingy winch refuses to donate any money to me, even though I was helping her drive. As much of a corporate, greedy, monopoly that bank has, it at least should have branches in the mid west. I finally found one in St. Louis. She has a nerve to complain about me needing to stop for money. Then the slut bakes me and her child driving though the boiling heat of summer with no AC. Her child cries from torture and I can't even sleep from disgust. She refuses to use the AC unless I give some money for gas. When it's my turn to drive, I stop at this diner and purposely sit at the air-conditioned diner for over an hour. Her child even stops crying from torture. Wild D complains that I'm taking too long.

When we finally leave its late afternoon and a bit cooler. The entire time Floyd calls and complains about the cat. I really see no problem, it's what you requested, a fat pussy. Of course, he wasn't as pleased. When we hit Kansas, Wild D decides to harass me by driving in a possible twister. It's pitch black and the best thing Kansas has is its borders to the next states. There's Kansas City, Kansas, which touches Kansas City, Mo. There's also Leavenworth prison. Perhaps the best thing Kansas has to offer. As for gas stations and street lights, no good. As we drove I begged to stop because it was a major lightning storm. I wasn't sure if a twister was about to start or what. It was lightning so hard that it lit up the whole road which other wise was pitch black. Wild D tries to blame me for stopping for lunch and spending an hour for us driving through the storm.

We stayed in Denver 2 days and she got irritable that I drove 8+ hours at a safe and normal speed and she ended up driving the rest of the way back. She said that she'd never do that again. I asked what. She claimed drive to Denver. She expected me to drive more than 8 hours, and I did. Denver is supposed to be a 30-hour drive. It took us that long because I drove a lot and we got lost. This really is her trip to drop off her child. We didn't even go the Denver Mint. I talked much of the time she drove to keep her up. She claimed she needed someone to not just talk to keep her up, but to actually drive. She balks, "If you're tired, conversation won't keep you alert. Another driver will." Well I helped her drive while baking with her child and being tormented by the pre-twister lightning storm en route.

Once back, Floyd complained about Fat, in which he did the entire trip. She was scared and hiding in his closet. He claims the roommate's big evil dog harassed her and that she slapped him in the eye. Luckily I never declawed her, even though I still think about it to this day. He also claims that she allegedly crapped in his roommate's shoe. He called me on several occasions complaining that she kept crying. She was scared, and like any baby, wanted her mommy. He also did not enjoy sharing his pillow with Fat, who cried and walked around his pillow and head while he tried to sleep. He wishes never to meet any more fat or skinny pussies from me again.

THE INSANITY AT BERKLEY

After Filthy left, Myro moved in. She was kind of my last resort. She wasn't a student, she was an escort who wanted to use this as her business and live at her DC home. Of course, I wanted someone who would live here, not solely use it for some horny perverts who know where I live while she is still safe in DC. Filthy and Linda left the apartment in ruins and his bathroom looked as though a volcano erupted. Ash and dirt covered the sink and tub, not to mention clothes, food, and books covered the floor. Even though the place was shot to hell, I was in. Thanks to the shiftless management and God, I slipped through the cracks. There was a waiting list of over 50 people, and I wasn't even on a lease. Filthy told management that he would renew and thusly, I co-signed and got on the lease.

No one wanted the apartment and the few people that were willing to take it fell through so I was stuck with Myro. She wasn't even too interested in the place either due to the jacked up conditions. She wondered when management would repair all of the damage. I guess she gave in and was willing to take the place. Thusly, I ended up settling for her to move in, I really had no other option compliments of the ragged condition the apartment was in. She even managed to replace Filthy and get on the lease—releasing the total burden off of me—compliments of the shiftless management. She also ended up permanently staying at the apartment and never returning to DC to live. In fact, because Myro wasn't a student, she stayed on the extremely shiftless management to get stuff done.

I told Myro from the top that I wasn't comfortable with her moving in because of her business. She kept assuring me, and still does, that her business or way of meeting guys off date lines, is no more or less safer than meeting someone in person. She tries to argue her point, but absolutely no one agrees with her. So far, the only person Myro convinced is herself. Soon Myro's boyfriend moved in with us. I figured it was a bit more secure with a guy around but Myro had him hide downstairs or in my room so her clients wouldn't get scared away. I guess I was lucky to this point; the clients she saw were more scared than they were murderers. I still was never comfortable—and nor was her boyfriend.

In the beginning, with the exception of her clients who discretely came to her room and left without me or her boyfriend ever meeting them, she paid the rent on time and there was no real problem. Neither one of us had that much company and unlike most undergrad Americans who are loud, party, and have company constantly, Myro was quiet and stayed in her room. She played her TV, videogames, and her radio, but she did it with her door closed in her room. She ate a lot and when her boyfriend moved in she soon started cooking huge meals and left the dishes dirty for weeks. She was cordial and stayed to herself like me. I'm very cordial, quiet, and I watch TV but I'm not a loud drunk, and full of trash, dirt, and company. This is why I preferred a foreign or grad student. They are quiet, invisible roommates. When they are not at school they are in their room.

It was Vic and her boyfriend who got both of us hanging out. We'd quietly watch TV together and we'd talk but I wasn't that nosy and I didn't pry into her affairs and she didn't pry into mine. I wasn't intrusive or mixed up with what she did outside of Berkley. As long as the bills and rent were paid and the kitchen and living room was livable and non-disgusting, the rest was none of my business. Then her boyfriend met Vic and they began to hang out. Her boyfriend was Vic's biggest advocate and "bestest friend" and Vic was his. Unlike the privacy and space that Myro and I gave each other, Vic was completely nosey with absolutely no diplomacy or discretion. Vic and her boyfriend got us talking on many things.

Soon Floyd moved in because, for the second time, I tried to introduce him to someone. The first girl I tried to introduce to him was my one eyed friend whose mind and personality was just like his. Floyd didn't want to meet her cause of the eye thing, even though she had a nice body and stuff. I met Netira on the shuttle bus and we started going to the gym together. Being that I'm a cordial person, I listened as Narita spoke of her ex-boyfriend who broke up with her for some other girl. It's always mean for someone to leave you for someone else. It makes you ask, what was wrong with me? Wasn't I good enough? I didn't know Narita too well, for we were only hanging out at the gym for a month. During that time, she appeared decent and nice. Narita was intelligent, well to do, not a hood rat, and she seemed nice so I figured I'd introduce her to Floyd, who also seemed nice and wonderful to people.

Floyd came to visit Narita on a Friday, spent the night, and did not go home until 2 months later. Myro and I wondered when Floyd was going to leave. Floyd supposedly moved in to get away from his grandma. Perhaps that is quite true, but he moved in mostly for Narita. Floyd slept in our living room, used my bathroom, breaking half the stuff in there, and kept me from being focused.

The week that Floyd moved in, the frat boys decided to have a bar room brawl outside our apartment. Across the hall lived some really cool, fun loving, partying Greeks whose frat house was closed by the university for some binge drinkers' death. They were hot tempered, alcoholic drunks, who would spew fights out the window, so this was normal. We thought it was a WWF match. Myro looked out the door to see the rack of drunks yelling and fighting in the hallway in front of our door. I started to call the cops over this but I was nice this particular time. I wrote a note the next day but never got around to leaving it. It said, "Dear King Kong's, The next time you APES decide to get in a WWF bar room brawl fight outside my door, the cops will be called ASAP!!" I forgot the rest of the letter but it was along those lines. I never gave the note to anyone but I did ask Greek boy what the heck happened last night as the maintenance man repaired his door-knob. He apologized with his black eye and busted up door.

tHe cHaoS beGinS

Floyd claimed he wanted to move in many times before but since he never paid anything and made no moves, I figured he was just talk. Floyd claimed that he was going to move in and we—Floyd, Myro, and I—all agreed upon a rate. It took him a month to give me any money. It was the month of February and Myro was late for her rent too. It was the first in a long continuous cycle for late rent payments for her. Being that I lived there and paid my rent, that was where the problem came in. Floyd lived there as long as Netira toyed him along and he could tolerate Myro and her boyfriend's constant arguing, trashy dishes, and her boyfriend's blasting music. Myro's boyfriend had more visitors than Myro, Floyd, and me combined. His friends would come over, drink, blast music, and leave the house a mess. One friend couldn't even hold his beer and puked on the floor and couch. Being that neither Floyd nor Myro's boyfriend helped with the utilities, I was left with Myro—who was still struggling with rent every month. It became like the mad house soon.

Vic was trying to "seduce" Myro and Netira. Netira wanted to steal Vic from me and have Vic and Floyd battle over her to help build her self esteem. I guess Narita thought, "If I can steal Vic who's leading Lory on and not even trying to be with her in the first place; and then get him and Floyd to fight over me, I must really be someone special," which isn't saying much. Steal someone who is in a happy, or at least, in a real relationship, not someone wasting someone else's time.

Narita claimed that she wasn't physically nor mentally attracted to Floyd. Then why is she leading Floyd on and wasting both her and Floyd's time?! I know several people, including Vic and various tramps that Floyd dealt with, who would do this. I NEVER could understand the concept. I can see if he/she is a sugar daddy/momma and you're smiling and doing what you need to do to get your bills paid. The person most likely knows that they're being used for money anyway. Narita, however, was well off. She nor Vic used me nor Floyd for anything except our emotions.

If the only thing you're gaining by leading someone on is self worth, you need help.... .FAST!!! Is your self worth so shot to hell that you lead people on that you are totally not interested in? If so, then you need a therapist, counselor, witch doctor, priest, exorcist, something! What's the purpose anyway? None of them were ugly. Narita, Vic, and the few other guys and women I know, are attractive. It's Floyd and I that both need better self esteem. Me, Floyd, and many others I know

NEVER lead people on. As Myro and Floyd put it—and I completely agree—"If the only person that wants me is a fat wart hog, that makes it all the worst!"

I guess it's like those people who enjoy totally disrespecting their mates or friends by making them jealous. I know a lot of people like that. I'm not sure what someone gains when they tell their mate or friend how so many others want and desire them so much. How their ex is so sexy and still wants to spend time with them. How they have so much more smarts, money, goods, men/women, status, or whatever than you. How much more expensive their nice shoes and clothes are compared to yours. Perhaps it's some retart form of ego building. Unfortunately, it's hard to know if someone is wasting your time and just leading you on in the beginning, but the second you notice a mate—or even a friend—trying to make you jealous and revel in your woes.... RUN TO THE NEAREST EXIT, and leave all the baggage behind!!!!

aNOtheR maD hOUse

Again, I lived in a lovely collection of chaos: a constant flow of late rent, a pompous wannabe whore who won't leave, a toying slut, an annoying klutz, a loud scrub, and a kitchen full of filthy dishes. Not to mention a disconnected phone every other month. It soon wasn't too different from the mad house. I could never focus to get stuff done at the apartment!

Floyd wanted to permanently move in, and due to his problems with Myro's boyfriend, move them both out. He wanted to move out of the living room and take over their room. I offered sub lease options to Myro since she was late every month. Even though she can explain other wise, the landlord, paper work, and day the money finally came in, proves different. Myro didn't want to sublease because she said she didn't have anywhere to stay. I didn't want to get evicted let alone deal with the stress of constant late payments and disconnected phone. In the beginning the payment was fine but by the spring, it was always late.

I was willing to work with Floyd. However if Myro left, he wasn't going to move in. He was as irresponsible as her boyfriend, though he'd say otherwise. Floyd paid rent one time and then paid that late. The second time someone stole his ATM card and robbed his account. It just magically happened during rent time. Of course, if Myro left, I'd replace her with someone less responsible. To be honest and fair, she struggled for the initial money to move in but she paid the rent and utilities on time, and even flossed with fashionable clothes. It wasn't until the following year that the problems started.

Floyd decided to not take my suggestion, and stupidly sent a fax to the very shiftless management, who could care less about her escort services. As long as rent was paid, they turned the other cheek. Rent was still late! The maintenance man was more shiftless than Myro's boyfriend. The maintenance man would hang out in our apartment playing Nintendo, blasting music, and drinking 40's with her boyfriend. The maintenance man, of course, told them what happened. They thought I knew about it. I personally felt it was a dumb idea because as you can plainly see, nothing happened. I completely understand Floyd and why he did it. Myro's boyfriend, of course, even can see why Floyd would do it. Her boyfriend is embarrassed that the word is out about what she does and that he's dating her, however he's more upset that she never stopped. Myro obviously is not making too much money since the rent is late every month. It's none of my business what she does out in the street. As long as it doesn't follow her home to endanger me nor Fat, that's between Myro, God, and her clients. However, I was always concerned from day one with her doing it here. I can obviously understand why her boyfriend would have a problem with it too. Her boyfriend, however, never left her and dealt with Myro the entire time she did it. One would assume it shouldn't bother him too much, I mean, you are still with her, then you must accept it.

Well, Myro obviously—and her boyfriend due to embarrassment—were irate with Floyd. Myro was already complaining about him moving out without one months notice so they could get their monies together for that following month. Now under normal circumstances this makes since, but rent was always late. Outside of her boyfriend, the MAIN reason Floyd moved out is because he and Netira had an argument and didn't speak anymore. As I stated, the main reason he moved in was for her and when there was absolutely no chance of any relationship, Floyd moved back home.

Rent again was late that month! With Floyd spreading her business, Myro was ready to fight. Go figure, Floyd's plan was extremely non successful. He's supposedly an investigator. Floyd should know cops who could easily arrest her for prostitution, if that's what she did. They could simply pretend to be a client and if Myro did some illegal stuff, take her in. That may be cruel, but as Floyd and her boyfriend would say, Myro would see that this is not the best choice for her. It would be a hard lesson to learn, but nonetheless, a lesson. Her boyfriend even argued this situation when he first found out what Floyd did. That could be one effective way to stop Myro's activities, if they in fact were illegal, and put much pressure on her to change occupations once and for all. A harsh way, but quite effective. If what Myro did was actually legal, then that would just be anther client who just so happened was a detective or cop. Nothing would happen, no arrest, no departure of her boyfriend, <u>and still the chance of late rent again the following month</u>.

The most effective way with 100% results, no embarrassment, arrest, nor hard feeling is my original idea, **sublease**. I'd find an international or grad student who

146

is quiet, pays the rent on time, and Myro could move back home to get her finances in order. Boyfriend would have to leave, and as far as Floyd went, he was already gone due to Nerita not talking to him. I know Myro didn't want to move back home, who does, but if you're about to be taken to court for non-payment, you really have no choice.

Subleasing would help her rental credit history and mine. With some responsible person paying rent and bills early, it improves our credit history since both of our names are on the lease and her name was on the phone and utilities. She could decided what business or job she would do while living elsewhere.

On top of that, she'd been trying—with very poor results—to dump and ditch her boyfriend. He refused to leave. Who'd want to leave somewhere with free 20" TV, video games, sex, food, and drinks? If she subleased, not only would it build and improve her credit, but help Myro finally ditch her boyfriend once and for all. Her boyfriend would have no choice but to leave, someone else would be living there. Of course, to me the best idea, but as always, NO ONE ever listens to me. Thusly, Floyd's plan didn't work, she and her boyfriend stayed, and I ended up trying to move out. Like I said, by the end with the bombardment of insanity and cut off notices, it was the Mad House Part II.

Her boyfriend's biggest argument regarding Floyd's botched attempt was, "You should have never been doing this in the first place. You should have been stopped and changed occupations." I'm not sure if that's why he never paid rent. Of course her boyfriend never paid for anything. He used the phone more than Myro and I, and paid nothing on it. So as Myro said, he can't talk, he's not putting anything toward the bills. Floyd was mad because I did not take sides and "I have favoritism" or that I kept "playing both sides." I guess I should support him and be totally against Myro. What she does is none of my business. I solely want the rent and bills to be paid. If your 007 skills can get some bill paying results, then go ahead. They both did what they wanted and Myro got embarrassed and still had late payments and an attached scrub and Floyd got cursed out. What do you expect? I solely wanted bills to get paid. Going through management was the worst and least effective way. And if her escort business is going that bad, perhaps she should find other easy forms of money, which is much safer too, such as dancing and so forth.

Well compliments of Narita, Floyd fled to his home; and when summer came I tried to figure a way to find another roommate. Myro refused to sublease until business or money picked up, so I begged for another apartment. The manager went out her way to move me upstairs, to this much worst apartment. Myro wanted to know why I didn't want to stay, and she and her boyfriend had a nerve to take it personal. Her boyfriend questioned what type of friend am I? It's extremely stupid to me, to be mad at someone who doesn't want to get evicted and wants working phone service. I understood Belief's reasoning and didn't get mad at her for replacing me with her fully employed co-worker. In fact, if she never replaced me, I would have kept struggling with bronchitis, never conceived to take that Japanese class at NOVA, and ultimately never had that opportunity to work in Japan. Actually … that worrisome move could have been a better favor to me than either one of us realized!

Management even wanted Myro and I to sign a waiver with the lease saying if we're late one more time, we'd get evicted. That was focused at Myro but since we're both on the lease, I'd be out too. Because she did not want to sublease and her boyfriend paid absolutely nothing every month—because she was an escort even though he's still with her—I moved upstairs with someone who paid their rent in advance too. To top everything off, Myro ended up moving out less than a month later after I moved upstairs due to a restraining order on her boyfriend! I can never win for losing!! I can almost bet that if I never left, their comfort level would have never changed and they would still be there, late rent, and all. Her boyfriend even complained about the male foreign student—who is about studies unlike most American undergrads—is nowhere as enjoyable and fun as a female. As one guy said, 2 or more women is a harem to a man, it helps boost his manliness. He's the true man and king of the castle. Another man in his domain threatens his kingship. I asked why she left since no one has seen her boyfriend. Myro said that, "If I didn't moved out, he would always come around. Since he has no idea where I live, he's forced to leave and find another life."

MORE ANTICS WITH MYRO & SWAUTCH

That same year I took an audio production class at American University, the school that Swautch went to. He would come to the audio production studio where I took my class periodically through out the year to use the phone and internet on campus. I stole him a few times to help me in my production class. Of course, after every meeting he'd go to some club or party and I'd go home. That was a 2 to 3 hour class that I took after a rack of other classes that day so I would be exhausted afterwards. I'd reach my home via subway after 11pm on many occasions. The train was very slow during non-rush hour. On a few occasions he tricked me into going out with him.

The first time he promised me a ride home with this partying coke addict. She met us and took us to her hotel suite where she was staying. I didn't care except it was late and I wondered if she really was going to Md. for some party as Swautch claimed. Of course, I was stuck in her hotel suite. I kept calling Floyd for a ride. Of course he was wooing Netira and yelled at me for calling for a ride. After we ate I started asking if they would give me a ride home. Of curse not. They wanted a coke refill. I even contacted our addict Greek neighbors for coke to offer her, as an incentive to drive me home. They, everyone except me that is, went into the bedroom I guess to party. I gave up on Floyd's ride.

Swautch went on some run and I went with him. We took a cab to a hotel near his house and went to another suite where some guy from Kosovo was staying. There were some drug fiend whores in his room and I waited in the living room with Swautch. Kosovo apologized saying they felt uncomfortable using drugs in front of us. I could care less; I just wanted a ride home! Swautch got what ever he came for, we got some food, and he appeased me by getting me a toothbrush. I was still irritated, since I had to sleep on the short comfy couch, too small for me to even stretch out on. I was SOOO ready to go. The only reason I didn't take the train home, outside the fact that I missed it, was that I had a rack of bags I was carrying.

Another time Swautch and I met up; we walked to Cokie's place. She moved into an apartment. Swautch hoped Cokie didn't overdose. He said that the last time he saw her; she locked herself in the bathroom for 2 days and said she would never use drugs again. Of course that day she gave me a ride home because of more coke connections. Swautch wanted to go to a party inside my building. He was surprised that the party was actually across the hall from me. I could care less; I just wanted to go home. Being that everyone on our floor partied, it was no surprise to me.

Myro first met Swautch because she needed me to take her sister to the hospital because her sister's ex attacked her sister. Swautch wanted to go but since it wasn't a party, he stayed with Floyd. Floyd claims that after we left, Cokie, Swautch, and another guy laced our counter with coke and Floyd said get the eff out, not in here. Why Myro's sister didn't go to the hospital in some ambulance instead of my car is another question. We were there all night. The emergency room is slower than the management in our building. It's a great refuge from the cold for the homeless. They go in at night claiming something is wrong. Of course, they don't get seen 'til dawn. So they sit in the lobby with their withered duffel bag and ragged Trapper Keeper notebook (and I haven't seen one of them in 2 decades). The guards would tell them it's time to go. They would refuse saying, "Hell no, I'm still waiting to be seen!"

"Oh you're not going to leave?!"

"Eff you!!"

"O K, let me get the gloves!"

We busted out laughing. I guess they are so dirty and contaminated that no one wants to touch them with their bare hands. After talking all night, I finally decided to see what the heck was taking so long. By this time it was day.

Over the summer, Myro and I went to the French embassy for this free neo soul concert Swautch told me about. That's when she first hung out with Swautch. We did our usual, go to certain hotels for goodies. Myro, who used to work for one, was surprised but down for the goods. After partying all evening and scavenging all night, Myro and I were tired. Swautch refused to let me sleep and persuaded me to go to this club that supposedly has beds. It was this new 24 hours café and club. Being that it was loud and freezing inside the club compliments of their A/C, I hardly slept. Of course, people kept bothering me all night. By dawn I was cold, tired, and p#ssed. I had no good sleep and Myro couldn't drive any better than this plastic cup. Swautch, of course, wanted to keep partying elsewhere.

I asked Myro to buy me coffee and she claimed she had no money and so did Swautch. I'm mad cause I need coffee and no one will get me one, and of course, I have no money. Swautch introduced me to the bartenders and they gave me a free drink. The bearded one was kind of cute and both were nice. This lady, who was so high she couldn't keep her eyes open nor stand up straight, liked the same bartender. I called her Ms. Wong because she looks like an aged Ms. Wong from down the hall.

The frat boys at the end of the hall partied 4-6 days a week. Of course they had problems passing classes. They had many tricks to visit though. One high school drop out was a super addict and imitated Ms. Wong from Mad TV to Floyd. We pinned Ms. Wong to this girl never knowing or remembering her name. The addict from the club looks liked a withered and aged Ms. Wong. She claims she had a job but I figured she was just a professional addict. The texture and color of her face was equal to an aged brick. She claimed someone wanted sex from her in the bathroom. At this point, I was really soooo ready to go home. Myro and I left Swautch with Addict and another guy to continue partying.

Myro and I, had several other adventures with Swautch. We also had many adventures without him too. Another time Myro and I went to that same club, this Hungarian guy, who like most Europeans love blacks, wanted Myro and me. Of course, he was totally not attractive to either one of us. Later on, he also needed marriage for a green card. Here comes Swautch into this same club and we all hang out there. This cute Indian guy wants us to go to his apartment to party. Of course Myro isn't interested and I sure as heck won't go alone. I try to get her to go and she is really not interested. Of course, Swautch is ALWAYS ready to party, anytime, anyplace. Being that I was tired, and as always, was forced to drive compliments of no one else having a license nor car, I went home afterwards.

Another adventure is with this blind guy. I met him at this international gathering. He's Persian and blind since a child. He's like any other guy, ready for sex. He, unlike the last Moroccan who allegedly makes $5000 a month, is actually well off. He has his own business and a beautiful penthouse. I never asked him for money, even though he did offer to pay my cell phone bill once. I went over that day with my bill so he would help me. Of course, I took cock block back up— Myro. We went to some Spanish café (that would be Spain not Latin American where the food is delicious) that had cute music—sounding like the Gypsy Kings—and disgusting food. I wanted to go to this Italian restaurant but we got there too late. For some reason he ordered a lot of drinks instead of going to some liquor store and buying an entire bar for $50. I danced alone and a little with him. The bill finally came and it was $150. Of course he was shocked. I figured it'd be expensive since everyone kept buying drinks.

Well, after we paid, we left and I went to the gas station, I was almost on empty. Myro, who is scantly dressed on many occasions, was putting a sweater on since we left that Spanish lounge. Since he was busy feeling me up, I offered him the opportunity to feel Myro in the back seat. Of course, she was very pleased at this. Being that her outfit had no bra, he enjoyed the feeling. She requested him to wait until she exited the car fully dressed. Even though he was blind, he wanted in on the strip action too. "Oh come on now, equal access under the law." Of course I felt it was quite funny like him. Myro snickered but wasn't as pleased. He paid for the gas and some soda and we went to his place.

Myro and I chilled out there and I tried to get my bill paid but the lazy AT&T workers only work when they want to harass you, not when you need them. He was willing to pay over the phone with his credit card but you can only do that with the operator on the line. After chilling a bit, he was ready for some action.

Since he sat next to Myro to share the smoke and "equal access", she decided to go and retreat to his lofty bathroom. That made him move back to me. I knocked on the door, "Myro. Myro, are you coming out?!" "I'm straight," respond Myro. Of course this is not what I wanted to hear as he felt me up. After a bunch of knocking, she finally opened. I quickly walked in. I didn't see him behind me, but Myro looking out did. He was literally blindly walking with his hands stretched out behind me and looking for something, or someone, to grab. We quietly slipped out the bathroom as he kept trying to grab hold to us for some equal access action. We finally left because I didn't want my car towed, being that it says all cars towed after 20 minutes and we had been there at least an hour.

BaCKpacKinG oN thE ApPalAchIan TrAiL

Another adventure while I lived with Myro was when I was tricked into going on a hiking trip. I love camping—except the spiders and bugs—and I remember doing fun nature hikes in the girl scouts. Of course, me being dense as a brick, I somehow did not realize that this would be along the lines of Mt. Fuji rather than a fun nature hike. The book said for beginners and I've camped many of times. I expected paved paths with steps, similar to the paths up the mountains to the various schools I worked at in Japan. Japan, after all, is a very mountainous country. Of course, I was tricked again. No one lied to me; they just did not say you needed a certain level of endurance and skill to hike.

First it was the 50-pound backpack. That wouldn't have been so bad if I wasn't walking up unpaved paths of dirt and rocks for 15 miles. We drove down Skyline Drive. It is very beautiful.

> I would love to meet a man I'm interested in to take me on a romantic drive down this road and end with a picnic and perhaps camp overnight. Unfortunately, I seem to only meet fortified peasants, perverts, and slugs.

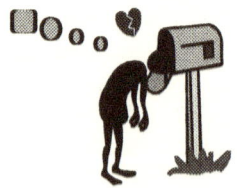

We camped the first night because we arrived late. The next day I realized what backpacking meant! It was VERY far from some gradually paved slope. Hello, is anyone home!? I really don't know why I was SOOO dumb to not realize that hiking in the mountains meant I would be going up a mountain!!! It was uphill on rocky gravel and down hill on rolling, slippery, rocks. At one point, I chose to slide rather than walk down the hill, to everyone's dismay. I begged to stay at one of the parking lots and for them to call the park ranger to pick me up. I would have happily waited for them in some lounge. They argued that a bear could attack me and they forced me on. They ended up needing to help push my fat tail up the hills and I fearfully walked down the rocky paths like a chicken. I literally sang the Hallelujah chorus the last mile back.

Of course, I was then in bed for 2 consecutive days due to muscle pain all over. I had pounds of Ben Gay rubbed over every aching muscle in my body. I sweat so much on that trip, I only used the bathroom once the entire day, I assume from the toxins leaving my body through sweat. Boy was I stupid! Hopefully, this would be the last time I'd be a stupid nincompoop and get suckered by some guy or situation!

ADVENTURES UPSTAIRS

I moved in with Anna, someone from Vic's Bible study. Her opinions are similar to Vic's. I also met up with Kong so he could help me move my stuff upstairs. I decided to help Kong move his junk from the woods near his mother's estate way out in Maryland solely because he asked me on the day of his mom's funeral. I got a moving van from school and in exchange of him helping me move upstairs, I'd help him get his stuff from the woods near his mom's home. I would even show him my dad's estate since he says he knows how to build homes from scratch and needs to store his junk. Besides, he paid for the van; it was just the mileage that ended up costing over $60.

While talking to Anna, I lost track of time and almost missed getting the van. I got to the rental office by the skin of my teeth, and got the van. Kong helped me move upstairs and I took him to some honky tonk blues concert in VA. The next day, I drove 3 hours to his mom's house to get his stuff from the woods. He had so much trash in the woods; including empty crates, which became housing for this baby raccoon. He actually ended up evicting the little thing so he could basically put the crate in storage. We were there until it got dark. While driving back it stormed violently, hurricane style.

At the storage, Myro called complaining about Kong's loud antics. After I finished cleaning my old bathroom for the new roommate, I took a quick shower. After all, my stuff was all packed up and I had no shower curtain. While I was in the shower, Kong playfully banged on the bedroom door making grunt sounds and calling my name. I was used to his antics and play, Myro and her boyfriend weren't. They were complaining because he woke them up and they thought he was actually trying to break the door down to kill me or something. "You need to tame your man! Why would you bring such a crazy person home?!" After they complained, I told Kong what they said. He took the phone and said, "I are guerilla!! I want banana!!" Her boyfriend responded saying, "You need to arch your back so all you need is a banana to calm him." I don't know about those two, but I thought that the entire episode was hilarious.

When I moved upstairs, the entire place looked atrocious. Seems like I can't win for losing! Like I said, my luck is non-existence! Downstairs had a new dishwasher, new cabinets, new stove, and due to the millions of holes in the wall, a new paint job and carpet. This one had old, disgusting cabinets, an old, barely working dishwasher, and is much worse than downstairs. My roommate did pay her rent in advance though. The apartment had dead roaches everywhere, and nasty junk under the kitchen sink. On top of that, the AC units worked horribly.

154

The lazy staff shifted the blame to everyone else except themselves. The maintenance guy finally came upstairs. He argued and complained about us being lazy because we didn't want to clean up the new apartment that we paid the $500 security deposit for. I guess the slumlord was annoyed that I kept calling about the problems of the apartment that she then complained about my illegal cat. She played tit for tat, you have a cat.

Following Floyd's usual routine, he, of course, liked Anna and wanted to date her too. However, like most men, he got tired of her really fast. She even molested and was all over him, showing him shivery and everything. Although he accepted it at first, he got tired of her and solely kept her on the back burner, as a security blanket.

AnNa and viC.

Anna is a female version of Vic. They both are fanatical in their beliefs of how people should be and have very little discretion. Many people I associate with have that "you do you" New York type of mentality. Being that New York experienced diversity by force via foreigners entering their land for over 100 years—with peo- ple coming from many different races, religions, ethnic groups, income levels, and every walk of life—they were forced to hold such a mentality. They were forced to tolerate and live near each other. This must be why New Yorkers have that "I live my life the way I want to, so you do you" policy.

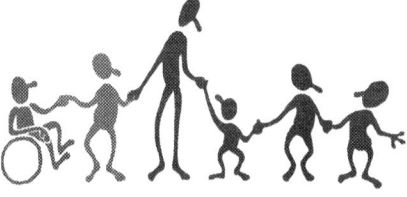

Like most zombified people who are not exposed to diversity, they expect you to conform and act like them. Anna and Vic seemed to question someone living life in an unfamiliar or different way than what they were used to—from bohemians to welfare recipients.

I guess birds of a feather flock together. I showed one supervisor my Japanese photos and he laughingly recited that quote. He said that I attracted hippies even in Japan. Many of my friends are definitely non-traditional like me. As you can see, I'm not a traditional 9-5 as someone oversees my work type of person. I guess, like the few other not-traditional Americans, I wasn't successfully programmed. I guess I'm too self-willed and stubborn to be programmed and zombiefied. Perhaps a "factory defect" in society's matrix. Zombies seem to have problems with people who are factory defects.

PEOPLE'S SUGGESTIONS w/NO HELP!!

Swautch's mom, Floyd's mom, my aunts and uncle, some church folks, and a few others suggest me living with my mom. (Even Swautch, whom I completely overlook because he DID make efforts to find me someone) "Why don't you want to live with your mom?" None of them live with their parents. Obviously if there is a flood or disaster, they would temporarily move in for emergency shelter. But this would be temporary. I see nothing wrong with someone living with their parents, siblings, and family, but 90% of the people that asked me don't live with their parents. I finally asked Kong's other sister who also suggested me move back home, why. After beating around the bush, she finally said it was a way to save money. I asked for what? Will after a year I be able to buy a house or will my credit and income still be so shot that banks will continue to be evil and not offer me a loan? Also, can my mom help me carry grocers, fix my car, enjoy a long road trip, or the likes? My mom needs help herself! This is the reason I suggested letting Kong stay with her so he could carry the trash, fix the screen doors, and OFFER A MAN'S HELP around the house!!!

What I REALLY want to know is why haven't any of these people from church, family, friends, and even their family *EVER* INTRODUCED ME TO ANYONE?! I know for a fact Floyd's mom knows millions of possible prospects due to her business as well as Swautch's family. No one has EVER set me up with anyone, introduced me to any nice man—from whatever country on earth—or even prayed for me to get a husband. Why should I remain miserably single, poor, and alone with no help-mate living with my mom as if I'm 10 years old when everyone else they know is either married or living in a halfway prosperous relation with some man?!

In fact, why does it seem like so many American Christian churches assume firstly, that anyone over 23 is married and MOSTLY, why do they REFUSE to offer prayers or any decent type of program for singles!?!?! People would sparingly help single men and then tell me it's not my time, I'm not ready, (BOTH ABOMNIBLE LIES!!) and to just wait on God! What an abomination! If you're a guy, lets encourage you and try to help you find a mate—or at least pretend to. Females, so what! What do you want! Shut up and become an old maid! This is a very backwards and ignorant mentality!! In fact, whenever I did ask someone to pray for me to get married, they always had some poor excuse! One pastor's wife rudely pushed me off to some prophet, and the prophet refused to pray for marriage and music offering some stupid excuse. Even in the Bible, if God told a prophet that He would curse a city and those city-folks begged the prophet to pray for them; the prophet would—and God would even spare that city. Several others flat out refused to pray for me to get married saying, seek God only and don't worry about being single, lonely, and not having a help-mate as your biological clock ticks away! Some **IGNORANTLY** told me to not even desire a husband! Excuse Me?!?! Some even **stupidly** had the nerve to ask me why do I want a husband in the first place! <u>Of course, each one of these abominable hypocrites are either married or dating!!!</u>

Wonder why is there a 200% effort via therapy, prayer, counseling, and mediation, to work on the shot to hell marriage situation in this country? Wonder why the divorce rate, even in churches, is over 50%? I'll tell you why! Try ignoring preventative maintenance and decent ways for singes to meet, instead of those SUPER STUCK-UP, VERY SUPERFICIAL, socials where if you're not some skinny blond or exotic international, just forget it! Don't be 10 pounds overweight, under a certain height, or without the right heels and make up on. What a wholesome, decent, group of arrogant Christian singles—I think I'll check out another mosque!! The American community, churches, and even many families ignores your needs, offers no help, and then plays catch up after marriage! Even those Christian internet message boards apparently do this. Playing catch up to some super obnoxious, emotional wreck you ended up marrying. Someone who's now causing havoc in your life because your sole reason for marriage was because she was a slim trophy with heels.

Outside of the fact that the institution of marriage in America is a JOKE, I've heard that in other countries, people play a much more active roll in finding a person a spouse. If that meant sending them to a certain area or country (such as sending me overseas), introducing them to suitors, or both, the church and community took an active roll in trying to find someone for that person.

For example, I believe that in some Jewish and European customs, the family and community take measures for singles to meet possible suitors. Also, several African women told me how they actively try to get their children married. If nothing more but to pray for then and constantly introduce them to possible prospects. Of course, most countries believe in staying married and trying to work your problems out as well! Maybe economics play some sort of roll in actively trying to find a mate for their child. I assume once married, the couple then would be able to financially help the parents instead of it being the other way around. Also, all mothers actively wait for a grandchild. Of course, America prides itself on one of the highest divorce rates on earth! Here in America, we take an active roll in playing catch up trying to mend the mess a couple got into since they based marriage on looks, a trophy, money, and other stupid things.

Kong's other sister said that she would rather be single than deal with a man—even with a second source of income and help around the house—simply for peace of mind. Of course she too has been married and have many suitors lined up waiting for her. Thusly, she basically has a "been there, done that, got the T-shirt" mentality. Perhaps that's the same mentality for many other divorced or separated women. If you have that been-there-done-that mentality, you don't "need any man, I can do this all by myself!" you of course wouldn't understand! You obviously can't conceive and don't understand why I—who's NEVER been married so how can can I possible have such a mentality—have a problem with being alone and doing **EVERYTHING** myself with **absolutely no one to help**. I guess like MANY Americans, people want a perfect mate when they themselves are NO WHERE NEAR perfect—and the perfect mate DOES NOT EXIST! She agreed and said that she doesn't expect to find a perfect man. I guess since 90% of Americans marry for status, money, a trophy, or some other retarded reason—the second the woman gets fat or wrinkled, or the man stops being perfect and rich, their spouse leaves for another mate.

As for peace of mind, I don't expect perfection, just a help-mate. A man I have chemistry with and at some level, physically attracted to, with a car and some form of income, I don't care if it's from washing floors. As long as he can help me carry groceries, drive around, know something about home repairs and auto mechanics, is not abusive, infested with disease, a raging lunatic, and not a walking whore, I'd be perfectly satisfied and fine as a wife! My standards have drastically lowered. I am completely different than the average needy woman. As long as he pretends to care—even if he's halfway lying—I'd be fine. Of course, I want to see guaranteed proof that he's not infested and has a clean bill of health. I'd have a million times more peace of mind from a husband who offers sex, money, and maintenance once a week and has "business trips" through the week over living in madness. I probably would get no more peace of mind living with my mom as I did with Kong and Myro.

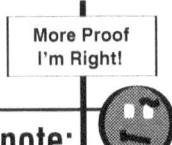

& One more post note:

Attention all of you holy rollers who hate gays, and such. Is it a sin? Of course according to the Bible, Koran, and Torah. In fact, many religions, I believe, teach this and feel this way. But here's the question, what do you do about it? I know Focus on the Family and several other organizations have outreach programs for gays, but our homophobic society overlooks and misses one crucial element.

Let's take a look at two groups in society. Groups that are against the social grain. Against the norms, values, and popular lifestyle of the average programmed zombie out there. The war protesting, green peace, save the world hippie and the save the black man from the white devil militant. Now mind you and remember that these groups are AGAINST the mainstream establishment. Let's check some basic things out.

The sloppy fat hippies apparently can only land a date with another sloppy fat, sloppy fit, or butch female hippy. Of course, the fit ones, no matter how many tattoos, dreads, body piercing, and sloppy they are, always has some guy. And as always, the man ALWAYS get someone regardless of how fat and sloppy he is. And don't think it's that different for the militant brother. He too, with his thick locks, Marcus Garvey shirt, and bean pie, has his beautifully fit African queen. Of course she has a natural or locks, and she can even be chocolate, but you can guarantee she won't be fat. At the most, she can be a fit 14/16 for those brothers who like curves, but not an inch bigger.

I even remember in Japan where this Canadian who was a cute blond with bright blue eyes only dated some Brit. And Asians LOVE blond white men and women. Being that she was short and squat, only Japanese fossils and cabbies flirted with her. Apparently no Japanese under 40 paid much attention to her.

Now if these anti-establishment, war protesting, green peace, save the black man, militant my brother would only date fit women—at the largest, a fit 14/16—**YOU CAN BET YOUR BOTTOM DOLLAR** that every other aspect of programmed society won't date them! What possible hope is there for "the fat girl" who isn't a size skeleton top model? Travel overseas to less programmed societies? Stay alone and single or solely be the trick to give head but never the public date? Go dike?

Now by all means, this is **DEFINITELY** not the only reason for going "dike" but I personally noticed and seen this for myself. All you have to do is go to any club, church, school, or university and see who has dates and who's left out. Especially in the more affluent neighborhoods where girls get nose jobs by 7th grade, you can guarantee that anyone over size 10 will be mocked and forgotten! They even have jokes on the comedy channel saying, "Bring Steve, he'll take the fat friend home!" After a certain size, you either are forced to go overseas or turn gay. Shoot, the only reason I'm not gay is cause I like men too much!

Now if a cute blond with blue eyes is ignored in Japan, and these anti-establishment activist seemingly only date fit women, **what hope is there for the rest of society?!?!** What can you do about it? I'll tell you what to do, change these **IGNORANT STANDARDS OF BEAUTY,** that's what!! How can you do that you ask? Check out the last page of this book, I'll tell you exactly how!!

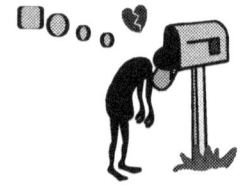

ANY COMPATABLE ROOMMATES

Can two females live together and get along? My mom answers this question when I constantly suggest renting the empty room out. She shouts that she doesn't want to live with anyone especially no woman. "Two adult women simply can't get along," she says. "A man can live with his mom and 2 adult men can live together but not 2 adult women." I don't totally agree with that. Two women or men can live in complete harmony with each other as long as there is no history between them. Two complete strangers can live together as long as their personalities are similar. The best pairs are quiet, reserved, and reclusive people, who respect each other, keep to themselves, and mind their business. Similar to how you are with your neighbor. You probably know their name if you lived in the neighborhood long enough, but that's about it. You mind your business and stay out of theirs.

If you have 2 people that try to become friends, problems can arise. Like your friend, you expect things from them. You have certain expectations. I'm sure every person has seen an episode of The Real World or some other insane reality TV show about horrible roommates. That's why I want to live with grad students or foreigners. They mind their business, are quiet, and are like invisible roommates. They're not up in your face, trying to socialize, hang out, and be friends. All of that is fine, but unless you both are mature, non-emotional, and mostly to yourself, it won't work out. Anna and Vic expected me to act and be like their "normal" family members and society conforming friends. I was too different, too hippie, rebellious, and non-conforming for their comfort. Something you could never find out about a person in Bible study.

WHY ARE YOU SO BROKE?!

I find it disturbing when people ask why am I so broke or why do I work there with a degree. If they are sincerely asking it out of curiosity or concern then I would entertain their question and hold a fair and reasonable conversation. If they, however, are asking it in a condescending and snide way, to judge and put me down, then it's none of your damn business. Why? What's it to you? What does it matter to you where I work, my age, what my budget is, or who I'm not sleeping with!? Critical people, who aren't perfect, criticize you for your faults or ways that they don't understand or find stupid.

No one is perfect. Every person living has some bad habits and addictions. Whether sex, junk food, drugs, cigarettes, gambling, what have you? If not, therapists wouldn't be rich (from millions of people with issues), Americans wouldn't be so fat (from junk food), and God wouldn't need to come and save us from our sins and problems. I don't feel sorry for an addict, drunk, or prostitute, but I would never stupidly ask why. Every person has problems. Problems are for the living. Each person has a set of problems specific to them. It's not my business what they are or why/how you got yourself into a situation. It's your personal, specific, problem, and it's up to you to solve and handle it. How someone handles it varies. Do they deal with their problems and life's circumstances with drugs, drinking, sex, binge eating, suicide, hustling, therapy, God, or what? Based on what they do and how they handle their situation will determine if they're out on the street, in jail, or in a crazy house.

Many folks don't understand why someone is homeless, stuck in a bad abusive relationship and won't leave, on drugs, poor, et cetera. Some nosy, critical, people ask stupid questions of why they are in that situation. When you invested time and feelings in a relationship, it's hard to just drop and leave, even if you know she's cheating on you or he takes you for granted. Obviously bad deals or stupid mistakes in life put people in bad situations. Perhaps it's not for you to understand. Instead of bashing and casting judgment on people, because only God can judge, try to listen, reason, help, and pray for them.

However many problems people bring upon themselves too. If someone is sick, in an accident, or situation that they had no control over, and it's just bad blows in life, then yes, I do feel bad for them. If they decide to use drugs, hustle, whore, do shady insurance deals, and such, then that's on them. If they get addicted, infested with disease, or caught, that's on them. I don't condone homosexuality, hustling, prostituting/whoring, and so forth, but I can understand why someone may be inclined to do it. Instead of me passing judgment and stupidly questioning why they live that way, I simply accept them as is. I may not be best friends with them, give them my keys, and such, but they are human. I'd rather talk and spend time with an addict or ex-con than some insulting, judgmental, wholesome, American citizen. At least they won't bash me for my faults and differences they don't understand or accept. The latter—like these ghetto co-workers at my job—thinks they're next to perfect and their way of life is golden, pure, and right. If you don't act and live like them, then bashing or joaning they will do.

pENINNAH sPIRIT

There was this really good sermon about shady, critical people and the favor of God. I wrote a lot of my notes down from this sermon as well as some good information from some excellent video sources I watched. Go figure, I saved my finished work a thousand times on 50 plus discs, and every bit of my material vanished!!!! I was stuck with a super unedited version of this book. After working on this book forever, I was almost ready to quit and start again at another point. At that time, I was also in a constant transition of moving, and Myro put her 40 pound laptop that she gave me in storage so I was unable to even work on anything any way. When I finally unpacked, found my discs, and made it to the computer lab—all which took an enormous amount of time due to my extremely busy schedule—I was very shocked and disappointed to not find my almost completed book on any of the discs. On top of that, they've been trying to delete my student computer account because I'm not currently enrolled. This would hinder my access to the high speed internet and decent word processing. Well anyway, this section came from my notes from this very interesting lecture/sermon.

The title of the sermon was, "Are You Really Favored?" It was about Hannah, this lady in the Bible, and her problems having a child and with Peninnah, the other wife. (Why so many wives in the first place?!) Peninnah had many kids and always rubbed that in Hannah's face. Although she had a rack of kids, the husband still favored Hannah. Obviously Peninnah wasn't pleased with this. In fact, Hannah means favor, and he said that one day of God's favor is way better than 1000 days of my labor. God's favor will get you noticed, open doors, and things that others struggle for. God's favor will turn bad things around. There will always be shady, critical, Peninnah types who question your favor in the first place and happily rub your problems in your face.

Peninnah spirited people like Mr. Hag(I'll get to him later) Vic, and many others can be extremely critical and negative. They get a kick out of your misery. In fact, after we left church that same day, Mr. Hag was balking about how I'm so fat and eat too much candy, though I eat WAY less junk food than him. I haven't really kept up with Anna since I moved out and as I mentioned, I washed my hands of Vic.

163

Mean, critical, or jealous people will always rub in your face your lack, faults, and shortcomings to put you down and make you feel bad. Saying that you might as well give up. If you're really favored where are your results and fruit of your labor? Where is your spouse, family, money, car, or house? It is obvious that you have no favor or any thing else and are wasting your time because your business isn't successful and you're still broke and alone.

To me, these are all very valid points and I personally would focus on that and want answers to those same things. It is extremely easy for everyday people—who actually look for goods, services, and things in the material universe to satisfy them—to get discouraged and jealous. If you're a super spiritual, psychic, meta-physical, yoga type, then material things mean little to you. You always seek and look for the spiritual things. I guess that's why some Buddhists abandoned mate-rial things and live a very humble, meager, life. If you're an everyday Westernized person whose use to having a roof over your head, food in your belly, and clothes on your back, such things would make you run and leave. Why would you stay where your life and situation is stagnant or gets worst. You want to seek a religion or practice which gives you a **better** lifestyle.

It's only human to ask and think that if this church thing and God's favor really exist with me, then why don't I have money, a home, closeness with my family, a car, a spouse, a good job, nice clothes, etc. You become envious over oth-ers who have what you don't. People with more money, better looks, bigger cars, nicer houses, and more stuff than you. Unfortunately, you will always have some-one better off, more lucky, or able than you. Also, there will always be someone much worst than you too. But according to my pastor, you still have God's favor. His response to the above questions is, so what, I'm still favored.

The pastor continued by asking who told you that? Who said you were fat, ugly, too dumb to succeed, will never marry, with credit so bad you'll never get an apartment, let alone a house? Who told you all of this? TV? Your friends and/or family? Yourself? God never told Hannah she wouldn't get pregnant and God never told you those things. No one likes who they are or what they have. Everyone wants something else and tries to be someone else. Men want to be women; blacks want to be white; whites get tans, big lips, and nose jobs. Asians get dreads or larger eyes; blacks get straight hair. Everyone wants to change their body. Take steroids to get bigger, operations to lose fat (which I want too) or to get bigger chests, even painful leg operations for midgets to get taller. Everyone hates the way they look and how they were made.

I guess God is disappointed that no one likes His subjective works of art, i.e. human diversity. You shouldn't listen to biased negativity, especially from shady Peninnah spirited people like Mr. Hag, Vic, (and at times even Anna and my mom), and especially **YOURSELF**—the most critical judge you'll ever meet!!

The type of people that say you must change absolutely everything about yourself to succeed. That you must become like someone else to make it.

Here are some good quotes taken from the video, **Never Too Thin** by Willy and Wendy Werby.

"First of all, the standards are very biased and slanted. Females, no matter how much they have to offer, are always looked upon as how beautiful they are. How well do you put yourself together physically. Men can get so much further with so little looks that looks are not even a factor."

Men are approved of by how much money, power, and clout they have. Their self worth is based on business and money. They can look repulsive and still book women. A woman can have a successful career, a nice house, and so forth, but if she is fat, single, or unattractive, then instantly people say something is wrong with her. A woman's worth is always based on her relationship—or lack there of—with a man and her looks. On top of that, she'd better look the way society deems sexy. Of course, men don't think for themselves and decided what they personally like in a woman, it's always based on the media and current trends in fashion, weight/size, and beauty.

The idea that one type of body, look, or style is good and the other type is bad is ridiculous. That's just as insane as the, "You have good hair" thing. Why is curly or almost straight hair good compared to nappy hair? Is it easier to comb? Sure. But braids and locks stay in nappier hair easier than straight hair. They're the easiest to manage of all. You just get up and go. In this same concept, society tells you what is nice, pretty, and acceptable. It would be all well and good if standards are based on body odor, something that makes you gag when you see or smell it, or something that infringes upon someone else. But basing it on a certain height, size, age, race, what have you, is very subjective. "What was considered beautiful throughout history is very different now. It's even different in non-Western countries where vast of the people are poor and being fat is only available to the wealthy. Being fat was a status symbol. It's only in affluent societies that the denial of food is a virtue and being thin is glamorous."

There unfortunately will always be a standard, and if you don't come to grips and accept where you live, work, how you look, and what you are, then you will always have problems. "There will ALWAYS be someone criticizing you for something. You're going to always not have the right cheek bone, nose shape, your hair's not going to be right, hips too wide, chest too small, it will always be something you're going to get hit with."

"Happiness and peace of mind should NEVER be based on someone else's acceptance. These things start from inside of you first. This comes from what you make out of life, the opportunities you take and make, and how you pursue your dreams—NOT conforming to someone else's standard. **Being a certain height, size, weight, etc. doesn't mean that you will be happy, satisfied, and content with yourself!** (Look at anorexic people and Michael Jackson, are they happy and satisfied with their body?) You rob yourself and miss the fullness of life when you try to become what everyone else says and wants you to be, instead of just being you—as is." As one lady said, "If you don't love yourself, it's harder for other people to love you. It's not the way you look, it's the way you feel about yourself."

"To get to a point where being short, fat, old, or some other trait, is preferred over another one, is no better than where we currently are now in society. It's not about saying one feature or style is better. Simply a basic acceptance of any shape, height, age, or however you are. [My hope is for society] to aim for self acceptance and for a society to accept all types and styles of looks and beauty, as just one of the many diverse physical characteristics of the human body and experience."—**Never Too Thin**

God said tHaT

On top of that, God never made you to change, mutate, and conform to become someone else. He made you just the way you are. This next section below was taken from a TV show, **YOUR DAYS ARE WRITTEN** that I barely caught. I recorded the tail end of it. It's from Danny Diaz, a pastor in California.

"Don't allow the world to define you. God already defined you. You're a king and a priest. Under the Father, through the blood of the Son. You're an heir of God and a joint heir with Christ. You're more than a conqueror. You've been called, justified, and glorified. For known and predestined [to be successful]. God sees us and the entire timeline of this material universe through a different lens. Your entire destiny was written in eternity past by the Alpha and Omega, the Beginning and the End. God sees your destiny and He created you specifically and precisely so you can fulfill that specific destiny deep inside you. Everyone should have a sense of value, self worth, purpose, and a sense of destiny. Everyone, not just the rich, successful, handsome, able bodied, people, but everyone.

God saw who you were and your ability before He even began to form you inside your mother's womb. He saw your potential and capability then formed you according to what He saw, not the other way around. God doesn't call the qualified, He qualifies the called. You may not have a PhD", 2 legs, long hair, be from America, or of a certain race, religion, ethnic group, or gender. You may not be rich with a tall, sleek, sexy body. You may not be slim, able bodied, or athletic. You may be laughed at, rejected, and sit alone for lunch everyday because stupid, small minded people overlook and dismiss you (but look at John Nash, the guy from a Beautiful Mind.) "But God doesn't look at the outward but at what's inside.

"If you have heart, desire, and passion you're on your way (to fulfilling your destiny and dream). You're on you way to that great somewhere, and I'm not talking about the great by and by, but in the here and now! Right here! Right now! There's a purpose for you. There's a purpose for you're existence. And there's a purpose for someone just like you. And God wants you to fill that gap. Don't allow the world to define you. There are many scriptures to define you. You became a new creation once you were saved. However old things pass away in a process, not instantly. And then you change, transform, and become new out of that process. **You are on a journey to become who you already are!** Through faith, you must learn to embrace the outcome of the steps you take. And it's going to take faith. And if God knew us before He created us; and He formed, created, and designed us specifically to accomplish everything He created us to accomplish, then He placed **everything within us that we need to succeed the entire way to the top!**

"**NO ONE is here by accident, and if YOU DARE walk out on what has been written and predestined on your behalf; then whatever you walk on will become yours!!** The only way to press toward your individual high calling is to stop living on Adam's time clock. We can no longer be limited to space and time. We must step out of time and into eternity.

People speak of the Great Exchange that took place at the cross. Jesus died so we might live. He bore our sickness so we can have health. He became poor so we can become rich. But He also stepped out of eternity and into time so we can step out of time and into eternity. The biggest way to succeed and move forward, is to stop looking behind you! Stop dwelling on the past. Stop even wasting time dwelling on your current situation. Stop viewing the past as if it's the present or you'll be stuck in that same stagnant rut year after year. Aim towards your destiny and future. Press, focus, gaze, and aim toward your future, destiny, and dream and nothing can stop you!"—Pastor Danny Diaz.

If you're going to listen to someone, you might as well listen to the Master Architect Himself. I guess He should know what you're worthy of and capable of doing. Surely, if you build something from scratch, you'd know how fast it could go, what things it could do, and so forth. Listen to God, not what people say. I may not have a fancy new car, 6-figure income, husband and family, big house, and such; but **I'm STILL ROYALTY AND A DIVINELY CREATED STAR!! Whether you accept and believe me, that's your problem!** When discouraging people wear you down with criticism and discouragement, ignore them the best you can. I've gotten good at ignoring idiots who take pleasure at harassing me.

Close your mind and ears to them and turn a deaf ear. Similar to how you hear someone speaking a foreign language near you. You have no idea what they're saying, so you completely ignore them.

My pastor concluded and said, "No matter what others say, don't let anyone make you lose your position of favor with God. That's the enemy's ultimate aim, for you to lose your position of favor with God. Once you lose your position with God, you lose your connection, protection, and blessings from God. Don't get so jealous that you get mad and hate God for the problems you have, compared to the blessings others seem to have. A person could easily say, "They have more money, bigger house, and all I have is a continuous cycle of late notices, bus fair, and no mate." But once you lose your coveted position of favor you won't be able to give birth to your God given destiny of health, wealth, and success!

The enemy doesn't just want to discourage you, but wants to make you quit and give up. To stop wasting your time with God, which is VERY easy if your disappointed at God and not successful. He doesn't just discourage you through any and every means he can find, (through your own critical self and through Peninnah spirited people) but also burdens you down. Then he destroys you once and for all. For if your destiny and mission is to cure cancer, help the homeless, or some uplifting and positive activity which would impact millions; it would be in the forces and powers that be best interest to rid you—and all traces of you—so your lovely message would never interfere with their plans.

After all, Hannah did finally have a child. Of course, Peninnah had a little tribe. Who exactly were her kids anyway? Hannah may have taken a decade to give birth to just one child, but he became a prophet and two books in the Bible were written for him, I and II Samuel. Peninnah came and left in obscurity, along with her rack of kids. I'm not sure, but I think I'd rather find one rock that becomes a diamond than get a basket full of worthless stones. After all, it's the quality not the quantity. Like the U.S. Marines, you only need a few good men over a million sloppy soldiers.

END TIMES PROPHECY

Many religions, especially the Abrahamic monotheistic ones, speak of end times. I'm quite interested in learning what various religions has to say regarding the afterlife and the end times. I'm not too sure of every detail, but I do know—despite wars, famine, and such, through history all around the world—Israel wasn't a nation until the 40's and DC never had earthquakes. I'm sure since the dawn of man, DC and other places had all types of weather and wars, however since I or my elders can remember, DC never had such weird weather. Outside of record highs in Europe or record lows in warm places, DC never had an earthquake. I always jokingly say that when DC has an earthquake, the end of the world is nigh. Myro said, "Floyd is cheating on a girl, I know the end of the world must be near." Whenever I finally get married—to a man I'm attracted to who actually likes me, doesn't try to constantly molest me, is sane, and not a perverted peasant scrub—the world will probably end within 10 days. Of course, just my damn luck. Habitually lonely and miserable, and the SECOND I finally find someone, the world blows up.

There was this big hurricane that came through DC. Several other twisters passed through leveling out a town one year, and killing 2 girls another. This, to me, is very unusual and freak weather. Well this hurricane really caused little damage in my neighborhood and the lights blinked only a few times. Of course, once it was over, the lights decided to blink out—for a week!! I hate the darkness. Shiftless PEPCO refused to offer me food vouchers for the meat and juice I lost due to the blackout. What the heck took so long? Why did it only go out AFTER everything was over? On the day the lights came back on, I went home to wash clothes. En route was when I got sandwiched between two cars. I was so distraught; I forgot to get the people's tag numbers or anything else. Thank God everyone was telling the truth. Through the girl's insurance, I got my car fixed—above and beyond damage from the accident, a rental, and chiropractor services.

After this incident, there was another more dramatic one. With all of my end time talk, DC had an earthquake. No one I know felt it except my mom and Swautch's grandma, but many others did. I'd better hurry and travel and find someone. Floyd, who is quite moody, had the nerve to yell and harass me for going to see his Chiropractor mom. He called me up complaining daily. I guess I'm supposed to ask his permission. He kept comparing me to some chick that asked his step-dad for help then dropped the case behind everyone's back. He also figured I'd ask for free stuff. I'm not ashamed to ask anyone—homeless to CEO—for absolutely anything, the insurance, however, was paying for my visits, so he had no grounds to argue. Thusly, I ignored him and made my appointment.

Earlier that month I planned a trip to see a speculator religious musical in Pa. called Daniel. I needed to see and critique 3 musicals, recitals, or performances for my music class that semester. Compliments of me STILL not dating any-one—or even meeting anyone this millennium that calls me more than once, isn't a raging pervert, lunatic, or difficult on the eyes—I have no one to take me on this wonderful date.

I look around for people I know with a car and spare time to go with me. I ask Floyd and his supposed girlfriend Anna if they would go. Anna is very interested and of course, Floyd claims that he's going, so my roommate Anna buys all three tickets. I pay her back for mine. Realizing that Floyd was most likely lying, even though Anna already paid for the tickets, (assuming that he'd feel some level of obligation) I started looking for his replacement. I told Floyd this assuming he'd get jealous and actually go. That worked to a point. He called Anna and com-plained about me to her. When Floyd refused to come over for sex in the raw with her, I knew for a fact that he was definitely going to stand us up for the trip.

I coincidentally got my insurance rental three days earlier so I was able to drive up without worry of extra mileage or wear to My Feather. I, however, definitely didn't want to travel alone, let alone waste two free tickets. Since I am so blessed to be alone with no one to take me anywhere nice, I called Swautch and a few others to ride with me. I finally found Myro, who wasn't working and had time to go.

Interestingly, she was newly into Christianity and learned a lot from the play. Her family, I believe, is of the Baha'i faith. On our way home, she coincidentally told me of her last E trip—a very bad trip—and the other events that led to her introduction to Christianity and her "Domino Pizza" miracles. Stuff happened, she needed immediate help, and she got immediate results—like pizza delivery, 30 minutes or less.

SWAUTCH LYING ABOUT MOVING TO NY

Swautch called me throughout the year to invite me and tell me about various parties. He partied continuously. I personally thought to myself, what is he on? How can someone sleep for less than 4 hours, then run errands, look for music, then party until dawn—and then do it all over again. Surely that is not healthy or normal. He called me in early October and said he was moving. He didn't want to tell me over the phone the details but wanted me to help him pack. The first thing I thought of was he's getting evicted. He confirmed it when we met up.

It was early October and he invited me to some N. African French party. I was tired and planned to rest that day. Being that I'm single and desperate, and Swautch claimed they were straight off the boat, I went and met up with him. As usual, I had no overnight change of clothes, toothbrush, nor underwear. Typical Swautch, he, of course, had something up his sleeve. He wanted me to help him pack. I agreed even though I had no change of clothes. Once we left the French party, we went to some hippie drum circle party that was just finishing.

I was tired of walking as well as partying, I wanted sleep! I went to his apartment and he went with some dude. Of course, not ONE item was packed. According to him, everything was packed. If you consider those crates of music up to the ceiling, yes they were. Like Kong, all of his junk is was crates, and the entire apartment was carpeted with wall-to-wall crates reaching the ceiling. He came back and of course nothing got packed. Some Jewish guy was to sublease and move there in 7 hours. I thought Swautch was mad! How was someone going to move here in 7 hours when absolutely nothing was packed or ready to move, let alone, do you have a van to move it. Well that was actually the last time I saw him.

Swautch played around about moving to NY for over 2 months and every time he called me he was in DC. Myro and I both wanted to help him move because she has never been to NY and I wanted to stay in NY to find a man. I begged, harassed, offered to rent and drive a van with his money—being that I had none and he couldn't drive. Obviously Swautch had none either, or he wouldn't be getting evicted. I used every bribe and plea to get him to hurry and move to NY. He called me Thanksgiving, again from DC. I was SOOOO disappointed. Myro got a job and everything, and he still wasn't ready to move.

Wild D left me a message on my cell about some news broadcast regarding someone she thought was Swautch. She said that she saw on the evening news that someone was murdered on Embassy Row with a name and photo similar to Swautch. Disturbed by this message, but assured that of course Swautch was absolutely all right, I called his mom's house to speak to him. I mean, I passed his building that Monday and started to stop by to see him. I felt that, of course, he wouldn't be there. He was supposed to get evicted in early October. Someone was supposed to sublease his place in late October. He's been claiming to move to NY for over the past 2 months. Surely, if he's moving to NY and getting evicted in October, there is no way he should still be in DC.

When I called his mom, she sounded a little down. She asked how I was doing. I said, "Fine, how about you?" She said, "I not doing so good." I asked why and she asked if I had heard what happened. I urgently asked what happened. She confirmed the alleged news reports. Shocked and stunned, I immediately inquire about the details. Then I asked his mom the same question I asked mine about where daddy was. I asked, "Where's Swautch?! Where's his body?" I mean; if he's in the hospital, then he might get better. There's a slim chance that he'll be OK. There's still that chance. Of course she answered that her husband went to identify his body. Well how lovely, like daddy, you usually don't send people to identify living bodies.

I was shocked, stunned, and in disbelief. My biggest question was why he never went to NY and stayed in DC in the first place. My biggest question, to this day is why. Why!? Why!? Why!? What could've he possibly done that was SOOO bad to warrant his death? Why was he so pressed to stay in DC in the first place? She asked me to call my mom, who looked at Swautch like a son. I didn't know how to tell her, so Swautch's mom said she would call. Obviously, she was overwhelmed and never had the chance. Unfortunately, my mom was falling asleep looking at TV when she saw the dreaded news about what happened. She must have seen the same one Wild D saw. Luckily I never saw it, so it was—and still somewhat is—not real to me. When she saw it she tried to contact some of our mutual friends, all whose numbers have changed. She finally called his mom who confirmed it. She called me crying on my machine, just like when she found Fuzzy, one of our cuddly and cute kittens that died a month before the Runt gave birth. We think she, like nosy and curious cats, sniffed and ate something bad.

It seems that every year from 2000 to now someone close to me dies. First daddy's brother Uncle Clarence in 2000, then daddy in 2001. Then Fuzzy, the kitten we rescued from the Prof. in 2002. She didn't even make it to be one. Then Swautch. Not in a million years would I expect Swautch to be next. Similar to dad's section, this is another section that I'm annoyed about writing. This section should NEVER exist. Obviously, he felt it was more important to dabble with drug fiends and get slumped in DC than to go to NY—where I could visit him for weeks on and off and finally find my husband!! **What kind of crap is this**!?

MORE RETARDED QUESTIONS
PEOPLE ASK!

On top of that, people would ask the most RETARDED, IGNORANT things. When I returned to Japan in lieu of my dad; Swautch, the YMCA manager, and even some Japanese friends, asked if I cried. Nancy and Myro even asked me this regarding Swautch. What would make someone ask such insane, retarded questions?! I was watching an interview someone gave regarding Johnny Carson, who just died. His comment reminded me of the above type of questions and feelings a fool may have towards someone who is very reserve and private. (You can also guess the date I'm writing this. I started in 1998, as I stated elsewhere in this book, and I hope to finish within the next 2 weeks). I actually never watched his show, my mom always looked at it. Carson said in an interview that even though he's an entertainer and speaks to millions daily, he was quite shy, reclusive, and reserve. Carson the performer and entertainer was very different than Carson the private, discrete person. Carson even said, on one of his few interviews, that he hates getting interviewed; it makes him nervous. And once he retired he basically left the public eye. Prince also seems quite reserved and very private.

They said that Carson spoke of a trip home, a reunion with an old teacher, and a ride in his dad's old car. They said that as he spoke, he began to tear up. This was something they had never seen him do, and it was then they realized he was very human with feelings. Now to me that is just insane! To assume someone has fewer feelings because they remain cordial and smiling with complete discretion; not telling you all of their problems or personal info (which is none of your business to begin with). I could see if they were constantly evil, mean, and nasty; sure, they are less human, humane, and are quite feelingless. But Carson was friendly, charming, and likeable.

Why would someone who is friendly but reserve seem feelingless to the point of being asked ridiculous questions or having crazy assumptions placed upon them?! I guess in the same way some imp would think some victim has no feelings and/or doesn't mind when a boss, co-worker, classmate, bully, or whoever, harasses and picks on them as they only smile or ignore it off. No! This definitely doesn't mean that **THEY** have no feelings or have the problem! **The problem is with the ignorant, obnoxious, bully!** Besides, the people who asked me those insane questions weren't even bullies. They were professional management staff or friends. I never once saw Myro, Nancy, Swautch, nor the Japanese harasses anyone. It was also a friend of Carson who saw him cry and made that comment. I'm sure if decent, respectable, people would think this way, then how much more would some lunatic, out of control, bully think?

Ever wonder what would make a Columbine or some school or workplace violence occur? That quiet, reserved, victim is the type that after being harassed to his limit, could possibly go off. Perhaps because their personality isn't the yelling, fighting type; ignorant bullies keep pushing assuming nothing would ever happen. And of course they may assume the victim doesn't care because they didn't lash out like some bully who's nothing but an uncontrolled emotional wreck! Does someone showing bursts of anger or telling all of their problems show feelings? To be honest, it just shows that they need medication, anger management, counseling, and are quite shameless with absolutely no discretion, diplomacy, or tact! Some folks have absolutely no discretion and would tell complete strangers all their info. From their weight, height, grades and GPA, to their income and family history.

DREAMS OF SWAUTCH

I had several unusual dreams about Swautch as well. Either before or right after his funeral, I was half sleep and I distinctly heard—very clearly—his voice. He yelled, "Hey!" or something along those lines. He said nothing else, but it was clearly a voice, not just something inside my head, and it sounded just like Swautch. I know I wasn't dreaming because it woke me out of my sleep. I have no idea what I was dreaming of, and I don't even think that I was sleeping that deep. When I heard his voice, I woke up startled and looked around my room for who was in it. Thank God no one was there and it was daytime. I'm also very scared of the dark.

The next dream I had was unusual and made absolutely no sense. I was most likely over his mom's house and sitting on her couch against the wall. He was sitting right next to me but he spoke to me via a cell phone of sorts. I wonder why he needed a phone to talk if he's right next to me. Well the connection wasn't even good. I couldn't understand a word he said. He just kept mumbling to me, like the adults do on Charlie Brown & Snoopy. We sat and talked, via phone, and there was shrimp on the table. There were 2 types of shrimp, some coconut looking fried shrimp and sautéed shrimp. There was a large photo of him on the wall. I kept waiting for that photo to turn, like every other photo in dreams and horror movies do. For some reason I started screaming, "NO! NO!" I'm not sure why I did that in the middle of the conversation, but of course, I must have lurked his photo on and of course, it starts moving and smiling at me—all while he sits next to me and talks via phone. The ironic part is, in real life he was too cheap to ever get a land-line, let alone a cell! Being that I made such a commotion yelling no, I woke up. Actually I tried to wake myself up, as if I was having a nightmare. I'm not sure why I was so scared.

The interesting thing is Floyd and I went to the Cheesecake Factory that same day. Of course he complained about my ordering and spending habits with his $40 coupon. After I left, I realized I hadn't checked my e-mail in over 2 weeks, if not more. This is not that unusual. I hardly check my e-mail. I check it about once a week, many times less, and send it about once a month. I'm a phone person; I check my phone messages at lease once a day, if not more. I didn't want to lose Swautch's final e-mail to me nor this other important message. My email always gets too full and starts deleting old messages. The computer lab, to my lovely inconvenience, was closed for another 2 weeks. Now what am I going to do? Me finding a way to retrieve and save these 2 messages was a dilemma in and of itself.

As I drove away from the computer lab however, I soon realized how my haphazard evening with Floyd correlated to that weird dream. At the restaurant we both had shrimp. He had seasoned battered fried shrimp, which is really good. Actually any form of shrimp is delicious. Anyway his shrimp looked like the fried shrimp in the dream. I had shrimp scampi, which is delicious, with giant grilled shrimp. That was the other shrimp in my dream. I was so surprised, I called his brother and told him of my dream. I'm not sure what the message was, other than I'm watching you or that I'm not that far from you. The 30th of December, I had another very silly dream with Swautch in it. This time we were hanging out on New Years Eve, like we did last year. We walked along and got into our usual argument over silly stuff. He harassed me to eat some cake in a bag and I refused to eat it. What a stupid dream, at least it seems that way for now. I however did ask him if the shrimp dream was a message from him. He confirmed it was.

Another dream started out with me over someone's house, perhaps Floyd. I was moving something into a long, big, black car, like a station wagon. I moved some folding chairs into the car and there was Swautch in the middle seat. All of his family then seemed to appear at that house. When I went back to the car, they were all gathered at the car crying. I forced myself to tell him what was going on. I told him that something very bad was to happen to him so watch out. Because his aunts and cousins were crying so much, he began to cry. Then he pulled himself together and said, "I'm OK." I contested, "No you're not! You're going to die! Why do you think all of them are crying so much? Why do you think all of them are out here in the car in the first place? They know you're going to die and they are sad." He said something along the lines of, "Look at me. Can't you see I'm flesh and bones? I'm right here. I'm all right." I believe I kept shaking my head no.

My last dream actually had him saying and doing something that I don't remember. I do remember me asking who killed him. I don't really remember his response. What I vaguely remember is somewhat like don't worry about it, or something along those lines. I guess it's not up to me to find the killer. Anyway, what can I do except call the cops and dodge the killers friends who may chase me for knowing too much. The only thing that I vaguely remember of the dream, except that he was in it, was that he apologized to me. Go figure. I guess it's not too hard to peek over and cross the thin vale that divides this plain of the living with the spirit world. I guess he, and others, could easily see how extremely disappointed I was. It's ashamed that I am so upset at him, and he's the victim. He didn't commit suicide, he was murdered. However—as if he could have stopped it or even knew about it—I am still very upset and extremely disappointed at him for not leaving this stupid city and going to a place a thousand times better—NY.

What if?!?!

I was always upset that God, or whoever, stole my dad from me without my marriage, a child, or even one more chance to see him again. I felt the same way about Swautch. I went pass his apartment that Monday and started to stop by. I keep wondering what if I went over. What could I do except call the cops or get beat down? I am as threatening as a delicate feather. However, I keep wondering what if I went over. Of course I never did, I mean he was supposed to be in NY. At the least, he would be staying over his mom's house. He was getting evicted since October. There is no way he would still be there two months after he was supposedly getting evicted. Besides, he was never home when I came pass anyway. I'd usually knock with no answer and I would end up leaving a message with the front desk. He was never there. Come to find out, they estimate the time of death that Monday evening. I passed his place that Monday afternoon.

I always wonder what would have happened if I went pass. And why couldn't God wait until I came home to see my dad again? Then my mom reminded me that she was upstairs when my dad died. She was at home with him and everything, and she couldn't do a single thing to keep him alive nor bring him back. I guess when it's time to go, absolutely no one can do absolutely anything about it. Is it easier to see someone die in front of you? Surely not. It seems easier to cope with their loss if they suffer and die a slow death than a sudden and unexpected one. It's easier to cope with their crossing and to realize that surely over there is hopefully better than their current physical state here.

It reminds me of Freda and Bob Marley. He got cancer of the foot—go figure—and as he was wasting away in the hospital, he looked in the mirror and said hurry up and take me. Freda was cripple for a lot of her life, and at the end, she was bed ridden and super crippled. She said she was so tired of the problems her flesh caused her, she wanted them to burn it the second she was set free from that wretch of a body she had. (This info was based on a Bob Marley documentary and the film Freda). I guess it's selfish and unfair for us to want them to hang on and suffer, even though you can prepare for their loss better. Another friend said that even if it's easier to let someone go after a long illness, you still ask why did they have to get sick in the first place. Belief's dad was in the hospital during his final days. They resuscitated him on several occasions. She said that when the doctor asked the family if they wanted to keep resuscitating him, her father mustered up a definite "**NO!**" No one, living or otherwise, should have to truly inconvenience themselves, linger on, and suffer due to our attachment and desire to hold on to them. Why must they anguish and suffer?

WHO DOESN'T BLAME GOD?!

Like most people, I automatically blame God and get mad at Him whenever some problem or tragedy in my life arises. I believe in the devil, but I—and many other's—don't really think of him except after some weird animal mutilation, horrible satanic murder, or at Halloween. Religious people quote the Bible saying there's a season for everything and that the Devil comes but to steal, kill, and to destroy. God—in the form of Jesus—came for people to have life, and have life more abundantly. However people, including me, immediately blame God for bad things—illness, death, destruction, problems, etc. God can prevent anything, but He chooses to turn the other cheek and look the other way. Which is why everyone seems to blame Him. Even if He did not personally attack the individual, He allowed the attack.

I still very rarely ask for anything "dangerous" such as, please heal XYZ, or something along those lines. It seems that whenever I ask Him for something the opposite occurs. I asked blessings for my mom, she gets a brain tumor and ends up in the hospital. I ask to lose weight, I gain it. I ask for a husband and marriage and my biological clocks rapidly and lustfully ticks away with me ALONE, MISERABLE, and LONELY. I ask blessings for my dad, and the next day he dies. Why would I, or anyone, keep asking for such things?!?! So for now on, I only ask for disposable things, such as time management, a relationship with Him, or help with a bill. Whereas, if it doesn't happen, it won't be a major crisis or loss. I guess He's not pleased with me not trusting to ask Him for bigger, non-disposable things. Anyone in their right mind would only ask for disposable things after prayer results like this.

I also hear that if/once you are in God's protection and under His circle, then nothing supposedly can touch you. I wonder does that protection extend for your friends, family, pets, car, and stuff as well. As long as you are doing some form of "work for the Lord", He'll protect you from disaster until you finish whatever He has planned for you. I assume to get under this "protection from God", you obviously need to be doing His will and obeying His word, like a good Christian. Why else would He "stick his neck out" for you and protect you all like that if you are acting and living a life against His teachings, will, and the Bible. He might as well protect Satan worshipers and witches for that matter. On the other hand, you can ask—such as I do—why do all of the presumably evil and greedy people of the world seemingly have so much power, protection, money, and apparent grace from God? Perhaps Satan grants it to them?

mY joB

I must detour for a moment (which is not uncommon for me, as you have read) to accurately answer this question. I was at lunch when I just so happen to stumble upon the answer to the question above. An answer that I really didn't know nor put much thought or effort into finding in the first place. I'm sure any devout Christian knows the answer back and forth, but I didn't, just as I'm sure many others don't. This is for you, and me. But to tell you the answer, I must actually start from the beginning.

You probably realized by now that I've been writing different parts of this book at various times over the past 5 or so years. A little while after I dealt with Mr. Computer Genius/AKA/worthless Boston Market peasant (from The Worstest section), I went and bought a voice processor on my own. I'm not much on writing. I actually bought a voice processor to speak instead of type my papers and stuff. This dinosaur is too old and slow to load it up however. So is my mom's computer. Thusly, I'm forced to type.

Being that I'm super busy all of the time—mostly running in circles like a maniac accomplishing nothing—I must allocate time for this book. I also got discouraged after my dad passed and my laptop was stolen from the mad house, among other things. I finally am able to hopefully finish this 5+ year work in progress of my chaotic life. For health reasons, and my shear disgust of my shape, I need to lose weight. The doctor is concerned about my blood pressure. They've been trying to get me to draw blood to test my sugar and cholesterol. I hate needles and I know they both are probably high. I have a gut like I'm 8 months pregnant and I haven't even had the luxury of a man.

My discipline to go to the gym, practice my music, and even finish this book, is slim to non-existence. I'm also severely broke and have a hoard of overdue bills and money problems. Thusly I prayed to land a job where I sit on my butt for hours doing absolutely nothing. Forcing me to be productive to pass the time. Then, I can finish this book, apply for grants, and even sew my collection of holey pants to pass the time. I know of parking attendants, gas stations overnight, and security jobs where you sit around for hours doing nothing. The people pay you scraps since you are essentially getting paid to do nothing. Being that I had millions of late bills to pay, I hoped for a job that paid better than a gas station. I also asked to be put in a situation where I am forced to exercise. I couldn't think of any scenario except to work at a gym, be forced to walk to work, or something.

I actually smile as I write this because I realize even more how this lowly job actually is an answer to all of these specific needs. I basically do inventory in a warehouse. It's a lowly job but pays better than retail and a gas station. It probably pays similar to some security job or front desk attendant that answers the phone and buzz folks in the door ever 2 hours and twiddles her thumb the rest of the shift. The warehouse is huge and only managers are allowed to park near the door. I was irritated to park 5 million miles from the entrance—forcing me to walk quite a distance to my station and back to my car. I also need to walk just as far to the soda machine and the clean bathroom. There is this filthy truck driver's bathroom near me which smells like an outhouse at the zoo and a clean one far away. The only thing funkier is the professor's house, which smelt like raw ammonia.

I also help the handlers take down totes. It's not required but it helps get the job done quicker, it's a nice gesture—instead of letting them do all of the labor like a slave while I file my nails—and it is free weight training. In fact, it's paid weight training. If you don't know what free weight training is, it's a pun on words. Free weights, which is another name for bar bells or dumb bells, are those big iron weights people use in a weight room at a gym. Practically all gyms and personal training costs. You might find some rusted, broke down bar bells in a park that no respectable child would even use. You can also walk around a track field at a school or the mall for free, like many senior citizens do, which is about the size of this warehouse.

One of the handlers said she lost a roll of flab. I don't know how long she's been doing this nor how long it took her to lose it. Regardless, she lost it and that's all that matters. If she lost a flab of fat, and she is bigger than me, then surely I could lose a flab of fat helping them and working here. To top it off, between inventory, you basically sit around and twiddle you thumbs. In fact, I sit on my butt over half of the shift. The other half is spent going to lunch, waiting, doing inventory, listening to music, and talking. What a job. I started bringing Myro's 30-pound laptop to work to pass the time, be productive, and stay busy. Thusly, I get paid to not only do free weight training, but to write my book.

After I counted out my steps—compliments of the McDonalds adult get in shape Happy Meal step-o-meter which doesn't work—I walk over 2400 steps daily. Once I calculate my steps to and from my car before I even enter the warehouse, I walk over a mile. Since I get off at 3am, and the gym opens at 6am, I decided to get work done for 3 hours then work out for an hour. Thusly I'm productive, forced to walk, and I get my personal stuff done at work, all while getting paid better than peasant's salary. It's not a million dollars—yet, but it's something to help me with my bills.

Sorry to get so off track, but I wanted to explain to you this revelation and my unrecognized answered prayer, that I didn't even realized until I thought about it. Actually I was disappointed the first several month. It's un-air conditioned and stuffy, many co-workers are small minded, local, and very ghetto, and it's embarrassing to tell people. You know the kind that ask, "Why do you work there with a degree? Is that the best you can do?" Well once I realized how this was an answered prayer; I started finishing my book.

geTtiNg fooD & $ bY reaDinG thE Bible

A pastor said that you can get money, rent, and food, solely via reading the Bible. I of course wondered how can someone get money, food, or some material thing just from reading a page in the Bible. When rent is due or your car is about to run out of gas, is a verse in the Bible going to produce money out of thin air? I wondered this and wanted to question but never got around to it. He explained how God looks out for you and goes ahead of you. God and the spirit realm is not limited to time and space. God goes before you and He is not bound by the material universe. Since God is obviously not stuck on human's earthly time clock, He's able to go to the future for that particular crisis that you'll need help with. God goes ahead of you in time to prepare whatever is needed for you in the future. Then the pastor gave several examples like folks giving them money or clothes when they were down and out.

Well, as usual, I was broke, on E, and hungry. It was lunch and I hoped one of the package handlers would donate a $1 hot dog to me. She explained how she was strapped with only $5. I then searched my car hoping to find a miracle or something. Nothing. I commented to God about my current need for gas and something to eat and I of course mentioned—as if He doesn't know—that I did read the Bible that day. This actually is a rarity; I never spend time reading the Bible. I decided to ask this guy for $5 for gas. He gave it to me without trying to take me out, get my number, or say how he was broke. I figured he was just more mature and generous since he was a little older. As I continued to read the Bible, I ate sunflower seeds for my filling lunch. I grumbled the above question on how food and money appears out of the Bible. When the staff returned, they asked me not to eat out on the floor; I guess I'm a bit messy. She asked if I got my hot dog. I lied because I was too embarrassed to admit that I didn't even have one dollar.

Later, she asked if I like steak. I'm not a steak eater, however they said they had some steak and maybe chicken in the break room. I thought someone got some food and didn't eat it all, and was giving me the uneaten leftovers. They said there was some luncheon in the break room. Oh really?! I'm not a steak eater but I am hungry and broke, I'll be right back. I rushed to get my free meal on. They were grilling steaks outside and had potato and macaroni salad upstairs. They even had fruit, candy, and soda. I asked what was the occasion. The only answer I got was, "Your steak is burnt." Or, "I knew you'd get some food." I'm like, "And what?! So, you're eating too." I never figured out the reason, but I sure did pick through that burnt steak and ate dinner. I even took 2 sodas home. Hey, it was free. As I was leaving, on the bulletin board right in front of my face was the answer to the above question, **Who Really Rules the Earth?** What an interesting coincidence.

WHY DO EVIL PEOPLE KEEP MONEY & POWER?

Getting back to the above question, why do all of the presumably evil and greedy people of the world have so much? They seem to have plenty of money and riches, and the seemingly most wicked folks of the world seem to hold the most power. This is from a track titled, **"Who Really Rules the World?"** Many people assume God rules the world, including me, but this leaflet says it all.

"Jesus said, 'The ruler of this world will be cast out.' So the ruler of this world is in opposition to Jesus. Despite the efforts of well-meaning humans, the world has suffered terribly throughout history. This causes many people to wonder. David Lawrence wrote, 'Peace on earth—nearly everybody wants it. Good will toward men—almost all people of the world feel it toward one another. Then what's wrong? Why does war, evil, and terrorism exist despite the innate desires of people?' It seems a paradox doesn't it? When the natural desire of humans is to live at peace, they commonly hate and kill one another—and with such viciousness. Humans have used heinous methods to torture and slaughter one another mercilessly.

Do you believe that humans, who long for peace and happiness, are capable in themselves, of such gross wickedness toward others?" (Certainly I personally do, but anyway.) "What forces drive men to such loathsome deeds or maneuver them into situations where they feel compelled to commit atrocities? Have you ever wondered whether some wicked, invisible power is influencing people to do such acts of violence? The Bible clearly shows that an intelligent, unseen being has been controlling both men and nations. It says, the whole world has been laying in the power of the wicked one.'(1 John 5:19) Jesus was even tempted by the devil. Why would the devil tempt Jesus if he didn't already rule over what he offered? Think about this. Satan tempted Jesus by offering him all the kingdoms of the world and their glory, and said, 'All this I will give you if you will bow down and worship me. Jesus said, Get away from me Satan. For it is written, worship the Lord your God and serve him only.'(Matthew 4:8-10) Would Satan's offer been a real temptation if Satan was not actually the ruler of these kingdoms. No, it wouldn't. And notice that Jesus didn't deny that Satan actually had power over these worldly governments. Jesus would have pointed out to Satan that these governments that you offer me are not yours to begin with. I already own them. So Satan really is the unseen ruler of the world. The Bible calls him 'the God of this system of things.' (2 Corinthians 4:4)." Again, this very helpful quote came from a religious pamphlet titled, **"Who Really Rules the World?"** by the Watch Tower Bible and Track Society of Pa.©1992.

MORE PROBLEMS WITH MY LIFE

Greedy Bank of America stole thousands from me, is currently holding my paycheck hostage, and even had the nerve to send my info to check systems. Leftist and hippies protest Wal-Mart and McDonalds when I hear absolutely nothing about greedy, corporate banks, evil cell phone companies, malicious credit boroughs, and demonic credit card companies.

Why?

If these anti-Wal-Mart protesters are so angry at capitalism and corporate greed, then they should use an Enron or greedy bank as their capitalistic mascot of evil and corporate greed. I know they love to target Nike and other expensive name brands for their South Asian sweatshop labor, but what about the Mexican and Central American migrant workers; aren't they America's current "slave labor"?

I as a consumer see absolutely nothing wrong with Wal-Mart. If some third world country wants to try capitalism and open a McDonalds, what's wrong with that? At least they have the Ronald McDonald house and other community and social warfare programs for orphans and sick kids. They hire seniors, minorities, have many franchises, and the cheapest prices in town. Besides, how else can you eat and drive. Fries are easy to eat when driving, unlike a salad or soup. And if you're like me and ALWAYS, ALWAYS, ALWAYS, ALWAYS driving and doing ABSOLUTELY EVERYTHING yourself with ABSOLUTELY NO HELP FROM ABSOLUTELY ANYONE, then the convenient, unhealthy, fatting, fast food drive through with cheap prices is the best way to go. Is it the best tasting? Heck no! If you want to lose weight, everyone knows cheeseburgers, pizza, and ice cream isn't the way to go. But it sure is convenient.

As for Wal-Mart, I love Wal-Mart. As a consumer, the only thing I think and care about is variety, quality, and prices. Most mom and pop stores have very limited variety with expensive prices. I guess that's the reason the Home Depots and Wal-Marts took over. When I shop for food I want something fresh, a good variety to choose from, and a cheap price. When I buy gas, I want it durable without water or some filler that hurts my car and makes her sick. But I also want it cheap. And as for toiletries and everything else, I go to Wal-Mart. It has everything, except cute clothes. I even buy shoes there. It has all the made for TV stuff. It even has adult tricycles. Especially the Super Wal-Marts, what other store can you buy everything you need?

As for corporate greed; many banks, love to swallow up and monopolize the industry. The only convenience is that they would have ATMs everywhere. And unlike Wal-Mart or McDonalds, demonic credit cards charge you what ever they want and constantly screw the public over! Like that cell phone commercial where they rip you off with their contract and then screw you over while you have the phone with horrible service. And if you don't like it, find another company, they'll mistreat you just the same!

You would think these corporate protesters would target greedy banks, shady insurance companies, demonically wicked credit card companies, unscrupulous credit bureaus, and rip off cell phones over McDonalds and Wal-Mart. After all, I can visually see how Wal-Mart and McDonalds's try to help the local community. I can also see as a consumer, how these other greedy corporations, rip off customers and screw them over with very little options to turn to. Especially those credit cards!

REGINGERFACATION OF BERKLEY

Being that I had so many non-existent opportunities to buy a house, (which is equal to my non-existent spouse) most of my living took place in rented rooms. I lived in a hand full of apartments compared to the rooms I rented. Outside of 2 apartments and the Baltimore mad house, every other place was via work or school. Of course universities, internships, and study abroad will put you up in a place "in your name" but you don't go through some landlord and have them pull your credit. Once you're accepted to the school, job, or internship, they give you housing. I prefer it like that or in a room where there is no credit check and security deposit. Less money for me to pay and put out and way less hassle. When a landlord asks for my credit, I usually leave and move to the next vacancy. I slipped through Berkeley's cracks compliments of it being run like a very shiftless dorm. It was very badly managed, which came to my benefit. Obviously, it was also losing money. Thusly the corporate owners finally sold it, and thus, sold us—the tenants—out.

The new management company will remodel the building and raise rent to almost twice as much. Of course, 99% of all students and residents can't afford it. Ironically, some of the addict's mommies and daddies can afford to keep them here, to vandalize and all. The reason people, such as I, stay here is because of the fairly reasonable price for the size. You get this huge bedroom with your own private bath. Each room had their own A/C and heat unit that you could turn on and off independent of your roommate. The only thing you shared was the huge living room and kitchen. There was private parking, $1 laundry on each floor, a study lounge, elevators, and a free Univ. of Md. shuttle to the subway and throughout campus. And you're literally across the street from the main campus gate. Thus, the reason students mostly occupied it. You had drunks, grads, and PhD's. Compliments of the regingerfacation process by the new management, there has been an exodus of students daily. What student, freshman to Ph.D., whose stipend, scholarship, or financial aid is their only income, can afford this?

Because of this, and the fact that to date I have yet accomplished what I initially enrolled in school for, I temporally dropped out. My goals were to establish and build my business, lose weight, publish this book, and work towards a master. I distraughtly have yet to lose a pound, finish this book, or build my business to any sustainable level. ☹

CrackHead HooKup DowN thE DraIn

Well compliments of the eviction, and the fact that I've been trying to buy a home forever to absolutely no success, I looked into building a Virginia cottage. I told Daddy that I wanted to build a house on the farm back in '98. He said, "Go for it, just don't ask me for any money." That was usually his response to most things I was going to pursue. Compliments of a redneck squatter on the land, and the toothless, redneck judge—who most likely was his brother—we lost 5 or so acres of our inherited family land. It is only my aunt and Tony on the land and 10 or so acres unattended. I want to build a cottage there simply so it will be inhabited and attended to. My dad died trying to get that stolen land back, to no success of course thanks to our very fair judicial system.

Like I mentioned, I've been living on my own somewhere since I went to college. I never was evicted and my phone very rarely gets disconnected. I'm not rich and I live below check-to-check, but I am responsible enough to pay my basic bills and expenses. Evil banks refuse to work with people who never held the same job for several years, which is ridiculous. You can be responsible, make decent money, and always pay your bills and they would give you a very hard time. Being that my credit is horrible, my income is minuet, and the longest job I had was my 1 year contract which they tried very hard to get me to quit, no bank would dare give me a chance.

When I went to see Swautch's family who lives near mine in the country, I went on down to visit my family afterwards. I went to see my great aunt, and her neighbor talked to me about construction and buildings. He referred me to this seemingly divine hook up. He said this developer would work with me even with horrible credit and on welfare. Wow, this is definitely a divine hook up.

When I first spoke to this developer, he said he was willing to work with me, and he would clear the land, create a water and septic system, and build a shell for $25k. I would put several thousand down, pay him monthly, and hopefully pay him off within a year thanks to some hopeful grant money. He claimed that he could even clear the land and build the shell within a month. He seemed down until I called a month later to meet in person. Then he threw shade and kept speaking of some dreaded and horrible bank loan, as if any bank would EVER give me a break. He said he didn't do in house financing anymore. I asked about the first conversation and he claimed it was a misunderstanding. What?! Then he shadily told me to drop $25k and we can talk. What?! When I tried calling him and my great aunts neighbor back, nether answered their phone. How lovely!

MORE CHAOS IN MY LIFE

When Myro left her boyfriend, she moved in with her friend Nancy and Mr. Hag. His looks, cigarette-smitten voice, and attitude are all equal to Hyattsville's mom. He even has skills to scare off telemarketers. Now you know that takes major skills to make annoying telemarketers run. Myro stayed there until a few weeks ago when she couldn't take him anymore. Well she cursed him out and left, and I let her crash in the living room for the time being. I assumed she would only stay away a few days to cool off. Everything was completely up in the air. It just so happened she landed a nice job on campus so staying with me was very convenient for her.

Compliments of the free shuttle around campus, Myro would get free rides to and from her campus job. While living with Mr. Hag she received a gift from our church. It was a nice car. It has good pickup, runs smoothly, and simply needs a few repairs. It does smoke like a chimney however. She allowed me to drive her car to work since she now can take the free shuttle and I work 3000 miles away in Gods country/AKA/UFO land. My Feather is sick of driving a million miles a week.

Less than a week later I receive this cease and desist letter. In super legalese it said to cease and vacate you apartment and leave in 30 days or renew and pay the lovely $1550 a month. I immediately called the leasing office to figure out what was going on. The irritated secretary said that they were doing major repairs to the entire floor and it was a safety hazard to have anyone living there. I had no choice, I was being forced out. I questioned the notice. The secretary was quick with me saying unless I renew and pay $1550, I must leave. No sublease, no relocation, renew or vacate in three weeks. What?! I asked what consolation was being made for me and the many other dislocated residents who were from other countries and cities and whose lease would be cut several months short.

They gave us a couple months notice that our rent would almost double, which is not enough time for anyone to find decent housing. It took me over a month to find Berkley—and me finding that was kind of a divine hook-up. For there was over a 50 person waiting list. It took almost an entire summer for a friend from church and her family to find decent housing in NY to do her residency. She found a hospital to be a resident in but I guess they didn't help find her housing. And if you think finding a roommate, house, apt., or any other type of living space is easy, ask ANY transplant to DC, NY, or any city. They will tell you; they hunt and search forever to find a decent place or decent roommate.

For students, the dorms fill up during the fall for that following year. If you didn't make your last minute reservations by spring break, you're short, and now it's summer. They told Anna that she wouldn't be able to leave until Sept. even though she found a possible place available mid July. Now they said, get out or renew. No wonder there's an exodus of students every day. Myro asked what was my plan B since my welfare hook up fell through and I knew I had to move out for several months. Being as organized as I am, of course I had no plan B.

AN ODE TO THE STRUGGLES OF FINDING A ROOMATE

And here's another post-note on the hectic curses in my life and an ode to the struggles of finding decent housing and a roommate. Being that I'm still single with no financial or physical help from any man, I decided to turn my den into a spare bedroom. Myro first gave me the idea when she very briefly thought about moving in. Being that I currently have an apartment to myself, I kind of gotten use to the space and privacy, but needing money, I posted a roommate ad.

I found Satan in the form of Josh Rainer. He was another last resort. He (and every other lunatic walking the streets being a menace to society) is the reason St. Elizabeth needs to revamp and open back up!! He claimed he was a Rasta and that was his excuse for his very weird behavior. He claimed he was a vegan and didn't eat anything that had a mommy and daddy. Outside the fact that he ate all of my food, he spoke of stoning gays and dikes saying how they are a sprain on the human race. How he appeared to be allergic to whites and if he was in line at a store to buy some food and some "negative" person looked or said something to him the wrong way, he would return the food and leave the store. How he could not put something to his mouth or skin (i.e. toothpaste, soap, food, etc.) that some drag queen, white, or gay/lesbian person touched or handled. I asked how does he manage to eat out if he's "allergic" to all of this? And more so, is this actually Rastafarianism; or some type of homemade religion based on some psycho-somatic condition he has? He even admitted it was probably some type of mental, psycho-somatic condition he had and he added all of that stupidness to his wannabe beliefs.

Being that he asked for his money back and told me to find his replacement 2 days after he begged me for this place and paid me his rent (via some girl who had pity on him) I eagerly started searching for another roommate. As I mentioned, he was the very last resort. Being that again, I was extremely tight on cash and needed some rental help, I accepted his offer. If nothing else but his female friend bailing him out on rent, I would not want him. Is she also going to bail you out next month too? What if she's mad or broke, then what do you plan to do for rent? Being that he said he'd rather be homeless and sleep in his car than have a place with no food, he requested his money back. Being that I already used his money to pay rent, we agreed to find his replacement and pay him with the next tenants money. I told him of soup kitchens, food stamps, and food pantries. I guess he either was not that serious or interested in eating. At first I just thought he had some weird religious and ethical beliefs. He actually acted and appeared like those peace-loving, "Yo my brotha/sister, peace man, vegan eating, dreadlock wearing" types. I completely did not realize how crazy he was—and I COMPLETELY learned my lesson on not doing background checks. As I mentioned above, I would hate the hassle of someone asking me for some credit and/or background check for simply a room. If they would hassle me on this, I'd leave and find another room. I now have learned my lesson though.

Being the lunatic he is; I guess he forgot he told me to find his replacement. He started to act very weird. He never said much which was fine, I'm reserve too. But he would rattle the extension cord, slam his hips on the floor, flicker the lights on and off, or knock on the wall whenever I would be in the kitchen or something. If I went to "investigate" this noise, he of course would stop and pretend to be sleeping and not know anything about it. I actually caught him in the act, which is why I know what he was doing.

For some reason, he and many others like him are free to roam the streets of society while St. Elizabeth's and the police ignore the problem. While the publics stays politically correct by not enforcing lunatics roaming the streets, refusing to take their medications to normalize them, and hospitals, nuthouses, and the government ignores this problem, how can anyone expect to have a safe society?!?!

At least people who suffer from depression—which life automatically serves you—may unfortunately be a danger to themselves but are not a threat to others. It isn't exactly fair to lump all folks who have learning disabilities and are slow, physical disabilities and are considered handicap, and folks with depression or even mild anger issues—which life also throws at you—in a similar category with raging lunatics who are threats not only to themselves, but to innocent citizens as well. For depressed people know they feel shabby. Lunatics actually think they are fine as they try to kill the giant pink elephant that just entered the door—and thus another unnecessary shooting or murder spree.

When gun lobbyists insist on keeping certain groups with as many guns as possible, (with HORRIBLE gun control and many restless lunatics) St. Elizabeth's and the government insists on releasing every psycho that enters their care within a few days, and society as a whole ignores this problem, you end up with this:

- Demonic Amish schoolhouse murderer.
- Mad teen gunman that opened fire outside a Fairfax, VA police station.
- Lunatic accused of crashing SUV through barrier and underwent mental evaluation.
- The snipers who terrorized the Washington DC area for three weeks in October 2002.
- Crazy murderer who killed the pregnant mother by slicing her belly open and stealing her unborn baby and then drowning her 3 other kids and stuffed them into a washer & dryer.
- West Islip, (Long Island) N.Y. lunatic accused of killing his mother.
- Mad Pennsylvania woman who kills her 3 children and boyfriend, then kills herself.
- Adan (17) and Policarpio (22) Espinoza murdered their 3 nephews by trying to behead them.
- Insane lady who gruesomely murdered a pregnant woman by snatching the baby from womb.
- Lunatic who doused his girlfriend & 3 kids with gas & set afire as he drove and crashed, killing everyone.
- Biswanath Halder who goes mad and then on a shooting rampage on a college campus.
- John Hinckley, Jr. who enjoys the luxuries of St. Elizabeth.
- And the MANY school shootings, such as:
    - Lincoln County High School in Fayetteville, Tennessee
    - Heritage High School, Conyers Georgia
    - Columbine HS, Littleton Colorado
    - Heath High School, Paducah Kentucky
    - Pearl High School, Pearl Mississippi
    - Red Lake High School, Minnesota

When I finally found a roommate, I told him he could leave, since a friend figured he was being an a'hole because he wanted his money which I spend on the rent. I told Crazy I had his last month's rent money so he is free to go (and spend it on his crack). Well now he didn't want to leave, cause as several friends, including Kong said, he was homeless and really had no where to go. It took me writing a 30 day vacate/eviction notice to be served by the cops, spending $75 to change the locks with Kong packing his trash up and throwing it out the door. He had the nerve to bring the cops to me for his "$7" and his illegal eviction. Obvious he was friends with some cops who made me either pay him $250 to officially leave or give him the new key. I ended up paying this jerk $250 and still having his rancid *ss hang around my building waiting for his mail. I of course, kept some mail and sent the rest back to sender—wrong address! He bribed me with $50—that he never paid me—to meet him and give him his paycheck.

rACIST reDnecK cOP

Then you have A'holes like Lee who post ads announcing basement apartments and rooms for rent and then allegedly get his girlfriend to leave her contact info, call the people, and be the point person. She seemed cordial, gave me all types of info on her, her boyfriend, the place, them being police, their neighborhood, even their pets. She invited me to check it out. The basement apartment was WAY out, even past my job—which is also way out. It was actually only 15 minutes to my job from their place, which is why I considered it. She even said that if I was satisfied with it and all went well, I could pay the day I visit the place and she would hold it for me. I agreed and needing a place, I left a check with them to hold the room.

She was very cordial and nice when she greeted me and showed me around. Even her cute doggie was nice. She seemed to have no problem with me moving in. I thought it was weird that she wanted me to write the check out to him. He was quite standoffish and never really said much. He asked if I planned to stay 6 months or a year. I requested a month-by-month lease. Then he said he would make a month-to-month lease since I only planned to stay there as short of a time as possible. Basically until I found something a little better since it was furnished with their living room furniture and I really had no space to put a lot of my non bedroom items (such as my kitchen and living room stuff).

It basically was a last resort place, but I figured I'd better leave some money just in case nothing else came through. Surely this is a way to hold my space, similar to how I did Linda at Berkley Apts. I gave her a post-dated check to hold my space for the following month while I went to San Francisco. She didn't even cash it until after I moved in. This is how it is supposed to be done. I should get my check back if I don't stay there. Thusly, I left Lee a check and moved whatever boxes I could fit inside my car there.

Obviously, she wasn't good at screening the people. This racist, redneck, pig gets her to tell me that they're selling the house within a week of me leaving my money—and he still hasn't given me all of my money back! She explained how they allegedly had a huge fight (obviously for her not being wise enough to not let some niglet move in and how could she not figure out that I wasn't white over the phone.) They allegedly weren't speaking and were breaking up over this fight. I guess she, who was a Capitol Hill police, was more interested in the money and a decent tenant. He, also a Capitol Hill police, obviously cared more about skin color and hair texture. He allegedly was trying to move deeper into redneck country to become a sheriff for Charles County, MD. People like him fuel the stereotype that all America cops are racist and enjoy police brutality and profiling. When they have wholesome bigots like Lee on the force, he gives the police a bad name!!

On top of that, he has **absolutely no landlord business ethics**! Outside of him advertising his place when he only wanted a certain type of person to move in (which is illegal), he should never accept business money from a potential client/customer if he isn't going to follow through on his part of the business deal. He owes me over $150 and has yet given me all of my money back. He tells me to take him to small claims court, which I plan to do after I expose this to as many concerned, decent, citizens as possible.

PaycHecK heLd hosTagE

After this, Bank of America decided to steal my check and hold it hostage for 3 weeks making it impossible to pay my tithes, let alone my rent. While I waited for this bank to release my check, I got rescheduled at my job from the hot, dusty, desert warehouse with weekends off to the refrigerated, slow moving produce warehouse. On top of the fact that it's cold—I hate heat—it's not full of dirty, dusty, crates that I'm forced to sit on but an air-conditioned break room with a table to sit this laptop on. Thusly, I'm sitting at a table for much longer periods of uninterrupted time in A/C over some nasty old crate in a dusty, hot warehouse with massive noise, commotion, and distractions. Hopefully, I will finish this book within the next 2 weeks.

However with the transfer, I went from having the weekends off to Sunday and Wednesday. I prefer 2 days in the row, whatever day it is. I'm so busy, I have no social life. I think the last oh so lovely date I went on was with the lying "millionaire" Moroccan who took me to the parking lot instead of the coffee house over a year ago. If I have several days off in a row, I rest, relax, and recuperate from being SUPER SONIC BUSY. Even though this isn't two days off in the row, God must have something in store for me; there's church on Sundays and Bible Study on Wednesdays—which I haven't been to this past summer compliments of my old work schedule.

Later that day I went home to check the mail. Finally my check had been released. Compliments of Nations Bank, I was over a week late on rent. On top of that, maintenance constantly needed to enter the apartment for one reason or another. I kept hiding Fat. Who knows, they possibly noticed Fat one time or another. When I went to pay my late rent and give management our vacate forms, I figured I'd ask for some sort of consolation due to the unfair and untimely exodus of the residents. The chances were slim to none that any consolation would arise, but it sure as heck doesn't hurt to ask.

The leasing office was being relocated and her entire office was a mess. She had chairs, trashcans, boxes, refrigerators, etc., all over the place. When I gave her my rent and forms, she put them in a desk. No filing, organization, or anything else. Unfortunately, kind of like my filing and organizational system. ☹ They were so unorganized and in a state of chaos, she said absolutely nothing about my late rent, let alone any late fees or illegal cats. When I explained my sob story and situation, I asked if there was any way to relocate me at least until our lease is up. I still have neither place nor plans for Sept. but that's a month away. Hopefully, through the miracle and grace of God, I will secure a house and move there by fall. But anyway, back to sad and unfortunate reality. I didn't expect anything but amazingly, she worked with me. As much as they seem to want to vacate all residents unless they renew a pay twice as much, she said she'd relocate me the following month. Go figure!

GOD SPEAKS THROUGH MY CHAOS

I know and have seen a lot of people, young and old, black and white, who are quite charismatic and somewhat entertaining. I never thought they were crazy, I just figured they felt something that I, and many others, didn't. I never wanted nor craved for what they had. In fact, it's all well and good for them, and as they say in NYC, "You do you." But as for me, I am perfectly content without making a spectacle of myself in doing these antics. Sometimes it is quite a spectacle, but other times it is subtle and seemingly more convincing. For if someone starts sputtering around and foaming at the mouth you wonder whether to call 911, shout also, or pray for them. If someone, however, subtly and in control claps or shouts like your team just scored a goal or point, well you figure that whatever the pastors is speaking on, they must really relate to. For why would you shout and cheer like at a soccer game over a sermon or speech? I personally don't see anything wrong with that, I mean, if you really feel that sermon, then you shout. I am more subtle, however. I do take notes though. I bought a cute, tiny, kid's notebook from the Dollar Store that I put all of my notes in.

Even if you are a devout religious person and not an atheist, you may question why someone would start jumping all over the place, yell, shout, and roll on the floor embarrassing themselves. I mean, when you go to church, there are many bystanders wondering what is it that these folks feel to make them act that way. Is there something wrong with me because I sit aimlessly and don't talk in tongues and run around, or is there something wrong with them? Maybe I should say another prayer for myself so I can get these super Holy Ghost actions, movements, and miracles. I personally was always the bystander and not some fanatic religious person by any stretch of the means, as I'm sure you, would agree. In fact, I probably would be dead or stoned if I had to follow strict rules as they have in some religions. Some say I'm quite a slacker—though I personally disagree, I just hate hard work.

Some religions, beliefs, and traditions require strict discipline and 100% obedience. Now Anna and Myro, who have Marine Corps discipline, would come out excellently. If it was all or nothing for me to succeed, I wouldn't even waste my time trying. Some diets say you can lose 10 pounds in a week if you follow it. Of course it's a complete, disciplined, 100% effort and if you cheat and don't follow through just ONE time, forget it! Now what the heck is that all about?!?! I'm not a machine. I know I'm going to fail and cheat one of those days. If I try to follow some strict, stupid diet of eating only a carrot and grapefruit all day, drink 70 cups of water, and run 10 miles, I'd fall short the FIRST day! I know there are many disciplined machines around who can follow this and other absurd strict plans completely to the T. I'm just not one of them. Unfortunately, I'm one of those lowly, lazy, loser types—i.e. a human being and not a cyber.

QUICK RANT ON MYRO, SWAUTCH,
 & MR. HAG

And speaking of weight loss and fatness; the skinniest people I know—Myro and Swautch who are the size of a twig, and Mr. Hag, who is very slim with a beer potbelly—are the main ones haggling me on weight loss. I can see if they were fat and then lost weight, but they couldn't gain weight if they tried. Mr. Hag confirmed that he was scrawny most of his life. I assume sweets, age, and his sugar condition are the reason he even has a potbelly. Swautch tried numerous times to gain weight—along with Floyd who is much bigger—with protein shakes and such, to no success. Of course for a female in this stupid society, skeletons are gorgeous. Unlike the others, Myro can out eat everyone I know. Like Ms. Pac Man, she can eat like a pig and drink like a sailor, and not gain weight nor get too drunk. I, on the other hand, can drink one cocktail and have a buzz and eat one hot dog and gain 10 pounds.

Now there are people who overeat like a pig and never exercise. Of course they would get fat. There are also many people like me who are fat but eat **NO MORE** than any slim person, and move **NO LESS** than any slim person. It's just our metabolism is slower than a slug. We need to eat <u>WAY</u> less and move 1000 times more than the average fit person to ever see results. An atrocity in my sight!!
And you always get these ignorant fools who know **ABSOLUTELY NOTHING** <u>about health, fitness, nor weight loss</u>, and stupidly assume that fat people are fat because we are lazy pigs. Like idiots assume someone is homeless or poor by choice. Things happen and you lose money, but I NEVER met anyone in my entire life who wanted to be homeless and poor when they grew up.

And unlike those people who were athletic kids or teens, got lazy after college or childbirth, and started eating like a hog and never exercise—I've tried everything to be fit! I also know MANY others who try to eat right, count points and calories, exercise, and still not lose weight! It is extremely retarded to assume everyone who is fat overeats and never exercises! And most of those idiots who assume that (or assume folks want to be poor) are neither fat nor poor. They ignorantly speak on what they know ABSOLUTELY NOTHING ABOUT!!!

I find it insulting and ironic that the skinniest people I know get on me the most about my supposedly overeating and exercising habits. I know for a fact that I always try to exercise. I go to the gym way more than Myro, Swautch, and many others. I also never eat breakfast, (which is very bad) skip lunch many times (which is worst) and always try to eat healthy. I love health food stores, salads, aerobic classes, and such. Myro commented more than once on the lack of tasty, normal foods in my house. Saying, "How are you ever going to keep a man? What man would stay with only some carrot sticks, nuts, soymilk, and rice pellets around? Unless he's a rabbit, no one would stick around for this. You never have real food such as fried chicken, mac and cheese, greens, and stuff. Always some weird tofu nuggets, rice  milk, bee pollen, and odd foods that most people don't even want to taste, let alone eat."

I personally don't want or need steroid filled, cloned meat and factory made vegetables. I, however, have horrible time management and never seem to find time to cook up meals for the week and exercise daily. They, however, assume I'm fat because I overeat and under exercise, all which is a lie!! I know I have horrible eating habits but I very rarely pig out on junk food, fast food, and stuff. And I would out dance Swautch in a second. Swautch would always want to leave the dance club early. As I stated earlier, I would go to some clubs when they open(around 8pm) and be one of the last to leave when they close(around 4am). Of course later on, Swautch out partied EVERYONE. He was very hyper, however he never danced, he'd just hang out and socialize. I would dance and try to actually enjoy myself. I love dancing to almost any type of music. He would just talk to everyone.

I guess America has more humans than zombies after all; we're the fattest nation. I guess a majority of the population is also busy, weak, and undisciplined. Oh well. Perhaps they will finally develop something for us. Like stop super sizing and over processing white sugar, flour, and every processed piece of high fat, high cholesterol, massively high simple carb junk/processed/packaged/prepared/frozen/carry out/fast food on the market. And get rid of the steroid, antibiotic, cancerous, fatting, heart attack causing, factory-farmed meat. It's perfect to make you unhealthy and fat. And look, that's what we are, a nation of fat, unhealthy, super unexercised, walking heart attacks.

bacK tO mY poinT

Because of my human nature and character, super strict regimens, religions, diets, et cetera, don't work. If it's an all or nothing point, I'd just choose nothing. I know I'm no Holy Roller machine; I'm quite human and imperfect. The reason I seek the easiest way out. If my weight loss or getting to heaven was based on something like that, I'd be one super sized, 500 pound, hippo headed straight to hell.

I have personally checked out as a visitor, guest, or even a curious student; Buddhists, Wicca/metaphysical, Nuwaubian (and their supreme leader who over- stands), Islam, a voodoo priest, my Orthodox Jew neighbors, Scientology, and many others. They have all types of rituals, activities, chants, charms, spells, incan- tations, prayers, poems, and everything else you must practice and do at certain hours, days, and locations. They also could never give me concrete answers and absolutes regarding the results of these rituals. Is this spell, incantation, or what have you guaranteed to work? If I must put money, time, and effort into these can- dles, incense, and oils, I want to know that this cute guy I want will be crawling at my feet. Of course it was a spell for a man, what else. Well I would definitely do one for fame and money if that was guaranteed to work also. They, however, could never offer a 100% money back guarantee. What after a month it didn't work? Try again? And why waste my time and money with you and your practice or religion if it's no guarantee? It appeared meta-physics/new age declared the best results and guarantee, but somehow fell short on presenting results.

Meta-physics and new age could be anything from Astrology and Wicca, to some Buddhist/Hindu/Shaman fusion. That's all well and good; it just seemed to slightly go against the mainstream monotheistic religions. Outside of that, new age would be the easiest choice. There appears to be no hell and not really much accountability—except karma. However, several meta-physics I know seem to not be able to get results. One claims skills to travel throughout space and time, yet can't get a landline phone. In fact, he only has some pre-paid cell. What type of power and results is this? Another constantly struggles with money. If you claim high skills to harness the powers of matter and the universe, at least own a landline and some money!

Forgive me for saying this, and I know every practicing Muslim and Jew will dispute this, but even Islam and Judaism didn't have a guarantee on entrance into heaven. Maybe it's privileged information for only practicing Jews, not curious visitors. But when I asked, they always referred and focused on life here not the here after. I asked this one guy in rabbi school and he said that they always teach you how to correctly do the rituals and act here on earth and they usually don't talk much about the afterlife until later on in rabbi school. I thought that was real interesting.

The Muslims have very graphic descriptions of all the types of punishments and hell and what you can do to get there. If you don't breast feed you go here, if you complain when your husband beats you, you go there, if you sneeze and don't talk to your 3rd wife you go here. It wasn't these exact descriptions—except the girl did use the breastfeeding one. They however did list a million and one types of punishments and ways to get punished, but no guarantee after years of obedience, ritualistic prayer, and such, to get to heaven. I heard via right wing conservative

Christians that the men get Haurá's or many young virgins to have sex with. What about the women? Don't they at least get one sexy guy to show them gentleness, chivalry, dedication, and romance? I guess if you obey 200% and never complain you'll make it to heaven.

SomeThiNg oF InTeresT

All in all, because I'm an undisciplined human rather than a Marine Corps machine, I seek the easiest solution with the biggest results. If there is one diet that says I must starve on mints and gum to lose 14 pounds in a week (as one MLM diet group says); and another diet that says I can eat as much healthy grains, produce, and fish I want to lose 5 pounds—I'M THERE!!! So far, I haven't quite found one that easy. They usually limit the amount of one thing or another and want you to exercise for over an hour and do weights. This is all great, well, and good. I love dancing and fun dance style aerobic class. I also love stretching afterwards and have absolutely no problem with weight training. It's just my schedule is chaotic, hectic, and shot to hell. I can't even seem to find time for flossing my teeth and taking my daily vitamins. Which is REALLY bad.

On that same note, if one religion offers a guarantee of heaven, health, prosperity, and protection for you, AS IS, without requiring some machine like all or nothing set of daily rituals or upfront costs, I'm there. Scientology, for example, asks for money up front before they offer you a series of classes to take you to the next level, then more money for the next level, and so forth. Like I said, lazy or not, I need the easiest way out.

Here is some interesting stuff I found off the internet regarding <u>RELIGION verses a RELATIONSHIP with CHRIST</u>. It's from this informative site called **10 Reasons To Believe** (<u>http://www.gospelcom.net/rbc/rtb/3rsn</u>). Go figure for their long site name.

"Religion is believing in God, attending religious services, taking catechism, being baptized, and receiving communion. Religion is tradition, ritual, ceremony, and learning the difference between right and wrong. Religion is reading and memorizing Scripture, offering prayers, giving to the poor, and celebrating religious holy days. Religion is singing in the choir, helping the poor, and making amends for past wrongs. Religion is something that was practiced by the Pharisees, those Scripture-loving, conservative, separatist, spiritual leaders who hated Christ enough to call for His death. They hated Him not only because He broke their traditions in order to help people (<u>Matthew 15:1-9</u>) but because He saw through their religion into their hearts.

"Jesus said, 'Woe to you…. hypocrites!' (Luke 11:44). What looks better than being dressed right, attending religious services, and doing things that mark us as decent, God-fearing people? Yet how many religious scholars, ministers, and faithful followers withhold honor and encouragement from their wives, attention from their children, and love from their doctrinal enemies? Jesus knew what we often forget: What looks good may have a heart of evil.

"Jesus spoke to religious extremists who had a passion for detail (Luke 11:42). Jesus saw our tendency to make rules and to focus on "morally correct" behavior instead of keeping our eyes on the bigger issue of why we are trying to be so right. While the Pharisees were big on knowledge carried out to its logical conclusions, they forgot that God doesn't care how much we know until He knows how much we care. It was this greater "why" that the apostle Paul had in mind when he wrote, 'If I speak in the tongues of men and of angels, but have not love, I am only a resounding gong or a clanging cymbal…. .If I give all I possess to the poor and surrender my body to the flames, but have not love, I gain nothing' (1 Corinthians 13:1,3). One of the greatest dangers of religion is that it distracts people from the Word of God and from a "right heart" by unnecessary activities of denomination and traditions. Rather than leading people to God, religious people shift the focus to themselves and their own rules. Religious people are those who trust the beliefs and actions of their religion to do what only Christ can do.

"Because religion cannot change a heart, it tries to control people with laws and expectations that are not even kept by the leaders who interpret and apply the rules. With this in mind, Jesus said, '…. .you load men with burdens hard to bear, and you yourselves do not touch the burdens with one of your fingers' (Luke 11:46). Religion is good at outlining high standards of right behavior and relationships, but poor at giving real and merciful help to those who realize they have not lived up to those expectations.

"Christ is more than a system, tradition, or belief. He is a Person who knows our needs, feels our pain, and sympathizes with our weakness. In exchange for our trust, He offers to forgive our sins, to intercede for us, and to bring us to His Father. He cried for us, died for us, and rose from the dead to show that He was all He claimed to be. Conquering death, He showed us that He can save us from our sins, live His life through us on earth, and then bring us safely to heaven. He offers Himself as a gift to anyone who will trust Him (John 20:24-31)."

HelL InsuRancE

Many folks simply get "hell insurance" and get saved at one of those open-air revivals, TV evangelists, or street corner preaching sessions. You can go to any prison or Christian youth camp and have the kids or prisoners saved from going to hell by the end of the program. Somehow I always wonder how effective those quick 1-minute prayers are. For I never felt anything while I prayed it nor afterward. I never ran, shouted, or got Holy Ghost fanatical at church. I never talked to God and actually heard Him respond. I mean, was this prayer successful? I prayed that prayer compliments of some lonely youth phone line I called via a TV commercial when I was 12. Feeling that it didn't work, I prayed that same prayer every night expecting some major difference. Somehow, I never quite got it. I'm not sure what happened; maybe I need to be super sensitive and spiritual (like some yoga metaphysic) or a preacher to understand? Besides, there seems to be over a million forms and denominations of Christianity and Catholicism, and each one is supposed to be different and the correct one to follow. I don't have time to dissect each one.

It's hard for me to understand and conceive how someone can live in modern day America—or any Westernized country where missionaries pour in—and not hear the over obvious call to salvation. Now I've been practically inundated with every form and sort of Christian way, doctrine, and call to salvation. Flyers/tracts, radio, TV, CD's and tapes, individuals approaching you in the street asking if you're saved and trying to witness to you and invite you to join them somewhere while you are in the middle of minding your business and going somewhere. Maybe it's just me, but it seems that here in America, every TV evangelist, pastor, Jehovah Witness, super Christian, or church person announces this plea for you to get saved.

I've been to churches where they would put people on the spot by asking them to stand up, raise their hand, come forward, or some other very obvious and embarrassing way to admit that you're not saved. Even if you're not, you don't want to be put on the spot—especially in a church—that you're not saved. You at least want to fit in and make pretend you belong and are saved. Now privately it's quite a different story, but publicly it can feel rather humiliating to parade in front of a church or group saying that you're some horrible sinner and—unlike every other goodie two shoes—you live a horrible sin filled life.

Since this is a book that I assume you are privately reading and not some big seminar to put you on the spot, you might be interested to read the following. The following quotes are from some Christian websites. Campus Crusade for Christ, www.crusade.org and this REALLY excellent Virginia church website, http://www.new-life.net/goodnews.htm that I actually found by accident. The Virginia church's site has a massive amount of info; from the history of Santa and Halloween to answers to why many Christians appear to be big hypocrites or why God allows horrible things to happen. They even have puzzles and optical illusions. I actually stumbled upon this site while surfing on-line optical illusions while at work. The only annoying thing is that, at the time of writing this, their site plays this REALLY AWFUL cheap keyboard music when you view it. As of now, I haven't figured out how to turn this torturous music off.

"False Salvation
You can't be saved by attending church regularly.
You can't be saved by believing in God. You must believe on Jesus Christ.
You can't be saved through religious activity.
You can't be saved by being a good person.

It's impossible to have any kind of relationship with God, if you don't come to Him through faith in Jesus Christ. In John 14:6 Jesus answered, 'I am the way and the truth and the life. No one comes to the Father except through Me ...' Someone must individually RECEIVE Jesus Christ as their own personal Savior and Lord. Only then can someone know and experience God's love and plan for their life. Receiving Christ involves turning to God from self (repentance) and trusting Christ to come into our lives to forgive our sins and to make us the kind of people He wants us to be. Just to agree intellectually that Jesus Christ is the Son of God and that He died on the cross for our sins is not enough. Nor is it enough to have an emotional experience. We receive Jesus Christ by faith, as an act of will. Prayer is talking with God. God knows your heart and He is not so concerned with your words as much as He is with the attitude of your heart. The following is a suggested prayer:

'Lord Jesus, I need you. Thank You for dying on the cross for my sins. I open the door of my life and receive You as my Savior and Lord. Thank You for forgiving my sins and giving me eternal life. Take control of the throne of my life. Make me the kind of person You want me to be.'

Does this prayer express the desire of your heart? If it does, pray this prayer right now and Christ will come into your life, just as He promised."

===================================

Now me personally, I prayed this type of prayer from a TV commercial for lonely teens to call. I wanted—and of course still want—hell insurance. If you are like me, the good better out way the inconvenience and bad. Me, and many others, are for peace on earth, good will towards man, recycling, etc., as long as it's no hassle. I have absolutely no problem helping someone or recycling my unwashed soda can or juice bottle in a very conveniently located recycling bin. However, if I must first wash it, then go the extra mile in my already extremely busy schedule to toss items in some recycle bin—in the trash can they will go. At least used papers get tossed at conveniently located paper recycle bins AS IS. Not washed, pressed, et cetera. Plastic and bottles are way too much a hassle in my all too busy life. I was forced to recycle in Japan. They actually expected me to pre-clean them and separate metal from plastic and so forth. Everything went to the recycle bin. Perhaps it was for papers, but someone will sift through and separate it at their end. I guess I'm some lazy, non-earth/eco-friendly type of person, oh well.

Getting back to my topic above outside this rant, most people have good intentions, just very busy lives. Helping others and the planet is great, and Christianity and the church thing is all well and good—until it starts infringing on the comfort of your life. No one wants to read the Bible, go to church—particularly at the crack of dawn—pray, and especially witness, tithe, and fast. These are things that would turn someone off of Christianity all together. You might be a bit more interested in God's salvation and hell insurance, God's help with your finances, health, life, and protection during these end times and days when all hell breaks out on the earth.

tRUE sATIFICATION oR nOT

Some say Christianity will satisfy you, make you happy, quench your thirst, and such. They say that, but when you look at many Christians, they seem poor, sick, down and out, broke, busted, and disgusted. Many are mean, conservative, closet bigots who hate gays, minorities, folks on welfare, foreigners, Muslims, and non-Christians. It seems like their life is centered on hate and bigotry. Others seem to be old, fat, women, with big hats who like to shout—then tell you off. Obviously, these are just stereotypes and not the case for most, but it does exist. Also, when one thinks of all of the rules—no pre-marital sex, partying, drinking, cursing, go to church, and so on, it sometimes outweighs the positive benefits and good. Christianity can easily seem to be a change for a miserable lifestyle over one that is allegedly enjoyable. I personally am not at that enjoyment phase yet either. I'm still lonely, broke, and single. So far, no scriptures in the Bible, church song, or sermon have changed this. I, however, do seek God's healing and protection in these end times.

hAPPY hAPPY, jOY jOY

Have you ever seen the cartoon **Ren and Stimpy** and heard their *Happy Happy, Joy Joy* song? If not, check it out on the internet, The Cartoon Channel, or something. The dog and cat would sing this silly jingle on various episodes of their show, along with their Powered Toast Man. I personally feel that people can easily get divided into two categories in regards to Christianity, what they seek in Christianity, or why they even got saved in the first place.

The first group can be called the *Happy Happy, Joy Joy* group. They can sometimes be described as "Oh God, I'm miserably confused, lost, and feeling really worthless, ashamed, and/or guilty." They're lost, confused, and been through some really tough times, and seek God's guidance, love, comfort, stability, and possible answers. Perhaps the difference between suicide or some mental hospital and peace of mind and sanity is God.

I assume this is the group that supposedly seeks Christianity as some form of emotional crutch. I personally have never heard anyone say this. I've only seen Christians on TV claim they hear this excuse from people they try to witness to as the reason not to believe in salvation or Christ. Even if this *is* the case, what difference would it make? If some emotionally damaged Christian uses God as an emotional crutch, what harm is in that? If someone who's an emotional wreck uses Christianity and seeks God to restore sanity and peace, no one should say anything bad about that. For salvation is far better and way cheaper than therapy, medication, and some insane asylum. These types of Christians seem to be good followers and team players. They appear to seek a form of refuge from the hell and emotional chaos of their life and/or personality. They got saved and seek God to be happy, fulfilled, complete, forgiven from their foul ways, and for the joy of Christ.

The second group is like me. Self willed, independent, head strong, leader types that are not necessarily good followers. We too have issues, problems, and hell within our life, but somehow we are a bit stronger. Maybe we cope differently and thus not exactly an emotional wreck. For whatever the reason, our reason for salvation is totally different. We're not seeking God for happiness, completeness, forgiveness, or joy. Perhaps we feel that we never were that evil to begin with. Or maybe we are more in control of our feelings. We seek miracles. Some material miracle. Money and wealth, marriage, healing and health, salvation from hell, protection from some disaster or accident, etc. We need and seek God for something physical and material, not emotional or spiritual.

AnTennAs oR nO AnTenNaS

I've heard Kong and others say how their spiritual antennas were dulled, out of tune, are revved up, active, and the likes. They're speaking of their intuition, 3rd eye, psychic powers, 6th sense, and ESP level. I guess if their antennas were turned down or out of tune, they would be like me and everyday people who walk the streets without feeling any special vibes and such. Obviously, if their 6th sense, 3rd eye, and spiritual antennas are revved up and on high, they just might see dead people too. Look out Ms. Cleo and *The 6th Sense*! Personally, my spiritual antennas are cut off at the root. I have absolutely no ESP level at all. Thusly, I'm about as human and non-spiritual as one can get. I would never survive as a Buddhist or metaphysics. I can't feel ANYTHING except the weather and rain.

sPIRITUALITY vS. nATURAL rEALITY

People say I'm selfish and of course no one's perfect. Personally, I feel that I'm more pessimistic than anything else. If you can't win for losing, every job and man you meet changes into the span of Satan, and you're the queen of bad luck, you'd be pessimistic also! Besides, to want, desire, and need is human nature. You, of course, want God to help, bless, and heal you just like He did for someone else. I see absolutely nothing wrong with that. Myro feels that I take things for granted and overlook many of my blessings. Perhaps I do.

At the time of writing this, she was sharing a fully occupied apartment with many visitors and deeply longed for her own apartment all by herself. She wanted something not so elaborate but decent where she can focus, meditate, and pray in her privacy. A car that actually ran for longer than a week without pouring money into it and her business to take off. She pointed out how I have all the things she desperately longs for: a place of my very own, decent transportation, and a business. She questioned why should God give me anything more when I don't appreciate what He has already given me? Stating that in the spiritual as well as in the natural, if you take something I give you for granted and don't appreciate it, why would I give you something else.

Obviously she agrees with me to some extent in feeling that it's human nature to want, need, and desire what God can do for you. If He blessed you, or healed her, or prospered him, then why can't I get help? I need help too! I guess she was pointing out that her focus is on God and serving Him and in turn, expecting and waiting for Him to fulfill all of her needs. With the little she has and as much as she desires—wealth, a nice home, etc.,—she said she is very content and satisfied. Focusing on God and dwelling on Him takes her mind off of her wants, desires, and needs. She says after praying, seeking God, and even fasting, it gives her comfort and makes her feel better. I guess that's what people mean when they say that when you get saved you feel this wonderful joy, satisfaction, and completeness that no drug, drink, man/woman, car, job, house, or money can give you.

NOW, SomeThinG oF InTeresT 4 "nOrMal" PeopLe

I will say for fairness sake for those who are like me and quite a bit more material and human based; Myro, her sister, (who's into Wicca and Metaphysics and is currently not interested in Christianity) her friends, and even her cousin are all VERY spiritual people. They're quite intuitive and spiritual. Some metaphysics or devout Buddhists (who aren't Christian, and if I'm correct, don't exactly believe in some absolute God) are very in-tuned to their inner self and very spiritual. People like me on the other hand, wouldn't recognize some spiritual, intuitive, supernatural sign if it dropped into our lap. So just to be fair, for "normal" people who have no antennas, a bit more grounded, (unlike me who's mind ALWAYS drifts off in space and dreamland) and are on the natural, physical, human realm over the spiritual, mental, supernatural realm, we sometimes need something a bit more tangible and real.

Perhaps that seems very selfish, ungodly, unspiritual, and absolutely faithless, but perhaps you are so spiritual and intuitive, you can't quite understand us. Basically you've lost touch with the human experience. Jesus had more of a human experience than you. It's quite impossible for someone who is no longer in touch with the human experience to relate and understand us. They are too far-gone. They probably are a few notches below Christ. The worst part is; they don't even realize it.

I hear people say that they got saved and go to church to get close to God. They want to know and seek God. That's great and perhaps true, but that is definitely not everyone. It is usually those folks who have lost the human experience that say, "Shame on you for getting saved and going to church and stuff for ONLY hell insurance, a miracle, or whatever God can do for you! You should go to church and get saved solely for God and to get to know Him more."

Well sure, but why did you *really* decide to go to church or get saved in the first place? To stop using drugs, partying, and whoring around so you can dive into church, the Bible, prayer, and fasting? I can almost guarantee, your motive was as selfish as mine and anyone else's. Like Myro and all of her super spiritual intuitiveness, you directly needed Gods help and an immediate miracle! Thus you got saved, went to church, and perhaps even started praying. This, of course, is still selfish. "Please help me out of this problem/sickness/accident/evection/poverty/or what ever emergency. God, the only reason I'm even giving you more than 10 minutes of my time is because this problem is more than 10 minutes long." The one and only thing you're thinking about is God helping you also.

I'm sure since most people have selfish motives, you might be a bit more interested in God's salvation and hell insurance, God's help with your finances, health, and life, and Gods protection during these end times and days when all hell breaks out on the earth. Your motive for salvation and wanting God, I'm sure, is quite irreverent. I guess whatever your reason, selfish or otherwise, I'm sure God—and the angels—are very happy when you do FINALLY call and give Him the time of day in your life. Perhaps even after you get delivered and receive your miracle, you might even start going to church, praying, and even reading the Bible and living for God. Although I won't hold my breath.

NOT RELIGION BUT RESULTS

All of my life I always believed in stuff and still do. I'm not superstitious but I definitely believe in UFO's, ghosts, psychics, and other paranormal things. Call me naive, I'd call you skeptically blind when all of the evidence is out there. It's not my fault that many people are skeptics. I'm not some religious fanatic and I personally believe there is truth in every religion—and bull in each too. I'm not sure if I want to 100% follow any particular man made religion, however I will obey the one religion or church that produces results.

I've been in and out of churches all of my life. Black and white ones, big and small ones, but none actually produced personal experiences such as I have since I started going to this small little storefront one. Most were either too relaxing(a nice way to say very boring) and formal or they would sing loads of good music and shout a lot. Even when they would preach a good common sense message, it was lost in all of that shouting. Or I would fall asleep if it was too long and boring/formal. Although all of the messages and music was good, it wasn't quite like this little, storefront church. This preacher explained how to pray, grow, and get results. They would also prophesy and lay hands on you. I see many churches on TV do that, but the ones I go to or visit were either too big or too formal. They either did not believe in healing, anointing, and supernatural things of some sort and were very formal, or they were so big they couldn't effectively reach everyone.

I want to go to a huge amusement park or party, it's more stuff to go around and do. If I'm trying to take some personalized class, I want it small. A super big church, dance, or language class, is almost as effective as simply watching it on TV. If you want personalized attention and results in a class, the smaller the better. A small class is almost like having a tutor compared to a big class where the teacher doesn't even know your name. It's good if you skip and slack in class but if you are actually interested in learning that subject, like a gymnastic, dance, music, or language class, the smaller the better. For you could practice what you learned and actually get personal attention to improve your movements, music, or speech.

Some of the speakers would also talk practical talk. I went to several FREE psychics (I'm too cheap to pay for one unless I'm guaranteed it's legit and really works, but free, hey what's the loss) who would "reveal" things that were somewhat or basically accurate. They never answered or responded to a direct question, complaint, or situation I had lurking inside my head or was dealing with. I seem to get some accurate and direct form of answer to my questions or complaints that I may have with God through this church among other ways. For example, one question I asked was why would God give me such a stressful, unfair, job in Japan. At the next church visit, the pastor answered that question. He said how the devil can switch things up in the night and you end up with something TOTALLY different than you started with. I guess the story of my life.

I wanT instanT resuLtS toO

Myro first invited me to her church for some seminar after our all night conversation about her bad E experience and her first church experience. Compliments of her pizza delivery instant miracles, I wanted and needed some help so I went hoping to get these instant results too. This church teaches how to get and build a relationship with God to get the results you want in prayer. As one preacher said, "Learn how to gain access to Heaven's storehouse to get unlimited blessings of money, success, health, and happiness." I even called myself helping with promoting the church by making a flyer for people searching for results and the truth. The pastor wasn't that thrilled with what I wrote.

He simply told me to eliminate most of it and only post this:

> **TIRED OF BEING BROKE, BUSTED, and OUT?!**
> **DRAINED and at YOUR WITS END?! NEED a**
> **MIRACLE and RESULTS?!**
> **Harness the presence and power of Almighty GOD**
> **in your living room, situation and life!!**

If you are curious what all I wrote, here it is:

> **There are many churches, synagogues, temples, gatherings, mosques, and religions where you can chant, pray, meditate, conjure, dance, sing, and meet a guy or chick. Just make your selection and take your pick. There's one on every corner. If you want entertainment, cheap tricks, and a new date ... enjoy. If you want a change—for the better—and RESULTS, check us out. We're a little off the beaten path—spiritually and locationally. We're next to the Amish Dutch Country shopping center near Laurel. We're a small international gathering who can each testify AND verify miracles within every person's life.**

Financial breakthroughs and miraculous money out from nowhere. Blessings of cars when the drivers didn't even qualify and should have never received it! A massive 4+ bedroom estate in a good neighborhood from an apartment—when the family didn't even qualify for the smaller home. Calls for good paying jobs—from out of nowhere—when the people were unemployed or under-employed, and they didn't even send out their resume. Having business grow from being dormant with unexpected clients. Having sight restored after being legally blind. Miraculous healing! Walking with a cane on Wed. and being healed to walk normal by that Sunday!! Having a 60+pound table fall on a foot needing crutches, and less than 48 hours later, was practically able to throw the crutches out with not even having a fracture! People being freed from nightmares, unwelcome visions/visits, and attacks by unseen forces in the nights. Having a shield of protection upon them allowing them to miss bullets, survive car accident without a scratch, and even escape from being gang raped—by literally blinding the rapists! This is literally just the tip of the iceberg and the icing on the cake!!!

Perhaps it's off the beaten path, but it gets results! Not some extremist, money swindling, judgmental, church, but one open to anyone, any age, any race, any religion, any culture. A church open to humanity, to human kind— just as you are! No one's perfect. If you were, you would-n't need to read this because you don't have any problems in the first place. If you are like the rest of us— tired and at your wits end with one issue or problem after another and you've tried everything else, check us out. One peek never hurts nor costs anything.

Learn practical ways to HARNESS the POWER and PRESENCE of the CREATOR HIMSELF to bring and create FAVOR, BLESSINGS, and OPPORTUNITY in whatever situation you are currently facing and going through!!

To be honest, I actually never got around to posting neither flyer due to my extreme limited internet access. Thus, one of the reasons I check my e-mail less than once a week. I'm STILL waiting for a laptop—or even a desktop—which would allow me to use a normal word processing version with spell check and such, as well as unlimited internet access. Since I am still currently poor, I'll wait to buy one. Especially since that damn Best Buy had the nerve to deny me store credit for a laptop. How dare them! Until I get a decent computer with internet access and such, a whole lot of things will have to wait. Oh well.

One quick post-note as I FINALLY do my final edit eons later, I now have 2 laptops! Myro donated her 40-pound laptop to me, and I bought a Vaio for less than $400. I also now have DSL & a friend GAVE me his desktop which is good enough for my voice processor!

ROYAL SET UP!!

As I mentioned above, Myro first invited me to her church for some seminar after our all night conversation about her bad E experience and her first church experience. Compliments of her pizza delivery instant miracles, I wanted and needed some help so I went hoping to get these instant results too. While there, this prophet was visiting, and she gave everyone a prophecy. The prophet was quite accurate for Myro, Nancy, and me. The prophet said God would reveal Himself strong in my life starting that night, after giving a brief but accurate description of me. I, of course, was quite paranoid by what she meant. What was going to happen to me? Was He going to appear like a ghost in my room scaring me? Was He going to knock on my door and say, "hi?" What was I to expect? After all, I only wanted some miracles—preferably instantaneous—not spirits, angles, and ghosts roaming around me at night.

a cOnsTanT neGaTive

As you might have noticed, I'm very pessimistic. Even to the point if someone calls or needs to talk to me, I immediately think of the worst. Who died? What did *I* do? What did *I* do this time? Am I fired? OK, I'm too fat, short, American,..... so you're dumping me? It's always this cloud of doom floating—wondering who's going to die, are they going to write me up and fire me, or how many checks did I bounce this time and how far am I in the red? It is ALWAYS something negative. It's my immediate and first reaction. I'm very cordial, and try to be subtle and never tell anyone my initial gut feelings. Nonetheless, everyone seems to always notice how negative I am. My co-workers, boss, church, family, friends, et cetera. I don't even see it most of the time. I guess I'm more noticeable than I think or try to be.

sNeaK-iN booTy caLl

Well, later that night, compliments of Nancy, I was disgustedly swindled and trapped. I ended up EXTREMELY UNCOMFORTABLE sleeping on the floor after getting complained at for making too much noise because they wanted to sneak over some guy's house. I was told it was some get together but found out it was a sneak in booty call of sorts, at my car's expense. And Nancy was even upset at me over something stupid afterwards. I would definitely call that one of my most uncomfortable nights of torment, along with that wretched un-air conditioned bus ride through the dessert with screaming kids and flies. Oh and of course, my horrible bus ride from San Francisco when I sat on that p#ssy seat.

Wild D's hellified car sauna. And let's not forget the many other times when I was tricked by some A'hole or something. As with all of the other scenarios I was tricked into, I'll never do this again either.

I'm sure she too had enough that she'd never invite me out again also. I embarrassed her and perhaps even got the boy in trouble for making too much noise looking for the toilet. Obviously—like my lovely "friend" from New Orleans—he wasn't in any predicament to invite people over. If he invited them and they wanted to sneak in and enjoy each other's company, that's all well and good for them. She should have been upfront with me, and at least let me know what I was in for regarding sneaking in someone's house—while their parents were home.

When I worked at Disney, I invited many folks down. Of course, no one visited me. I even had free tickets, which I ended up giving away to a family around Christmas, since no one came down. I, however, did give folks a heads up regarding my living situation. I lived with a roommate, and there were 6 of us in an apartment. You would have to sleep on the sofa or floor. On top of that, you would need to sneak in. We weren't allowed outside guests, as I stated earlier in this book. If anyone caught you, we all would be endangered of getting kicked off of the program. I assume that once I told people that, not too many folks were still interested. Not to mention, most folks I know don't travel all that often, unlike me. I'll happily travel at the drop of a dime if I'm able to, as you can see.

Even with all of that trickery and harassment going on, I still felt more comfortable over the boy's house due to the fact that I wasn't alone in my room or anything. After all, it was 5 of us in a bedroom, what ghost would bother me in these conditions. Ghosts and nightmares seem to only bother you when you are alone. I also only had the luxury of sleeping when I could get comfy on the oh so lovely hard @ss floor. However, after everyone else fell asleep and I finally fell off to sleep, I had my first batch of unusual experiences with what I assume to be God.

FIRST DREAM AFTER BEING TRICKED

In my first dream, I dreamt I was sleeping inside that exact room, and above on the wall the street lights made a marquee sign moving across the wall saying something along the lines that "Christ was the only way." I had to look twice to make sure I wasn't hallucinating and this moving sign was being cast across the wall via only the street lamps. After I sat up to see if I was seeing what I thought I was seeing, I felt it was extremely unusual. I woke up right after that to realize I was only dreaming and the room was back the same again. In my next dream, there was this light from above in this dark room pulling me from my center as I vibrated. My tummy felt like I was going down in a roller coaster. I actually seemed to have lost my breath in that experience. I immediately woke up because it was quite unusual and very intense—enough for it to take my breath away. Time I laid my head back on my pile of clothes made into a pillow, it immediately happened a second time. Those were my first batch of odd experiences. I told the pastor's wife and she said it was amazing and was a message from God proclaiming Christ. I'm glad somebody thought it was amazing; I was quite terrified with it.

From then on, it only seems to get weirder, if you will. Perhaps more divine for some. It was from this point in my life, that unusual luck—which I am the QUEEN of BAD LUCK—and blessings starting occurring. Blessings such as; me getting unexpected money for school after they told me I didn't qualify for it, slipping through the insurance cracks, and even saving ware and tare on My Feather, and carpooling with a student who needed extra credit. The student even had a recording studio to video tape this Baltimore basketball game I needed for this school project. The students videotaped the game using their high quality digital camera—since my camera that I took some really great photos, including the I ♥ Lory , vanished with out a trace.

Unusual weird stuff started happening also. Such as when I sliced my hand closing the window, and it wasn't even hard to close. Not one piece of the glass was cracked. How do you slice your hand doing a mundane chore like using the remote, washing your hands, or closing the window?! My money also seemed to vanish.

frUgaL, noT cHeaP

People have the nerve to call me cheap. I'm not cheap. I'm poor so I must be very frugal. I am the extreme opposite of those stupid people who get a huge sum of money one day and a week later it's all gone—with not ONE responsible thing paid for. It's one thing to treat and reward yourself. I am definitely for that. No job, man, or anything/anyone else will do it for me. Everyone needs to be treated. There is, however, a VERY definite difference between treating yourself, and wasting your money. If you spend all of your money on stupidness, gambling, shinny cars, rings, and flashy stuff that's ignorant. In two years, 90% of that stuff will be worthless. I guess I'm like a Russian Jew or Japanese businessman; I invest in things that will grow in value, not just stupidness to waste my money.

When I finally got a job in Japan paying something, I still lived frugally. While everyone else was enjoying life and getting to know each other at the beach, bars, and such, I paid off my bills, paid on my student loan, sent money home, and invested. I know Bruce wondered why I was so cheap—always calling me a cheap Jew—as he bought a rack of stuff for that small apartment. Surely he could afford it and probably had no bills or debt to pay off. In fact, I spent my money to incorporate my non-profit and pay the IRS non-profit filing fee. I did buy two things. I bought a radio with a mini disc solely for an interview I did. I also bought a phone with an answering machine because I wanted to record my own message in English and the phone I had only used Japanese. Outside the fact that clothes were made very small, I didn't want to waste my money on anything unnecessary.

I'm VERY thrifty. After all, I have to live like a pauper. I must stretch $100 for all of my groceries—since I have no more food stamps—toiletries, cleaning supplies, cat food, transportation, Starbucks, and more. How do I do it? Very thriftily. However over $400 vanished—like my camera—out of my account. The statement said I used $400 on Starbucks, Wal-Mart (which I only bought a water pick $30, panty liners 99¢, and about $20 worth of stuff), the $1 Store, and eating out. Perhaps it's magic. Perhaps it's like slicing my finger while closing the window, and when I say slice, I mean three cotton balls full of blood slice. Perhaps it's in the same place my disposable camera and missing pairs of socks are. Like David Copperfield, it vanished like magic.

Also, as I watched this TV evangelist (who many try to throw off the air because his show focuses on faith seeds and tithing) 3 wood chip men appeared on the wood on my door. Because it produced good results, I always look at him. He said there was a demon personally assigned to attack my finances and other areas of my life. Me?! I'm poor as a church mouse, as my Dad says. He might as well assign himself to some homeless guy. What an idiotic demon!

1st WeD. thIs sumMeR

The first Wednesday off since my new work schedule, I went to Bible study. The pastor just so happened to talk about ways to go far in health, <u>wealth</u>, success, and life. It was just like the faith seed I sewed to get a decent job and out of debt when I lived in Va. The first Wed. back in church, God had a personal and specific message just for me. Later, the pastor prayed over everyone. When he got to me, he prophesied and prayed for me to have organization, discipline, and focus. This is something that I REALLY struggle with. I've been praying and asking for discipline, focus, organization, and financial help.

Later, pastor explained how you must deposit or put something in before you can withdraw something out. I remember Myro used this analogy regarding finding a date en-route to seeing the play Daniel back when she first told me about her instant miracles from God and took me to this church. I explained how busy I was as the excuse of why I never got around to calling any of the few numbers I received from the different guys I had met. "If a guy gives you his number and you only call him once in 2 months, most likely he'd forget about you." I said they most likely have my phone number and flyer. She said that being that I'm never home nor do I answer the phone when I am home; they probably did call and just didn't leave a message. Many people get confused with my voice mail message. They may think it's a business line or my work number, or feel that it's a wrong number all together. Nonetheless, they don't leave a message. She said way back then—the same way in the spiritual as in the natural—you must put in some effort and time to get anything back. If you like them, call then. Actually try having a phone conversation to see if they have enough sense to speak for over 10 minutes and not repeat the same 4 questions.

People say that you can only withdraw and take out blessings if you deposit time and tithes and offerings. I will vouch that when I did do that 21-day prayer campaign and sewed a faith seed (I don't even think I paid it off) that in less than a year I got my prayer answered. Even if this TV evangelist is a scam, snake charmer, or Satan himself, God—or somebody—listens to him. I did it in 1999 and in 2000 I got results.

DEATH & LOVE HAVE NOTHING TO DO WITH EACH OTHER

I always hear people saying, "God said this" or "God told me that." How is this? Does He call you and talk via a phone? Does He send you a letter or e-mail? Is it in your dreams, which is the most believable to the average layman? When you fellowship and spend quiet and intimate time with God does He knock on your door and hang out with you in your room? Do you both sit together and have tea? Perhaps these are haphazard insane questions, but the average person—Christian and non—probably would like to know. People would say "God said this" but I never quite had that type of conversation with Him. It was always one sided. Dear God, thank you, forgive me, and please help. I think this church showed me how to get a relationship. This relationship is totally different than being religious or saved just to go to heaven.

I'm sure anyone who has a relationship with God has experienced many conversations with Him. I heard this speaker on some radio show compare conversations with the Holy Spirit to A/C vents in your house. The more worldly you are, the more the vents would be clogged and closed. The more spiritual you are, the cleaner and more open the vents are. Therefore granting you clear and good conversations with God. Thusly, I would assume a lot of Christians must have many chats with God. For me, this is all very new.

Unlike many others who seem to talk to God daily, I never had unusual chats in my head before. This experience was quite unusual and slightly disturbing. I mean, I hoped I wasn't going mad. Perhaps lunatics who normally talk, argue, and debate with themselves, feel quite at home with this. Lucky for me, I'm sane (contrary to what many jokesters might say). I assume only lunatics argue and have debates with imaginary folks or demons in their heads. Or perhaps very spiritual folks with sharp antennas or powerful meta-physicists with their spirit guides would have successful 2-way conversations within the spirit realm or God. I guess similar to how you would talk with another person. Perhaps this is all very normal for some, however for me, this was quite the opposite. I am not super religious, a median, psychic, metaphysics, nor am I crazy. This conversation was quite the event for me I would say. It's like the icing on the cake of all of the weird and unusual stuff that started to happen.

I woke up one morning/afternoon—I'm a late sleeper—and nothing seemed unusual. It wasn't raining, no earthquake, no nightmare, I don't know what triggered this chat with what claimed to be God inside my mind. Just out of the blue something deep inside my mind, within my deepest thoughts, started this conversation about love. What the hell?!?! I was fully awake and listened as it answered my questions. I have no idea how the chat started but I do remember where I took it. "If you are God, then why did you take my dad and Swautch? Where is my disposable camera with the important film and the I ♥ Lory photos? Why am I single and lonely? Why am I broke? Why do you refuse to answer my prayers? Better yet, why do you let all of these horrible and evil things go on in the world? If you are really God, what type of God are you to do such mean things? Why do you take little kids and babies, if you speak of love so much? Why do you let all of these people die?!?!" He claimed death and love have nothing to do with each other. Excuse me?! I COMPLETELY DISAGREE with that. To me, death, life, and love have everything to do with each other. He repeated that comment several times and kept throwing out how He died for people.

I repeated my battery of questions to Him. Then He said how He came down and died for people. I said, "Well if you are really God, you are supposed to be everywhere, including on earth. If you are God, then you already exist in the spirit world so the most that coming to earth in the flesh, and dying for us was to you, was a major inconvenience. (This is before the Passion of the Christ came out) You already existed. How is dying for us when you are already supposed to be here on earth—omnipresent—show love. It just shows how you were willing to be inconvenienced for man?" He said that I never read the Bible (in which He was quite right) and that I had no idea what I was talking about. That I should read the Bible before I blindly talk.

He said that He loved people and me. He claimed that my questions and prayers were stupid. That I should pray for diligence, focus, etc., instead of material things that I could buy whenever I do become focused and diligent. He said that is just like someone praying for a nice dress or a pizza to eat and then it's gone instead of knowledge and a good job so that they will have a continuous flow of money to buy many nice clothes and all types of food, including pizza. He said my requests were silly and that I was a mess, which is why I was single. He said that I was lazy and had unlimited access to the gym, music practice rooms, and computer lab. Why was it that I was too lazy to go the gym and practice rooms yet complained that my prayers for weigh loss were never answered? "What's stopping you from typing and finishing your works and books? What's stopping you from exercising? Do you have organization and money now to take care of yourself, let alone a family? No, then whose fault is it? Did I say be lazy, procrastinate, misplace your camera (like you do with everything else, lose it, them blame someone) eat like a pig, and get nothing done? I don't think so. So why do you blame Me for not finishing your book or losing weight, when you, with all your free will, sit around and lazily do nothing?" Of course, I had a rebuttal for that and tried to plead my case, but He had a very good point. I had access to those things but never got around to going. Something ALWAYS came up and hindered me, and thusly it never got done.

I was quite skeptical since I do have a very active imagination. How can I be sure that I was really talking to God and it's not my overactive imagination? "You could be the devil pretending to be God. How can I be sure that you are God and not the devil or that it's not my imagination?" He then pressured me to get out of bed and read His book. I said, "Why don't you call me now and once the phone rings, prove to me it's you by letting me hear your voice over the phone. Or send me an e-mail." This must have been stupid to Him. He said, "Why should I use the phone? Do I need a computer or phone to communicate to people? Am I human or am I God? Why don't you use the computer to finish your book and phone to make your business phone calls? How dare you ask me to do such a stupid thing as to make a phone call to you as if I'm unable to communicate any other way. And you actually think I need a computer to write a letter when I created the whole universe and my Bible with just a thought. Please, why don't YOU get up and read MY book. Why would I type some measly letter on a computer when I created an entire collection of books, 66 of them, for you to read? So get up and read, since you blindly speak on what you know nothing on. Get out of bed!"

Of course I ignored this command assuming it was still my overactive imagination. I was just getting entertained with my active imagination and still hoping that I wasn't going mad. Then He said, "If you don't get up now, I will have to …" Even though I was still skeptically questioning how real and accurate this experience was, I wasn't going to play with my life. In the event it was real, I got the heck up out of bed before He rebuked His wrath upon me. He told me to go open the Bible and read His word since I didn't know what I was speaking about. The first page I opened to when I randomly opened His book was **Acts 2**. It's in that book and that section that it speaks of the Holy Spirit landing on the apostles and them being able to do miracles. To me that was quite a sign and confirmation since this voice inside my head kept saying that He was the Holy Spirit, the third part of God's trinity. God the father, God the Son—Jesus, and God the Holy Spirit. I told the co-pastor about this and she confirmed it was indeed the Holy Spirit and many people, including her, have similar conversations.

SpiriT = minD, souL = HIM, & bodY = fleSh/M&M's

God explains stuff to me very well. He explains how that everything in the material world has a duplicate in the spiritual.

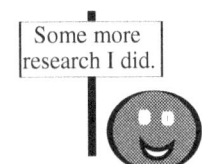

Coincidently, I heard about this interesting theory today, which basically confirms what God explained to me several years ago! I also just so happened to be editing this particular section of my book today. This theory is very new and quite confusing to me, however very interesting. For you physics and science buffs, there is this amazing theory (which I'm sure you are familiar with) by David Bohn. I believe it's called "quantum holographic universe principle". Physicists' hope that the findings of this surprising holographic universe principle will be a clue to the ultimate theory of reality. (Scientific America, August 2003) From what little I could understand, I believe it tries to explain psychic powers, ESP, time travel, black holes, parallel universes, and many popular metaphysical topics. The physical universe is nothing but matter and energy.

Between Einstein, some other scientists, and some discovery in 1982 in some French university; David Bohn concluded that their theories are just like a hologram. A hologram of, lets say a cat, can be cut up, and unlike a photo, STILL show and produce a **complete image** of a cat, and not half a cat like a photo would do. He also said a mouse brain could be unraveled and dissected and would start forming new brain cells. Somehow this all ties into the fact that:

- There is some connected material, string, (I guess similar to the String Theory) or something that connects every person, place, and thing—and even different time periods throughout history. How this connected thing—perhaps God—is like the Blob or a giant bubble connecting all matter, past and future. This is why psychics can perhaps know the past, future, what's going on in China, Russia, with their mom, son, dog, on the moon, Mars, Pluto, whatever. Distance and time would not be a problem, because like God, this thing connects all of space and all time periods. This "divinely" connected thing is in each and every piece of matter in the material universe—and thus all people ARE REALLY CONNECTED to each other. I guess this would be a problem for bigots who hate minorities, feminists who hate men, people who hate animals, or even atheists who hate God. If it's a part of you, then you firstly, hate yourself. And also, unlike liposuction or some nose job, you can never chop it off and get rid of it. For it's a part of every cell and atom in your body so now what can you do?

- Perhaps this "quantum holographic universe" theory can offer some scientific basis—and some more understanding and enlightenment on the trinity concept. For this "quantum holographic universe" theory acts and behaves like God. The Torah, Gospels, and other religions know God as eternal, all knowing, and all-powerful. This "quantum holographic universe" theory supposedly connects ALL physical matter in this material universe—as well as throughout the ages. Thus offering hopeful scientists a way to not only better understand ESP, but other galaxies. If simple humans can know what happens in some other place, time, or person, then why wouldn't God who's WAY MORE SKILLED at using His brain, psychic powers, and 3rd eye?! I.E.—**all knowing**. Besides, what other figure, creature, or being known, existed from the beginning to the end of time? I.E.—**eternal**. This "quantum holographic universe" theory even offers scientists chances to better understand and attempt time travel. The fact that everyone knows God is <u>all-powerful</u> does not need to be mentioned here. Besides, this theory offers no support regarding God's omnipotent ability.

- This "quantum holographic universe" theory also sounds like God being omnipresent! This is where the concept of the trinity could possible have some minute form of scientific validity. If this "quantum holographic universe" theory covers the ENTIRE material universe— basically all of existence—and it says that all people that ever lived (throughout the ages)as well as every other piece of matter is connected (perhaps to God) then why would it be that difficult for God, who is EVERYWHERE ALL AT ONCE, to hang out inside humans as the Holy Spirit? If you waste ice water in your gym bag, that liquid pouring off of your clothes is STILL H2O. Why would the liquid soaked through your clothes turn into coffee or something? Water can still be in your water bottle AND also soaked and dripping off your clothes, it is STILL water. And just like this water, and this "quantum holographic universe" theory, God should easily be able to manifest Himself inside humans if He ALREADY is EVERYWHERE in the first place. How can a God/AKA/the Holy Ghost who covers all of time and space, have difficulty living inside humans who are nothing but a microscopic piece of this material universe?! As for God becoming flesh as Christ. That should be even easier. If He can simultaneously live inside ALL humans as the Holy Ghost; then how much easier would it be to simply manifest Himself into flesh via some virgin and live as ONE

222

person?! Seems like living as one person and being in only one place at one time is 1000 times easier than being inside every human simultaneously.

- On top of this, if God—like this "quantum holographic universe" theory—transcends time and space, it would almost make it IMPOSSIBLE for Him NOT to somehow be inside, influence, and touch every piece of matter. If a slug and street thug can leave a trail of slime and evidence on everything they touch and everywhere they go, why couldn't God leave His "fingerprint" on this material universe?! In fact, one of the websites seems to have some Christian, or at least divine Godly slant. And coming from a scientist, this is borderline blasphemy. That's almost like a pastor going to some satanic ritual or an atheist teaching Sunday School!

- And even just as interesting, researchers "found" the duplicate/ghost/copy of matter. They said that when they tried to split atoms in some super big magnetic machine, particles would form. Scientists always thought nothing existed inside or in between subatomic particles. They now discovered that there is this type of invisible, ghost, exact duplicate particle existing in the middle. This ghost/duplicate particle is inside ever piece of matter.

To me, all this sounds like something right off Star Trek and the Sci-Fi Channel! Just FYI, NASA allegedly is supposed to be working with some scientists to build warp speed, space travel machines using these concepts so I guess it must have some form of validity. Again, I interestingly just heard of this concept today—and I also just so happened to be editing this particular section of my book today. This theory is very new to me and quite confusing, however very interesting. It also fits exactly with this very conversation I had with God SEVERAL YEARS AGO. Go figure. Check out these few sites I found online.

www.science-fair.spiritworld.info &
www.science-fair.spiritworld.info/natures-mind.html

Back to my point!

Well anyway, God explains how that everything in the material world has a duplicate in the spiritual. There is me in the flesh and Casper the friendly me in the spirit realm. The real me is the spirit part. My mind, thoughts, emotions, feelings, desires, dislikes, etc., are all part of the spirit. It is the spirit that actually sees the images that my eyes capture, hears the sounds that my ears capture, feel the pain, taste the flavor, and smell the fragrances. It is my spirit that holds my personality, baggage, and emotions. It is the Casper the friendly me inside a candy/flesh coating. You know like M&M's, chocolate inside a candy-coated shell.

He explained how it is your spirit housed inside your candy-coated flesh that has this space for God to enter and live. Like an invisible, life size, hallow, plastic mold of you or me. Before you are saved and ask Jesus in your life, the hallow, invisible, plastic mold is an empty vase or vessel just waiting for occupancy. Once you're saved, Jesus enters and fills the space inside the hallow mold of you.

He said He gives you 100% of Him. The reason you don't feel His power is that you are dirty. People speak of growing in Christ. He explained it's not literally a growth. You don't get 20% the first week and after you complete some prayers and rituals you get another 30%. Once you successfully pass and elevate all of your spiritual classes, within a few years of hard work, you finally get 100%. No, you get 100% of God—complete and all at once.

The more you grow in Christ, the more dirt washes off you. The more you backslide, the more dirt gets on you. The more dirt and sin you wash off, the more He can shine through. Give Him you and once He got you, He got you. Once God has you, He has you. Who can fight against God? They may try any and everything against you, but if He got you, God takes over any battle and situation and shines right through you. The clean, shiny, washed off Casper the friendly you. And again, if He got you, who can be against you?

aN activE imaginaTioN getS acTivE conversaTioN

This is something I believe He said in response to why I personally hear Him and He responds to me often. It seems that He talks to me seemingly more compared to others. Seemingly, even more than people way more knowledgeable in spiritual matters than me. I asked if there was something I did or wrote or if that lady prophet put a special anointing on me to have conversations with Him.

He said that it was nothing in particular I did, or that someone gave, or put on me. He is always waiting patiently for people. "Waiting for them to open the door to their heart and give Me the time of day and chance. I came all the way down here to die, not just to save you from hell, but also to actually have a personal relationship with you. Unfortunately, most folks put Me on the back burner until things happens and stuff hits the fan, and then they remember Me and pray for My last resort miracles and grace." He said that I was curious and inquiring so He revealed himself to me.

I made this Dear God list of things I needed help with. I haphazardly threw on the list "knowledge about God and a relationship with Him" out of obligation. I was somewhat indifferent in the matter. I just kept getting bombarded with, "You need Him" and, "Seek Him first" that I felt that if I didn't throw that in my Dear God list, He wouldn't answer it.

I tried to explain to people how I was very aware of His existence but He was big and distant not some personal friend or God. His power was very evident but as this massive, powerful force. Obviously people who speak to Him or even go to church and are very religious couldn't relate and had absolutely no idea with what I was speaking about. On the other hand, any person—religious or not—who isn't this super holy roller, should easily be able to relate.

Obviously unconditional love for God and your common man is much easier said than done. The second someone becomes a jerk, that love changes. And as soon as what you prayed for or someone or something you care about is hurt, sick, or dies, you quickly turn on God. Most people quickly boast of how they love and know God. I wonder if they talk to Him a lot and if He actually talks back to them too. If so, then obviously they must really know and have some relationship with Him. I feel people say this because they are supposed to, just like everyone knows that God is love or the sky is blue. You can easily say that you know and love God and that you know He is love, but when stuff happens, do you still love Him and do you still actually believe that He's love, or is He some evil, unfair, God?

I—as well as any intelligent, non-atheist, human being—know that God is massive, all knowing, and very powerful. I understand that He is love, Jesus died for us, and everything else you were taught in Sunday school as a kid. Even a parrot can recite and repeat words. How real are these words though? It is one thing to aimlessly recite prayers, Bible verses, and what you are expected to say and know, compared to what you actually believe. When stuff happens, danger falls, or you think this is the end, what do you say or do? Does that repetitive prayer or verse actually make you feel better or do you solely shout, "Oh God, please help!!" Usually followed by, "If you help me this time, I promise I'll go to church and pray." You know, some lie along those lines. Of course, at the time you're serious.

That's if you actually have enough thought and time to say and think that. Of course, no one is ever in their right mind when they think they're about to die, their car is stolen, or any emergency.

To me, God was like lightning. You know it exists, you see its power and might, but it's not some fuzzy rabbit or cat that you can snuggle up to and love. Is lightning—and God—powerful, fearsome, and huge? Yes. Are they snuggly, loveable, and consoling when you're depressed, lonely, or need someone to talk to or a shoulder to cry on? For the average person, I don't think so. Now of course, if you're super holy and live next door to God and have lunch with Him daily, sure. The average person knows God is this omnipresent, all knowing, extremely powerful creator and force who made them, died for them, loves them, and has a battery of prayers and Bible verses that they can memorize and recite.

Perhaps because He was so distant to me, He revealed Himself strongly to me in a way that I could actually get to know Him and that I could personally relate to Him. I guess He revealed Himself in a way to appear closer to me and less distant. He said that all of the things I needed and asked for would only be possible through Him so He had to reveal Himself to me first in order to work on all of the other concerns and problems I have. God doesn't choose the richest, smartest, or most holy. He chooses a dedicated few. I guess like they say, it's not the quantity but the quality. And we all know what the U.S. Marines say, a few good men. This verse in the Bible popped in my head. 1 Corinthians 1:26-29, "My dear friends, remember what you were when God chose you. Most of you were not wise by human standards. Most of you were not influential people nor came from important families. But God chose the foolish things of this world to put the wise to shame. He chose the weak things of this world to put the powerful to shame. What the world thinks of as worthless, useless, and nothing at all, is what God has used to destroy what the world considers important."

I decided to ask God during one conversation if He talks to everyone just as much as me. The answer I heard was this. "I came to you the way you needed me to come. Some only need subtle thoughts or My answers to come to them through others. (TV, pastors, the Bible, other people, et cetera) Some need me to come through even stronger. To come to them via angel visits and straight up visions and visitations. For you, visions, visitations, and audible conversations is a little disturbing and much. On the other hand, messages through others are too subtle for you. You are very poor at picking up hints and noticing things. My conversations to you are what you need to relate to me and make me your personal friend, savior, protector, and confidant. The more I talk, the less distant I am to you. The closer I get, the more you can relate, rely, love, and trust me.

All anyone has to do is ask. I patiently wait. 'God, show and reveal yourself to me. I actually want to get to know you. I want to know who and what you really are. I want to know you for more than some far off cloud or burst of lighting and electricity or some far off source of powerful energy. I want you to reveal yourself as the loving, protecting, faithful friend you are, not just hell insurance.' For this relationship and level of closeness will determine your safety, protection, and kingdom access compared to isolation, desolation, and sole survival when all hell breaks out on this planet."

EnTrancE tO God's waRehouSe

After watching several TV evangelists speak about the same topic, transformation and changing your mind, I started thinking about success and access to God's unlimited warehouse—which will supply all of your needs to unlimited health, wealth, happiness, and success. This is what the Holy Spirit said to me.

"I am not a Jeanie in a bottle/Bible. Do and live in sin, shut Me up inside the Bible, and when stuff happens, 'Oh God, pray and open the Bible!' Then poof and all is well. 'Oh thanks so much God, now get back inside this Bible until I need you again.' And then you close the Bible up until the next emergency." God is not some AAA God.

"The only time you'll help is if it would be totally rude and mean if you did-n't. For instance, if you don't hold the door for someone with a huge package or do a nice gesture as a thank you if they do something nice for you. Don't DARE let it be an inconvenience for you to help someone, such as give up a good parking space to be nice. What's the chance of that? Slim to none. And yes, many people are like that, but I am not. Remember My first and most important commandment above all other laws and commandment. Love Me first with all you heart and love your neighbor as you love yourself.

"You put out less than 50% effort and want 100% results. No! Not in nature, not in history, not in life! Everything costs, even salvation. Outside of Me dying for you, you must do more than just believe—for even Satan believes in Me—but you must also inconvenience yourself and change from your old, comfortable, sinful ways and repent. You will die in the wilderness if you don't change and transform. After all, I came and died to be with you and have a relationship with you, not just to be shut up in a Bible only to be called when stuff happens.

"I came to give you prosperity, health, happiness, and a life more abundant. I died in vain if the only thing a Christian becomes is a broke, lowly, human. Even pagans live better than that! You're an embarrassment to Me and to Christianity when you don't improve and stay broke and beneath the levels of decency and progress. But you can only progress once you leave the wilderness of your sin. And you must change and transform to leave that wilderness and enter My prom-ise—the land of promise, wealth, health, and happiness.

"For not even mortal man will help a person and give them money, marriage, a business, and the likes, and not demand their loyalty. What's in it for them? For if a guy gives a lady some money, and so forth, and she spends it and ditches him, then he wasted his money, trust, feelings, and time on someone who only wanted to use him for success, money, or what have you. Any human with 5 brain cells would only help someone when they have—at some minimum level—a guarantee that the person would be loyal to some extent. For in that case, they could give their money and goods to just anyone.

"If mortal man has enough sense to do this, surely I, who created existence, have enough since to hold back My blessings and promise. I'll hold back until I know that when a person gets My promise—access keys to heavens storehouse and the promise land—that they are loyal to My word and Me. That no matter how much life, the devil, or whatever shakes them up, like Job, they would never leave. That they are firmly planted into Me. It is then, and only then, when you are so deep rooted into Me that I'll take you out of the wilderness and into my promise. Otherwise you'll live and die in your sins, lies, and old ways out in the wilderness. Only a fool would do otherwise.

"I love you more than you can understand and conceive but I won't give you anything here. You're not rooted, you're wishy washy, and not loyal. You, and people like you, want everything for free. You all want the "magic gift shop robot God" to serve you, but you won't serve anyone, except by force. You all curse and complain way too much and your sinful flesh must die and be transformed before you can get near any key to my storehouse.

"I want you to come here into my promise. I want to bless you abundantly because I love you and you have a lot to offer people. You're very special and everyone—from animals and kids to old people and CEO's—like you. Your personality is great. Your attitude is bad and full of sin. I can't be near sin. I'll end up destroying it, and you along with it. I need to be with you and near you, for you to get privileged access to enter My warehouse. For you can't go into My storehouse without Me, for I AM the warehouse! For you to come near Me you must be changed. You can't bring your old, sinful, flesh nature near Me without getting destroyed.

"You wonder why I'll leave all of you Christians in the wilderness so long. First of all, I'd be a fool to give you access without your loyalty. Secondly, I'd destroy you. You would get destroyed once you came near Me. I can't be near your old sinful nature. I love you. I died for you. But for your own good (and anyone with common sense) you'd be in that wilderness for life. You won't progress one inch toward My promise until you change, transform, and get rid of that sinful, rotting, flesh and become new in Me. Once you transform and become new in Me, then, '*Welcome to your land of promise, here is your personal set of keys to My storehouse. Help yourself.*' For by then, like Job, you're not going anywhere.

"I will provide for you while you are in the wilderness. That's My job as your father. I'll protect you, that's My job as your God. The Israelites shoes and clothes were in tact and fine for 40 years. They always ate and drank. I kept them safe, with food, shelter(a tent), protected, and clothed, but they never progressed. They never even got a new pair of shoes, for 40 years! I made sure they had shoes and clothes; I stopped the material's aging process. But you can guarantee, they did not get 1 new pair of shoes nor did they step 1 toe into that land I promised them. Why? They refused to change, repent, obey, and serve me. Thusly, they lived and died in their sin, lies, and lack, out in the wilderness. And the 2 that did transform and change entered that promise land. Read the book, it will tell you the whole story."

thE Rock

Today at church a guest pastor talked about evangelicals, which I never studied on. He spoke mostly of the church but he did mention a major key and coincidence—time management! Anyone who knows me for more than a day know how unorganized I am and how horrible I manage my time. As always, I was running late and God was really getting on my case for some unknown reason. After all, I'm always late. At church the guest pastor spoke of respect for God's house, the man of God in charge of the house, among many other things—including coming to church on time.

He began his sermon on time management and how it's important to keep yourself productive and busy and not just sit around and get nothing accomplished. He particularly mentioned how if he had just 1 minute to wait in line or at lunch, he'd read a self-help book and now he's getting a small New Testaments to read. He also mentioned how several well known pastors—among millions of other writers—would write a book in whatever time allotted to them, not wasting even one moment. And how if a writer sold a million $10 books he'd make $10,000,000 (ten million dollars, I had to actually count the zeros cause there are so many). The entire message was on being productive, making good choices, and managing your time. The last part was kind of confusing though.

Well this interesting thought popped into my head. After the guest pastor spoke about respecting God, your church, arriving on time, being productive with your time, and even used the example of the book (all of which I have issues with: time, tardiness, and being focused to finish this and another book) he answered my question. He actually spoke over my head and I really didn't quite understand so I just sat there and listened. It wasn't 'til dinner that God urged me to write this and reminded me how it actually answered my question, without me even understanding the answer. In Matthew 16:17-20 and Isaiah 51:1 it speaks of a rock and God. The pastor explained that the rock was Jesus and that the Christian church was build on Him.

He explained that we/I am not just a nobody. Some nobody that aimlessly and worthlessly exists. I am special, created in God's image, and a chiseled piece of God off His rock. You know the saying, a chip off the old block. He said that Rock(Christ) and His word is here to make you destiny bound. I am a piece of Christ but I am nowhere near finished. I am under construction and I am a work in progress. I am a piece of God's Ultimate Rock (Christ) being chiseled and molded into a final and ultimate piece of work. That I am being built. I am also being established by God and when someone is established and self-sustaining, they are wanting or needing of nothing. You aren't that welfare neighbor—like me—begging for an egg, oil, or milk. You are self sustaining and anything you need you are more than able to get even before you run out of the supply you currently have.

Now I always heard from childhood that God is love, we are all children of God regardless of your race or religion, and God is everywhere. So hearing this Rock that I, and every other piece of humanity, is being chiseled from, didn't sound all that different. It was, however, that not everyone is part of God. The chat in my head with God is this. Even though every human is created in His ultimate image and likeness, we are not all in Him nor is He in all of us. He loves everyone regardless of race, religion, creed, sex, or whatever (that's why He came down in the flesh and died for us, so He could have a relationship with us, not just "hell insurance"). Everyone has the chance to be saved and He wants a relationship with all of us, but not everyone is in Him nor is He in all of us. Not everyone is part of this special anointing. This is a special anointing in Him and through Him for grace and protection.

aN aNOINTING of pROTECTION

This must be why some people seem to be able to go to war and in the mist of danger and return with only a scratch. (Like me? Not sure.) Others can't seem to go down the street without ending up in the hospital. Some seem to have all types of miracles, opened doors, and slip through each and every crack, even if they are not super religious. Others like me, must work hard for absolutely everything they get. God said that He loves everyone and looks over their life even when they are far from Him, are atheists, or don't even know Him, but it is only through grace, not obligation. It is only the chosen that have His special anointing.

Breakthroughs and allocations that others seem to work so hard for and never quite get (such as myself), drops easily and quickly into the lap of those anointed people that God is with and they are actually with Him (maybe this is my problem—perhaps it's a 2-way effort). "It is through My grace and their loyalty that I bless them and they prosper in health, wealth, and success." And it is through those select people that can—and do—make a difference in all aspects and areas of life. They make positive uplifting differences in life even if it is not through a particular sect or denomination of Christianity—perhaps like Rosa Parks.

It is those chosen people that can make a huge, positive, impact in life that have the special anointing. For it is also those folks that usually need that special anointing of protection. For the devil works overtime to not just discourage them and have them fall away by any means necessary, but to also ruin and get rid them so the work that they personally would do, would be halted. For if something happened to an uplifting and positive speaker, researcher, teacher, or entrepreneur, then their venture and business would never happen. If their business, class, or invention, would impact millions, it would be in the *powers that be* best interest to rid them—and all traces of them—so their lovely message would never interfere with *their* plans. But greater is He that is in you and me, than he (Satan) that rules this earth! For the created (Satan) can never be greater than that which created it (GOD).

WHAT AN IDIOTIC DEMON!!!

I know there's a personal attack on me. Why, I don't know. What idiot would need to go out of their way, in the natural/material or spiritual realm to personally attack and keep me broke and unsuccessful? Like the unusual spiritual happenings earlier in this book talking about a demon personally assigned to my broke-ness to the 3 woodchip men appearing on my door. They might as well assign themselves to a crack head or homeless man. I have no money, clout, and no one listens to me. Why are they personally interested in harassing me?!?!

The funniest thing is that I'm sure you've read how I feel like the curses of hell and earth are upon me. The most retarded and insane things and events keep happening to me and it ALWAYS seems that I just can NEVER win and end up successful no matter how many struggles I go through and how often I lose! I just can't win for losing. Seems like there is a constant cloud of bad luck and doom upon me. Most people (except Anna, she'd happily rub my bad luck in my face) think I'm over reacting and making things up. Perhaps I am being dramatic a bit, but you yourself can see my constant streak of horribly bad luck. You can read the mounds of chaotic things that keep happening to me, and insane situations I keep getting myself into. How I just CAN'T WIN for losing!

For example, I mentioned above how I gashed my finger open soaking up three cotton balls full of blood simply by closing the window. You would think I cut myself on a knife or glass. Another example is how my gym clothes magically moved down 15 plus lockers and mysteriously appeared in another locker to be cut off and held hostage. No one, including the employees and myself, figured that one out.

Also, a few weeks ago I went down the country to visit my family after picking up some things from Swautch's family. I stayed the weekend, and before I returned, I paid my respects to my grandparents, uncle, and others at the family plot. I said hello and talked a bit. I then asked my uncle what he said or did to my dad since it was only one year from my uncle's death that daddy died. My dad supposedly started talking to him and drinking again. After I left I got into my car to drive home. I went to clean the windshield and the stupid windshield wiper handle broke when I pulled it toward me to wash my window. Now I've used this lever as well as the light/high beam lever a million times. Why would it decide to snap this time? And isn't that a very difficult piece to break? My cup holder via Kong, sure. My delicate door (which another geo owner told me breaks easily) breaking from misuse via a moron, sure. A windshield wiper handle? How unusual is that!?

In fact, that whole weekend was something. It was forecasted to be heavy rain the entire weekend. How great, My Feather has such suspension problems that the mechanic wouldn't perform my alignment. Of course he probably wanted to squeeze money from me like a sponge. A road trip on wet roads would be havoc on my dainty feather. However it was quite hot and sunny the entire day. I went shopping after I left Swautch's family, then finally made my way to my dad's estate. Once there, my aunts, Tony, and I even went out to dinner. The ground and car was wet when we left the cafe. The radio reported twisters that night, however I only saw the remnants of the wet ground. That entire weekend was nice, until it was time to drive home. Again the forecast was for thundershowers for the entire route to DC.

With my lovely broken wiper handle, and the eternally long roads of 20+ miles each until you get to an open gas station, I figured I was truly in for some bad karma. I was, of course, quite upset and irritated at the attack on my car. It appeared to start raining the entire way, and of course, every gas station was closed. I passed five closed stations on the 30-mile stretch to simply get to the main intersection—and the only open gas station on a Sunday night. Let's not mention that it was pitch dark. I am driving on a 2-lane country road with no street lights, stores, or apparent civilization. When I finally arrived at the station, I really didn't know what to do. I mean, they were simply cashiers and sandwich makers, not mechanics. God kept telling me to not worry; it would be fine. I ended up using a pencil, which I currently still use since I have yet had the chance nor money to fix her.

God brought it to my attention saying how desperate Satan is, being that the only thing he can do is harass me with a broken wiper handle or my gym locker. Satan is obviously searching and picking at straws for ways to harass and get me. I assume God and the angels are working overtime to hinder the forces of darkness against me. Perhaps they do such an excellent job watching over me, the only thing Satan can do is cut my finger—which healed within a week, hide my gym clothes—which I got back and can only marvel and laugh at, break my wiper handle, and attack me with a spider. I HATE spiders!!!!!!!! Unfortunately, he is doing a hell of a job keeping me single and broke! Surely, I will have to break out of this curse of single-ness and poverty with some positive and lasting results—perhaps via going to NY or overseas.

NOW DON'T FORGET THE GOOD STUFF

God also wanted me to write down some of the positive occurrences that has happened. Such as, me slipping through the cracks on this insurance settlement ending up with my car fixed "for free." Including additional much needed repairs not exactly associated with the accident. Getting a **free** CD player with installation in my car—which formerly had absolutely nothing compliments of the worstest, Hyattsville! I also "lucked up" on buying a high quality DVD/VCR player for only $25! Wal-Mart and Sams don't even sell it for that! Anna paid more than twice that simply for a VCR. I received a used laptop for free from Myro and Swautch—since my first one was stolen via the mad house in Baltimore.

Also, this engineer called me out of the blue. I placed a ***Volunteers Needed*** notice on a campus community site about 2 years ago. He calls me from that site saying that he needs volunteer hours and is even interested in my organization. He also said he could arrange to bring bands to perform for free and help host an open mic music fund raiser for FREE where my organization could keep most, if not all of the money made. WOW!! He also has his own recording studio.

Furthermore, I actually lucked up on a Sony Vaio for less than $400 and a free desktop which supposedly has enough RAM to work my voice processor I bought over 3 years ago—as well as Photoshop and/or Illustrator. The same friend who gave me this desktop and sold me the DVD/VCR, talked me into re-enrolling back in school, to be exact, enrolling in grad school.

The only reason I did it, despite his constant badgering, was so I could get the loan money. Unlike undergrad where you only get loaned so much from Uncle Sam, grad school gives you almost $10,000 a semester! Particularly since a conventional bank loan is nearly impossible, I have no spouse to help me, I don't have a decent paying cozy desk job, no millionaire diplomat friends, or as of yet, any type of corporate sponsorship or grant; I basically have no other way to raise money for my business, resident community center, or any other venture I am trying to pursue. Now that's a lot of money—to pay back *and* use!

I plan to invest in my music and aspiring book publishing business—being that I have a thousand stories and songs collecting dust just waiting to be written and made. I also plan to use this money to finally travel to Europe, Egypt and the Holy Land, and stay in NY (or maybe even in Europe somewhere). The friend that convinced me to enroll is also enrolled and studying abroad in Europe to be with his girlfriend. This way, I will get to travel as well as sell my books and music (since foreigners LOVE American music and will buy American stuff WAY QUICKER than Americans—look at Macy Gray, Michael Jackson, and even David Hasselhoff. Did you even know he had a CD?)

And lastly, surely I'll find a mate! If nothing else but some sexy guy needing American salvation and a green card. And I am actually passing my very first semester of classes—go figure. By the way, all of the classes in my discipline are on-line. This means I can stay in NY or Rome and study, all while investing Uncle Sam's loan into my hopeful property or business while I find my long awaited spouse.

ActuallY BlesseD ... froM thE starT

God also wanted me to mention and say what He told me regarding how really blessed I am, even with no money nor husband. How I really am blessed from the start. He formed me, and every other person ever born, before the foundation of the earth. Perhaps He knew my personality before I was born while I was still in heaven with Him. Perhaps He knew I wanted to live in the future—I am NOT the vintage/antique type but REALLY love futuristic things.

He blessed me with 2 wonderful parents and a result oriented church. My dad is a rarity, he stayed with my mom and took care of me when most Americans divorce and are single parents. Just like me, he was really interested in the origins of things—language, art, culture, and so forth. Mom had 2 miscarriages before me and 1 after me. I was a fragile pregnancy resulting in a C-section but was a successful one.

Even with the fragile labor forcing my mom to relax and stop working with me, I arrive with all my limbs and senses in tact. My mom also sheltered me. I'm an only child, although I'd love a twin. That would be the most wonderful—a duplicate of me! Some feel I'm a little spoiled. I don't think so, but I do question, when I can't get what I want or need. At least requesting a reason why the answer is no. I personally see nothing wrong with that. I am also VERY persistent, and via my dad, quite stubborn. Although I was lonely growing up, I guess I was lucky not to have the sibling rivalry and problems like that.

Also with the exception of a hernia at 6 months, going to the dentist to pull my teeth for overcrowding, a piece of glass stuck in my delicate toe from a broken beer bottle, and getting bronchitis in my precious lungs, I have NEVER been hospitalized or even had a broken bone!! Thanks be to GOD! I amazingly never even had cavities—as many sweets that I eat—nor any major injuries, illnesses, or hospitalizations!!

AM I FINISHED YET?!

I must stop writing somewhere or I'll never get this book finished. As you probably can tell, I wrote this book on and off for a period of over 5 years. I believe I started writing the outline of the antics and activities of my life when I worked at the gas station in 1998. I stopped and started continuously over the years. I started up again when I got the job in Japan. I kept myself busy at work by filling in the outline of my chaotic life. My evil boss should not have cared, I was required to be alert and show my presence at work during work hours, and I did. I stopped with my dad and started back up during winter break with Swautch. I called myself finishing up during spring break. Of course, I still haven't finished, and it's mid winter the following year. I am currently proofreading. Surely, I shall finally finish this within a week or so; I just need to stop adding things! I must stop writing or I'll never finish this book!

WEIRD FRIENDS

Practically everyone says this. "All of your friends are weird, except me." Naturally, they feel they are the normal one out. Of course, if you ask any "normal" person, they'd tell me everyone is weird, especially me. Most of my friends are hippies, geeks, gay, foreign, artsy, disabled, unique, weird, or wild. They may all be odd, but who is normal—or more so, what is normal? And who determines the norms of society? I'd personally rather have weird, unusual friends who are nice, help me when I need it, offer me a place to stay, are sincere, and enjoyable to be around; than some "normal", uptight, somewhat unpleasant, challenging person to be around. People say I have weird friends, I'm crazy, and so on, but guess what, they're still talking about me! They probably will remember and talk about me long after they meet me. That's staying power and the making of a household name!

LEAVING YOU WITH AN IMPORTANT THOUGHT

I'll leave you with this very important thought. Here's a concept I'm sure you are familiar with. The most precious and priceless resource is time. For money and material things can be replaced and repaired. For even your health can be restored and healed. Time is the <u>only</u> resource in this material realm that can NEVER be replaced. Once it's gone, it's gone! So always be productive and make good use of this most priceless resource.

I'll also leave you with this quote by some pastor, and one that I REALLY need to work on and improve myself. "Time is very important. The way you spend or waist your time will determine how soon you will get to your destiny."

ACKNOWLEDGEMENTS

I'd like to acknowledge and thank the following:

My Aunt Phyllis Moore for her patience and excellent editing skills. Editing for flow and grammar, she was the one who edited my chaotic mind to this basic flow you have here. My Aunt Gladys Wilson for her donation and financial support, as well as my Grandmother (who should be nominated for folks who don't look their age), great aunt, and a friend of the family who all sponsored a book so I could get this printed. My mom, who helped me do the mailings and for her support. Brother David Johnson who encouraged me and offered to help print this. My family for supporting me. My friends, here and abroad, for accepting me. Howard University for showing me first hand, a different side of black. Japan for showing me first hand, a different side of life. Pastor Sam & Cassandra Elliot and Power In the Word Ministry for a Devine Relationship. God and the angels for pulling me out of all sorts of insane predicaments. And lastly, myself for FINALLY finishing this 5+ year work in progress.

I hope you enjoyed this book and I hope my writing informed you and served your reading pleasure. If you have any comments, suggestions, or more so, complaints…. DON'T TELL ME!!! Do address all problems and complaints to the Correspondence Department. The address for the Correspondence Department is thus:

Correspondence Department
P.O. Box 33
Golden Street
Heavenly, Realm 33740

For if you don't like or agree with what you read, that's not my fault or problem. **You DID get your warning!** Don't complain to me, I'm just the victim of this system of things. Complain to the media, government, narrow-minded people, Satan, or God. If you wish to correspond with God—look above. If you wish to correspond with Satan, look around. And, if you wish to correspond to the media—help yourself. Feel free to send any comment, suggestion, and the likes to: The Washington Post, Washington Times, Washington City paper, L.A. Times, Miami Harold, NY Times, NY Time Bestsellers Book Division, Chicago Tribune, Pulitzer Prize Corp, Jay Leno, Oprah Winfrey, David Letterman, The Ellen Show, CNN, Fox News, and any other media outlet you know. I need as much publicity as I can get. ☺

COMING ATTRACTIONS

Check out these up coming books and attractions! Log onto **http://atsbooks. 50megs.com** to see the status of these and many other books and projects Imeh Smith or The Circle's Edge, Inc.™ is constructing.

- <u>Pieces of Me</u>

This is a coffee table art book inspired by this book, <u>Conversations Out of ChAoS</u>, and the authors life. It is a collection of poetry, essays, excerpts, and photos. It will be a beautifully designed full color 8½" x 11" book with an exquisite hard back cover. Here is a small excerpt from this book:

- <u>An unusual supernatural science fiction</u>

This book is a work in progress and is so new that it doesn't even have a name! This novel holds a very unique concept with aspects of suspense, action, horror, romance, religion, and a lot of supernatural. This is a short novel that will be a quick read that you will DEFINITELY NOT be able to put down!!! There is mystery, suspense, and action from the first page until the end!!! This novel will have a sequel coming out and may actually be part of a series. For a tiny synopsis you get:

Fleshless demonic beings with great strength, abilities, intelligence, and skills to travel through matter and time, seeks humans to feed off of and control. An attractive, powerful, and unique young man with seemingly similar strengths and abilities to fight these demonic beings off. And a young, timid, lonely, virgin placed as the leader to prepare humanity in this futuristic time.

Be sure to stay posted so you can be the first to get this and many other book projects.

WHO IS IMEH SMITH

Imeh Smith is the founding president of The Circle's Edge, Inc.™, The Alvin T. Smith Foundation™, and daughter of Alvin T. Smith. She is a writer, artist, and creator of various programs and activities with similar missions as The Circle's Edge, Inc.™ or part of The Circle's Edge, Inc.™ itself. She realized growing up—and being a victim of it—that from grade school on up, there are no major programs addressing the root cause of being ostracized, taunted, and feeling left out. Since Columbine High, many administrators, social groups, and concerned citizens have implemented programs to address peer mediation, tolerance, among other things. She feels that the biggest reason for being ostracized and left out is misunderstanding, stereotypes, and myths, i.e. ignorance. What people do not understand, they fear and/or reject. She feels that once someone is educated of their ignorance, they will begin to understand. Once one understands, one begins to except and not ostracize.

She holds a Bachelors Degree of Art from Howard University majoring in Communications with a focus in Radio-TV-and Film, and a minor in Theater Arts. An avid traveler, visiting all over the US, Japan, and Korea, she plans to visit Europe and Africa this year. She was even groundbreaking in her travels to Onomichi, Hiroshima, Japan—in a one year English teaching and exchange program—by being the first participant like herself (Afro-American) in that city on the JET Programme. She is currently perusing another degree in Cultural Anthropology and Linguistics. She is a connoisseur of music and—like her father—enjoys exposure to all types of culture, art, music, dance, science, religion, history, and language. In the past, she studied Chinese, Italian, Swahili, French, Korean, and Hebrew. She currently has a working knowledge of Japanese, Spanish, and American Sign Language. She is presently working on several books, CD's, and a collection of footage she gathered and recorded while in Japan. And if you're reading this out of her book, congratulate her for FINALLY finishing her exhilarating and whimsical book—inspired by her own life—on a eccentric, naive, curious, single, female.

Log onto **www.ImehsCollection.com** or call the office for speaking engagements of her educational and very entertaining presentations.

THE CIRCLE'S EDGE, INC.™

The Circle's Edge, Inc.™ is a non-profit art organization about cultures, ability levels, and acceptance. I started this concept and idea about 10 years ago over a debate with my mom about school. From grade school on up, there seems to be nothing focused for people who feel left out, bullied, lonely, and have few friends. This was way before Columbine High. Being an artist and hanging around Gallaudet Univ., I incorporated art into my vision. I feel that one of the biggest reasons there is so much strife, pressure, and loneliness is that people dislike what they aren't familiar with. For a person doesn't choose their ability, race, age, sex, looks, where they are born, how much money their parents have, their height, or size. It's ridiculous for people to be picked on, left out, harassed, or attacked for being different. I wanted to educate and expose people to various types of ability, diversity, and culture through entertainment and art. The mission of The Circle's Edge™ is to dispel myths and stereotypes about culture, ability levels, and self-image, through education and art. We offer meetings, programs, and events as a way for people—in particular those who feel left out—to get involved and belong to something with no niche attached. Our meetings and activities offer a way to foster the belonging aspect of our mission. Log onto **www.circlesedge.org** and check out our info line **(443)451-0130**.

The Alvin T. Smith Foundation™

The Alvin T. Smith Foundation consists of an Historical Collection, an Associate and Scholar Program—an opportunity for volunteers to not only fulfill volunteer credit, but also get public recognition as well—and the Memorial Fund, a way to donate and help this cause.

The Alvin T. Smith Historical Collection consists of articles, essays, props and artwor, pictures, and much more. Alvin T. Smith—an honored member of the U.S. Air Force, a faithful member of the American Legion, and a friendly, open-minded, caring person—had a desire for research, knowledge, and the search for truth. This is a lifetime of research and work on all aspects of history. His research crossed the gamut of the spectrum. From Africa to the Americas. From ancient languages to the modern day pronunciation of American English. From religion and government to art and music. Log onto **www.AlvinTSmithFoundation.org** for more info.

PAST ACTIVITIES:

- Incorporated & received 501c3 non-profit status 2001
- Performed **AWARENESS PROJECT on TOLERANCE, ABILITY, & SELF IMAGE**™ at:
  - Roots Alternative Learning Center 1998
  - Model Secondary School for the Deaf 1998
  - Heartland nursing home 1998
  - Culture Café 1998
  - Presentations in Japan showcasing American culture and dispelling myths 2000 and 2001

....Now if a cute blond with blue eyes is ignored in Japan, and these anti-establishment activist seemingly only date fit women, **what hope is there for the rest of society?!?!**

What can you do about it?
I'll tell you what to do;
<u>CHANGE</u> these
IGNORANT STANDARDS OF BEAUTY!!

How do you do that?
HERE'S HOW....

THE AWARENESS PROJECT ON TOLERANCE, ABILITY, & SELF IMAGE™

- What's missing in today's society that causes so much hatred, terrorism, and harm?

One of the most prevalent and overlooked problems in modern society is intolerance, human neglection and our constant need to be accepted and belong. Many times people are cast out because of being different: disabled, race, religion, age, size, and such. A person does not choose their race, size, ethnicity, ability, and so on; they are born that way. The biggest reason for intolerance and exclusion is ignorance—unfamiliarity, stereotypes, misconception, and so forth. What people do not understand, they fear and/or reject. Once someone is educated of their ignorance, they will begin to understand. Once one understands, one begins to tolerate and not ostracize.

Millions of problems exist because of intolerance, non-acceptance, and rejection.

Because of unfair biases, standards, and myths on many sub-groups of people, vast feelings of being incomplete, unattractive, unable, as well as many other negative feelings exist. This makes people desire to physically transform and try to change who and what they are, to hopefully be tolerated, accepted, and to conform into societies myths and biased standards. This, and other Industrial/Western societies, place unfair, incorrect, and harsh standards regarding beauty, levels of ability, culture and customs, how someone walks, talks, sings, acts, and the like on people. These extreme biased opinions only apply and bene-fit a few, and negatively affect the masses. Because tremendous intolerance to dif-ferences exist, the very fabric of this—and other countries, is permanently stained. Wars and crimes of intolerance started. Murder, hatred, teasing, con-tempt, and scorn have occurred to the victims of these stereotypes and mythical standards. Great loneliness, depression, and sorrow occur within the victims, which only produces additional negative outcomes.

What the SOLUTION?

1. JUST BE YOURSELF. The more you try to be someone else or please others the less you stay yourself! And you can NEVER completely satisfy humans—there is ALWAYS something you just can't to right. Why, because NO ONE is perfect!!

2. IGNORE negative people and be around positive people as much as possible.

3. You can do and be whatever you put your mind and will to.

4. If Rosa Parks, Dr. King, Mother Theresa, and many others can make a difference, SO CAN YOU!! You can start out by volunteer & working with The Circle' Edge, Inc.™

It only takes one amazing act to create a change!!
Look at the major societies in the world. From Gandhi to Mandela,
it all started with one!!

COME HELP MAKE A DIFFERENCE & CHANGE THE WORLD
while you're at it!!

You can further help this cause by joining, volunteering, offering in-kind gifts of a much needed item, money, or service, or even a referral. Donate an **in-kind gift** of building materials such as cement, pipes for plumbing, windows, & electrical supplies, **advertisement space,** and/or a Pentium 4 laptop; **in-kind services** of, plumbing, carpentry, electrical help, & much more for our **Resident Community Center & Artist Retreat!**

Do you know of any business, organization, school, corporation, or civic group that may be interested in the _Just Being Me_ presentation, Corporate Sponsorships, Cause Related Marketing or Co-sponsorship?

Just Being Me is an excellent presentation for high school and college students, civic, business, and other social groups dealing with people who feel left out, ostracized, bullied, unpopular, and/or females (or anyone) with self image and identity issues. This presentation is geared for everyone regardless of faith, nationality, sex, class, age, or race!! This is a good presentation for youth & adults alike! It is free, easy to understand, under an hour long, and adaptable for most environments, we only ask for transportation costs. This presentation can be presented wherever you are, so book "**Just Being Me**" for your next program or event today!!

If you know of any company or group interested in Corporate Sponsorship, Co-Sponsorship, or Cause Related Marketing which would generate tremendous PR as well as lucrative residual income, please have them contact the office. Corporate Sponsorships, Cause Related Marketing, and even Co-sponsorship can offer their firm excellent promotional and marketing opportunities as well as creative strategies to assist in their taxing and business endeavors—which can even offer residual income! Contact the office at (301) 736-9460 for further information.

TO MAKE A DONATION OR TO BOOK "Just Being Me"; **E-MAIL, CALL, OR WRITE TO US VIA OUR SITES BELOW. WE WOULD LOVE TO HEAR FROM YOU!**

The Circle's Edge, Inc.™
P.O. Box 512 ■ Riverdale, MD ■ 20738 ■ USA

Also check out our sites and info line.
(443) 451-0130,
www.circlesedge.org,
www.AlvinTSmithFoundation.org, and
www.ImehsCollection.com! And our newest site,

ATS Entertainment:
http://atsbooks.50megs.com

BIBLIOGRAPHY

This is a bibliography of the books, some of the Bible verses, and some of the material mentioned in this story.

♦ Some of the **Bible verses quoted**:
   o First 2 chapters in Samuel I
   o 1 Corinthians 1:26-29

Some of the material mentioned in this book:

♦ Clueless

♦ India Arie http://www.indiaarie.com/

♦ Macbeth by William Shakespeare

♦ Mad TV featuring Ms. Wong

♦ *Richard* Scarry's *Best Word Book Ever* Giant Little Golden Book

♦ Saturday morning D.C. area kids shows
   o **Beth and Bower**
   o **Great Space Coaster** http://www.imdb.com/title/tt0170945 and http://www.tgscoaster.com/
   o **Kids Break** http://kidshow.dcmemories.com/kbreak.html
   o **New Zoo Review** http://www.otmfan.com/html/nzr.htm and http://www.landofthelost.com/forums/printthread.php?t=894

♦ Seto Inland Bridge http://web-japan.org/atlas/architecture/arc22.html

♦ *The 6th Sense*

The Bibliography

♦ **BLUBBER** By Judy Blume Published by Yearling

- Bob Marley documentary http://en.wikipedia.org/wiki/Bob_Marley
- Campus Crusade for Christ, www.crusade.org
- **Freda** Directed by Julie Taymor 2002
- Articles on **Johnny Carson** http://sfgate.com/cgi-bin/article.cgi?file=/c/a/2005/01/24/CARSON.TMP and http://en.wikipedia.org/wiki/Johnny_Carson

"Despite decades on television, Carson was never open publicly with the details of his personal life. 'Nobody got to know him,' said comedian Joan Rivers, who often substituted for Carson as a "Tonight Show" guest host. 'He was very private.'"

- **Never Too Thin** by Willy and Wendy Werby. Landmark Media, Falls Church, VA. 1992

"An overview of contemporary America's obsession with having a slender body. No female seems exempt from societal pressure or self scrutiny. From the average woman-on-the-street who wants to lose weight to the beautiful model who wants more slender hips and thighs, women evaluate themselves and are being judged according to their body size and shape" http://www.naafa.org/ The National Association to Advance Fat Acceptance

- **Power In the Word Ministry**
  15498 Old Columbia Pike
  Burtonsville, MD 20866
  301-421-1088 church
  www.powerintheword.50megs.com

- RELIGION verses a RELATIONSHIP with CHRIST. 10 Reasons To Believe (http://www.gospelcom.net/rbc/rtb/3rsn

- **Ren and Stimpy** *www.renandstimpydutchovengame.com*

- www.science-fair.spiritworld.info This site has information on the Entangled Particle Holographics theory/AKA/The Quantum Holographic Principal. This is the quote from their site.

"Entangled Particle Holographics suggests that all things in the universe are inter-connected informationally. It also maintains that underlying this unity or oneness is the mystifying and mysterious dance between all matter and energy and information. Simply put, the basic promise of Entangled Particle Holographics is that the most profound insights about our universe will be discovered among the most subtle, implicit, and invisible phenomena of the sub-quantum level."

- o http://colossalstorage.net also see:
- o The Holographic Paradigm and
- o Collective DNA Consciousness

♦ www.science-fair.spiritworld.info/natures-mind.html

This is another site that has information on The Quantum Holographic Principal. It was this site that I felt had some sort of spiritual/metaphysical overtone, and coming from science—that is borderline blasphemy. This is the quote from their site by Dr. Edgar Mitchell, Sc.D. of:

Institute of Noetic Sciences,
PO Box 540037,
Lake Worth, FL 33454
Fax: 1-561-641-5242
"Our Mission: Exploring the frontiers of consciousness to advance individual, social, and global transformation."

http://www.noetic.org/blog.cfm
Video quote: *"It's an obligation for science to begin to look, and look critically but open mindedly, at the possibility that our minds are more powerful than we previously understood."*

This paper presents a hypothesis for integrating into the scientific framework phenomena of consciousness which frequently have been considered beyond scientific description. Intuition, telepathy, clairvoyance and many similar information phenomena seem to be easily explained by means of the nonlocal quantum hologram. It is further postulated that from the point of view of evolution, quantum nonlocality is the basis from which self organizing cosmological processes have produced the common phenomenon of perception in living organisms.

- *Wellness: Concepts and Applications* chapter 8, Achieving a Healthy Weight page 240–243 McGraw-Hill Higher Education

- **Who Really Rules the World?** by the Watch Tower Bible and Track Society of Pa. 1992

- Virginia church website, http://www.new-life.net/goodnews.htm

- **YOUR DAYS ARE WRITTEN** by Danny Diaz
  http://www.dannydiaz.com
  http://www15.serrahost.com/dannydiazcom/StoreFront.bok

978-0-595-41637-0
0-595-41637-3